EXIT 13

EXIT 13

Oppression & Racism in Academia

MONTE PILIAWSKY

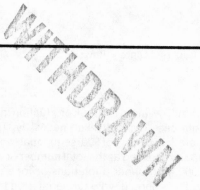

SOUTH END PRESS

Copyright © 1982 by Monte Piliawsky

First edition

Copyrights are still required for book production in the United States.
However, in our case it is a disliked necessity. Thus, any properly
footnoted quotation of up to 500 sequential words may be used
without permission, so long as the total number of words quoted does
not exceed 2000. For longer quotations or for a greater number of
total words, authors should write for permission from the publisher.

Library of Congress Number: 81-52707
ISBN 0-89608-096-x (paper)
ISBN 0-89608-097-8 (cloth)

Cover design by Lydia Sargent and Glober Graphics
Production at South End Press
Typeface is Century Oldstyle
Printed in the U.S.A.

SOUTH END PRESS/302 COLUMBUS AVE/BOSTON MA 02116

CONTENTS

v

ACKNOWLEDGMENTS

I am grateful to Winfield H. Rose for undertaking the herculean task of correcting my violations of the elementary rules of grammar and style. W.D. Norwood contributed significantly to the organization and tone of the work. James P. RePass was valuable in suggesting an analytical framework for the subject matter. An earlier draft benefited from the careful reading and helpful advice of Lloyd Dangerfield, William Cohen and my sister, Marilyn Cohen. My special thanks go to Henry C. Lacey and Shirley Bradway Laska for their encouragement during the entire project. The suggestions and criticisms offered by Lydia Sargent, my editor at South End Press, have been of invaluable assistance. I would like to express my deepest gratitude to my parents for their patience and encouragement of this project; without their support this book could not have been written.

One final personal note. This work is really the combined effort of the "Exit 13 team" which supplied me with both information and emotional support. Members of the group include: Murphy, Hugo, Gail and Stephen, Ellis, Jim, Bette, Ken, J.C., Margo and Wayne, Diana, Carol, Becky, Carolyn and Wes.

TO
BRIGADIER GENERAL WILLIAM D. MCCAIN
without whom this book could not have been written

"As I go about the campus, I have great difficulty in getting students to speak to me. I occasionally stop one who refuses to exchange greetings and ask for his name and station in life...One of these days a student who has refused to speak to me is going to appear in my office for help when in trouble with the office of the Dean of Student Affairs. I will then have the opportunity to remind him of his previous discourtesy."

—Brigadier General William D. McCain
President, University of Southern Mississippi
(1955-1975)

INTRODUCTION

Exit 13 is divided into two parts, a case study and five essays. The first half of the book is a case study of the educational experience at the University of Southern Mississippi in the early 1970s. The university was blatantly racist, an ideology symbolically exhibited in the person of the school's mascot, Confederate General Nathan Bedford Forrest, the founder and first Grand Wizard of the original Ku Klux Klan. Sexism pervaded the college community at USM. For example, a married professor of music was fired for having a baby, even though she did not miss a single day of work because of the pregnancy. Faculty members who challenged any university policy, or who expressed even liberal political viewpoints faced severe recrimination. By merely serving as a delegate to the Democratic Party National Convention, a history professor suffered a $1000 cut in salary. Similarly, USM students had no rights whatsoever. The administration cavalierly censored the student newspaper, prohibited anti-war rallies, refused speakers such as Charles Evers from speaking on campus, and on one occasion even abolished the Student Government Association.

Yet, as the second part of the book demonstrates, it would be incorrect to dismiss the USM experience as aberrant or dated. Racism exists today at *all* U.S. universities, even the so-called elite institutions. For example, in 1979 Harvard University had only five black tenured professors out of a tenured faculty of 352. And what are we to conclude when the new chairperson of the Afro-American studies department at Harvard declared in 1980 that "Afro-

American studies is not a valid academic discipline nor field of scholarly study."[1] Sexism, as well, permeates the elite institutions of academia. Women comprise less than 3 percent of the associate and full professor positions at the most selective Ivy League universities;[2] there are but twelve tenured women professors (3.4 percent) at Harvard today. The extent of sexism in academia is well captured by a former Harvard president's remark, "We shall be left with the blind, the lame, and the women."[3]

Faculty members who challenge the authority of administrators at their institutions, or who express radical ideologies are routinely purged from academia. Politically troublesome junior faculty are dismissed under the guise of "unbecoming professional conduct," a criterion which not only violates the tenets of academic freedom but also the Bill of Rights. College students are equally disenfranchised. Administrators at scores of uiniversities have imposed prepublication censorship on student media and have used their discretionary power to terminate student federal financial aid for political reasons.[4] The attitude of administrators toward college students received its most prosaic formulation in the observation by Columbia University's vice-dean of graduate studies that "whether students vote 'yes' or 'no' on an issue is like telling me that they like strawberries."[5]

The reason all universities resemble the University of Southern Mississippi is that the capitalist establishment controls higher education in the United States, *all* higher education. Because colleges perform the vital task of training the country's future employees, the capitalist elite demands the power to determine the course of higher education. The ruling class exercises this control through its domination of the boards of trustees of colleges. Board members consistently display a racist, pro-capitalist philosophy. M.M. Roberts, the president of the Mississippi College Board, has boasted, "I am a racist...I have no apologies for it, though. It's me."[6] But how different is his attitude from the actions of the "enlightened" members of the Boards of Trustees of the University of California and of Stanford University for firing Angela Davis and H. Bruce Franklin for their political beliefs, or the board members of the University of Maryland for refusing to hire Bertell Ollman because he is a Marxist? Indeed, a business philosophy prevails, and critics of the status quo, because they are perceived by those in power as challenging the capitalist "social" system, face recrimination throughout academia.

NOTES

1. *The Call,* 28 April 1980, p. 7.
2. Leigh Biensen, Alicia Ostriker and J.P. Ostriker, "Sex Discrimination in the Universities," in *Women in a Man-Made World: A Socio-economic Handbook,* eds. Nona Glazer and Helen Youngelson Waehrer (Chicago: Rand McNally College Publishing Co., 1977), p. 372.
3. Ann Sunderland Harris, "The Second Sex in Academe," *AAUP Bulletin* 56 (Fall 1970): 285.
4. Michael Miles, "The Triumph of Reaction," *Change* 4 (Winter 1972-73): 31-34.
5. James Simon Kunen, *The Strawberry Statement: Notes of a College Revolutionary* (New York: Avon Books, 1970), p. 140.
6. *Student Printz,* 11 December 1969, p. 1.

PREFACE

Alice: Yes, but where do I begin?
Chesire Cat: Why, my dear, you begin at the beginning.
                              Lewis Carroll, *Alice in Wonderland*

This book is not fiction. Every one of its statements is documented. Few readers will believe every episode, but then my two years (1970-1972) on the faculty of the University of Southern Mississippi in Hattiesburg, seem even to me like real life science fiction. Hattiesburg, for those who haven't been there, is a city of 40,000 in southeastern Mississippi, and is the county seat of Forrest County. Hattiesburg is exactly 70 miles from the Gulf Coast, 97 miles from Mobile, and 105 miles from New Orleans.

One-quarter mile south of Hattiesburg, as one approaches on Interstate Highway 59, there is a sign reading: "EXIT 13 University of Southern Miss. NEXT RIGHT." As soon as people make the fateful right turn at Exit 13, they unwittingly enter a twilight zone dominated by the Exit 13 syndrome, a place in which fact and fiction, fantasy and reality all become hopelessly entangled. The Exit 13 syndrome requires a sense of humor—one must laugh because otherwise one will cry.

What's so unusual about the University of Southern Mississippi, or USM? Many things: A special committee of the American

Historical Association in 1971 found that USM President William D. McCain "violated approved scholarly usage," that is, plagiarized, in an article he published in the *Journal of Mississippi History*.[1] USM is Mississippi's second largest university, with more than 12,000 students. While its library contains only half the books required for a fully accredited university of this size, it has what reportedly is the largest collection of children's books in the world.[2] During its first two years, the front half of the stage in USM's new $1.5 million Performing Arts Center could not be seen from any of the 218 seats in the balcony. Classes *are* held at USM on July 4th; according to rumor this is because Vicksburg fell to the Union armies on 4 July 1863, making the 4th a day of infamy. Five thousand copies of a cartoon in the student newspaper captioned "Love is never having to say you're hungry" were burned because a faculty advisor to the paper thought that the inscription denoted "oral genital sex."

This book, then, tells the story of what passes for education for those enrolled at a university which provides a "unique" setting for living and learning. One manifestation of this is the racism which pervades the institution. Although Black leader Charles Evers spoke on courthouse steps throughout Mississippi in his 1971 gubernatorial campaign, he was banned from speaking at USM. Such hospitality is also afforded certain whites with "questionable" political affiliations. While flags throughout Mississippi and the nation were at half-staff during February 1973, in memory of former President Lyndon Johnson, the USM flag was flown at full-staff at first and, after a few days, was removed entirely. When President Richard Nixon ordered the flags back to full-staff on February 14 to honor the returning Vietnam POWs, the USM flag immediately reappeared. Prominent individuals such as Mississippi Congressman Frank D, Smith, Pulitzer prize-winning publisher Hodding Carter, and the president of the Mississippi AFL-CIO have been denied permission to speak at USM.

Academic freedom or freedom of expression for students and faculty is virtually unheard of at USM. Professors who in 1969 merely signed a petition supporting the creation of a faculty senate were intimidated into removing their signatures. In addition to expressing opinions, it can be dangerous at USM, even to ask someone else's. For example, one professor was severely chastised by his dean for writing a letter in 1968 to Mississippi's attorney general asking for an opinion on the state's anti-evolution or monkey laws.[3] And, University President McCain boasted in a campus address: "Some professors lecture against my methods in class; perhaps they will not be present on the campus next fall."[4] They usually aren't.

Prepare to enter Exit 13, an experience which can best be termed "On Being Sane in Insane Places."

NOTES

1. "The American Historical Association and the AAUP: A Joint Inquiry into an Issue of Attribution," *AAUP Bulletin*, 57 (Winter, 1971), 529-32.

2. *Student Printz*, 29 September 1970, p. 2; *Student Printz*, 29 April 1971, p. 20.

3. Lew Powell, "Academic Martial Law at Southern: McCain Zips Dissenting Lips," *Mississippi Freelance*, I (July 1969), 1.

4. *Student Printz*, 20 April 1967, p. 3.

PART ONE

Chapter One

YOU ARE NOW ENTERING EXIT 13

It will be charged of course, that I am attempting to turn the university into a vocational school. Right. So I am...Literature and history, unlike money and possessions, will not bring their students solace and wisdom in times of disaster.

—*Charles W. Moorman*
Dean of the University,
University of Southern Mississippi

I arrived at the University of Southern Mississippi with expectations similar to those of any young academic, anticipating an opportunity to teach and a congenial atmosphere for research. But, after finding that neither was possible in the environment where I had accepted employment, I decided to do a bit of educational research on the environment itself, to make it the *object* of my study rather than the background for it.

As I began to write I recognized that the substance of my book had a direct bearing on the current controversy concerning the principal purpose of U.S. higher education. The history of universities in the United States records a continuing battle between those who regard the proper role of education as being the training of students for immediate jobs; and those who see education as preparation for moral excellence, which is attained by the ability to clarify values and to participate in critical inquiry.[1] In direct response to the demands of unprecedentedly large numbers of working class students, especially Blacks, entering colleges in the 1960s, the Carnegie Commission on Higher Education was organized in 1967. Chaired by Clark Kerr, the group, representing the leaders of the educational Establishment, produced twenty-one monographs and over eighty other publications over a six year period. The work of the Commission was decisive in restructuring U.S. higher education.

The overriding recommendation of the Carnegie Commission was that the liberal arts versus vocational training dilemma be resolved by stratifying higher education along a basically two-tiered structure. The Ivy League institutions and the major state universities would continue to provide a traditional liberal arts education to the privileged elite, while the community colleges would provide vocational training oriented toward the demands of local industry to working class students. Community colleges, the Commission said, "should follow an open-enrollment policy, whereas access to four-year institutions should generally be more selective."[2] The net impact of these recommendations has been to enhance the tracking system of higher education, in which Black and poor students are channeled generally to dead-end vocational programs within community colleges, while rich students are taught the "moral excellence" provided by the liberal arts education of U.S. elite colleges.

The Carnegie Commission was intent not only in protecting the elite status and function of the established institutions from the tremendous expansion in the number of students in higher education. In addition, the Commission recognized capitalism's increasing need for technical education, which led to its great emphasis on the community college as the major resource for providing off-the-job technical training, "flexibly geared to the changing requirements of society."[3] Not surprisingly, the business community itself has followed the Commission's lead in strongly encouraging occupational training at public expense at the college level.

What has been the role of the four-year secondary state college, like the University of Southern Mississippi, which occupies the intermediate position in the educational tracking system? As Samuel Bowles and Herbert Gintis point out, "the vocational orientation of the community colleges is becoming more typical of the system of U.S. higher education as a whole." They correctly predict that as the monetary crisis of colleges for financial support from student tuition and state legislatures intensifies, "the four-year institutions are likely to come under pressure for a rationalization of curriculum and educational method."[4]

Hopefully, this book contributes to the debate concerning the merit of a vocationally oriented university—the University of Southern Mississippi purports to be "the nation's most fervently career-oriented university"[5]—and also to a further understanding of the extent and nature of control and repression in our universities. For *Exit 13* is a case study showing how a procapitalist ideology permeates every aspect of college life and curriculum in a way that recreates a microcosm of the authoritarianism, racism, and sexism in society itself.

EDUCATION: BEST HOPE FOR THE "NEW SOUTH" (AND THE NATION)

This book has a second purpose: it tests from the vantage point of public higher education the endurance of Mississippi's "closed society," which Professor James W. Silver described in his classic study by that same name a decade ago. The essence of this closed society is the all-pervading doctrine of white supremacy and the silencing of dissenters from this orthodox view.[6] Since a university generally is considered to be the avant-garde of enlightment in a society, my hypothesis is that if racism persists and freedom of expression and inquiry is repressed by the Mississippi State Board of Education and at the University of Southern Mississippi, then Silver's closed society thesis is still viable.

I come by my concern with this issue more through personal experience than through pure academic interest. I am a Southerner and I have had an opportunity to study first-hand the much-proclaimed "New South" to assess its "newness"—the illusion or reality of its progress. As a native I am proud of many aspects of the South. I perceive that there are truths in the myth: warmth, civility, earthiness, religiosity, and family loyalty as some of the regional character traits which make the South unique in the U.S.[7]

But, also as one who has lived his entire life in the South, I recognize that racism has permeated the Southern experience. Has it lingered? If so, must we not challenge the proclamations of sweeping change for the region? And then must we not ask why racism has lingered, and what can be done to remove it from the

Southern condition? Such challenges and questions stemmed naturally from my experience as a professor in a Missisippi public
college.

Such concerns are not merely parochial. The ultimate test of
the character of the American people in general is their ability to
prosper from racial and ethnic diversity. Because of historical forces, the burden of the "American Dilemma" has always rested most
heavily on the Southerner, but cannot be avoided as a national
responsibility. In a 1972 *Saturday Review* article Peter Schrag
wrote: "The South is the last American region, and anyone concerned about the country's future must eventually return (or go for
the first time) to see what's changed, to test his own versions, to see
how it feels *down there* looking up."[8] Thus, an investigation of the
success or failure of the South in race relations can provide insight
into the national response.

In the early 1970s, the media celebrated the emergence of a
"New South" which was characterized primarily by the most successful advances in racial equality in U.S. society. Some observers
even viewed the South as the redeemer of the American soul. In
1971, Marshall Frady wrote in *Life*: "It may be the South after all
where the nation's general malaise of racial alienation first finds
resolution."[9] This dramatically changed interpretation of the
South was capped off by the election of Jimmy Carter, a Southerner,
to the White House in 1976.

Yet despite all the talk about a "born-again" South, the tone of
hopefulness which characterized articles written about the South
only a few years ago is changing. In mid-June, 1978, one could read
an article entitled: "Old Problems Persist in the 'New South' " in
the *Chicago Tribune,*[10] as well as a first-page article in *Time* entitled
"In Mississippi: The KKK Suits Up."[11] In October 1978, Tommy
Lee Hines, a 26-year old mentally retarded black man was convicted
and sentenced to thirty years in prison by an all-white jury for
allegedly raping a white woman in Decatur, Alabama, the city for
the trial of the "Scottsboro boys," an exactly parallel case forty
years earlier. Clearly, there is a need for an objective appraisal of
the South to measure exactly how much progress has been made,
and whether that progress is substantial or superficial. Where *does*
the South stand today?

The issue of the New South is partly a definitional one. Contrasted to the crude indignities of the pre-1954 period, racial conditions have improved markedly. In the most significant areas of the

Civil Rights Movement—political participation and access to public facilities—substantial progress has been made. Blacks have registered enormous political gains if measured in terms of registered voters and black elected officials. Specifically, between 1962 and 1980, three and one-half million Southern blacks were added to the voter registration rolls; the corresponding number of black elected officials in the South increased from only 72 in 1965, to over 2,000 today.[12] In addition, southern blacks have general access to public facilities. It may be, however, as Leronne Bennett, Jr., cautions, "wrong to extrapolate from these surface changes to changes in societal structures."[13]

For one thing, the impressive gains in black voter registration have not resulted in blacks holding political power even remotely proportionate to their numbers. In 1979, blacks constituted 20.5 percent of the South's total population, but held only 2.3 percent of the region's elective officers. Although blacks comprise popular majorities in over 100 counties in the South, only ten counties are effectively controlled by blacks, often because of ingeniously gerrymandered districts, designed to dilute the black vote.[14]

The net result is that the progress in black political participation has not transferred into an improved quality of life for most blacks. Many southern blacks live in towns where the electoral domination of the white merchants perpetuates racism. The continuing boycott of downtown merchants in Tupelo, Mississippi since the spring of 1978 by the town's black community in protest of alleged police brutality and job discrimination, well illustrates the intransigence of the "Old South."

Even the election of a black mayor can be an almost meaningless victory. Tuskegee, Alabama has had a black mayor since 1972. Whites have responded by establishing a separate sub-society, with their own private schools and even their own newspaper; many have moved to new homes in near-by suburban communities. Whites still own almost all the major businesses and both banks in the downtown area and totally dominate the economy of Tuskegee. As Professor Manning Marable concludes in his 1977 account, appropriately entitled "Tuskegee and the Politics of Illusion in the New South": "*De jure* segregation has ended, but *de facto* segregation and an ongoing culture of white racism remain pervasive."[15]

Another serious constraint on black city mayors is the power of the state legislatures. As white voters are losing political control of cities to blacks, they are increasingly dependent upon state legislatures to protect their interests. The current black mayor of New Orleans is desperately attempting to raise funds, but is hampered by a provision in the new state constitution which allows home-owners of residences assessed at under $50,000 to pay *no* property tax whatsoever. According to Julian Bond: "Because of population densitites, the South has elected more blacks to public office than any other region, but these mayors and aldermen and commission-ers often remain accessories beside the fact of actual governance of their towns, counties and states."[16]

This paradox of the New South—progress contrasted with underlying stagnation—is perhaps most dramatically exhibited in the area of public schools. The formal integration of schools masks a deeper and more significant pattern of resegregation. School integration has generally meant that white parents have pulled their children out of the public schools, leaving to black (and some poor white) children school systems which invariably are grossly underfunded.[17] The remaining white children often are divided from blacks by controversial tracking systems.

This pattern is followed closely in New Orleans, for example, where most whites send their children to private or parochial schools and no longer want to give the public schools their tax support. Although middle class whites have little concern about the quality of public education, they *control* the educational system through both political and economic power. Whether or not this non-support of public education represents racism, the net effect is that blacks have only inferior schools to attend.

The title of this section is meant to suggest that quality public education is the best means to improve race relations in the United States. This hypothesis contains one basic assumption. Scholarly studies of racism conducted by social scientists in the past twenty-five years have found that in a step-like pattern the more education people have, the greater their willingness to extend civil rights to minorities.[18] Since the overwhelming majority of Americans attend public schools, a reduction in the quality of public education could be expected to result in a more racist citizenry. Conversely, public education, if properly structured, can help clarify human values and direct human affairs "toward desirable and rationally justified patterns of action."[19]

Americans have always had sublime faith in the power of education. The eminent historian Henry Steele Commanger wrote in 1950: "No other people ever demanded so much of education as have the American. None other was ever served so well by its schools and educators." Americans quite properly have paid grateful homage to the success of the public schools in meeting the historic demands that society made upon them: to provide an enlightened citizenry, to create national unity, and to Americanize the millions of foreign-born.[20] Since 1950, society has placed another "historic demand" upon public education: to combat racism. The future of race relations in America depends upon its success in this endeavor; this thought was never far from my mind during my stay at the University of Southern Mississippi, and as I worked on *Exit 13*.

Chapter Two

GENERALISSIMO WILLIAM D. McCAIN

*The moment you say, "I am the president and you must obey,"
you have gone beyond logic and reason, and you are no better
than the leader of the most extreme student group.*

—*Arland Christ-Janer*
President, Boston University

What's the old saying—"old soldiers never die, they just retire
and run universities?" While unable to attract a magnetic figure
such as General of the Army Dwight D. Eisenhower, the University
of Southern Mississippi has nonetheless combed the ranks of the
armed forces in order to join the elite circle of universities run by
the military. From 1955 until 1975, USM was commanded by General William D. McCain and a junta of military advisers. When
McCain was appointed as the University's president on 1 August
1955, he named General Roger B. Johnson as his administrative
assistant. In Administration circles, however, General Johnson is
referred to merely as "Colonel." There's only one General at USM.

McCAIN'S MILITARY MANIA: "I HAVE TAKEN ON MY HANDS THE BLOOD OF SOME OF YOU."

General McCain's military bent is evident in his affection for
ROTC. "Would you go along with a student referendum on compul-

sory ROTC?" he was asked at a Student Senate meeting on 5 May 1969. "I don't follow the SDS line," McCain snorted, "Next question?"[1] Although the USM University Council subsequently voted to make ROTC voluntary, the General remained resolute in his opposition. Addressing entering students at orientation services on 7 September 1969, McCain said:

> I have taken on my hands the blood of some of you...The fact that some of you won't take military training means that you won't be prepared and some of you are going to die and your blood will be on my hands...I thought it was wrong but we have done it...It troubles me that I had a part in the fact that certain students will not take military training and will die as a result of it.[2]

General McCain enjoys telling his military anecdotes. On 17 July 1972, the General told 300 high school students at USM:

> When my son and I were called up for the Korean War, my son failed his physical examination and was not supposed to go. And I said, "Jess, get a new medical officer and examine him again." And he passed and went...And I had forced mine...of course he wanted to pass his physical. It took two of us to do it.[3]

McCain discussed his military experience at length in an article he wrote for the February 1972 issue of the *Journal of Mississippi History* entitled, "Some Reminiscences of the United States Archivist in Italy—Director William D. McCain on Military Leave from Mississippi Department of Archives and History." The following excerpts offer keen insight into this extraordinary man:

> I had an interesting trip to the north late in January, 1945, to check on plans for the spring offensive. I left Rome on the morning of January 25 in an open command car. The weather was quite cold. I had a British major with me who sat on the back seat and covered himself completely with a tarpaulin. He was surprised along the way to Florence when we hit a tree. An Italian cart was going south. We were going north. An Italian on a bicycle darted out from behind the cart. We smashed into him and left his bicycle a crumpled mass. We ended up against a tree. My right leg was injured and my trousers leg was torn. We left the Italian sitting in the road beside his wrecked bicycle. I instructed the driver,

"The next time you have a choice between me and an Italian, kill the Italian."

McCain explains his unauthorized firing at an Italian archivist this way:

> I knew the man who had been appointed to succeed Dr. Manganelli. I felt that he was a communist and I certainly did not trust him. I called the new appointee and instructed him to be in my office at ten. When he arrived, I stated in effect, "You have been superintendant of the Archivo di Stato for one hour, you no longer hold that position, and you are never to return to the Archivio di Stato." There was a great screaming and gnashing of teeth. I finally said, "If you do not obey my orders, I will get a plane, fly to Rome, and settle the matter finally." I could schedule a plane for Rome almost any morning in order to attend to business. The bluff worked and the man never returned to the Archivio di Stato. The fact is that I really had no definite authority over such appointments.

In his concluding paragraph, McCain explains how he accomplished his work as the U.S. archivist in Italy:

> The narrative of this story may not have given the impression that a vast amount of work was accomplished. I assure you that the achievements between May 1 and August 31, 1945, were somewhat miraculous. If anyone wonders how one officer contrived so much, let him remember that the officer concerned used Italians to do the work, even as he has always tried to use others to carry out the missions assigned to him.[4]

Those students who come to USM to stay out of the army are sadly mistaken, as Stephen M. Pike describes in a letter to the campus newspaper:

> Observations...such as guys marching around at 7 a.m. with wooden swords, Huey helicopters landing on Pride Field, and men in army suits climbing up walls of the stadium, led me to the conclusion that this is, in reality, a secret army base. The question is, what army is this a base of? This was a job for logical observations. Note: blacks in the lunch room have most of the clean-up work while most of the whites have the administration jobs. Note: the treatment of girls on campus resembles the super double standard of the Old South. Note: they play "Dixie" a considerable amount of times on the bells

and at football games. Conclusion: This is the last remaining outpost of the Confederate Army led by and under the direction of Major Major McCain...On to Gettysburg.[5]

MCCAIN'S FAMILY FEALTY

McCain has authored a 120-volume genealogical study of his family entitled "The McCain Chronicles." In the lobby of USM's new $1.5 million Performing Arts Building is a black rock which protrudes from a red brick wall. A plaque above the wall reads: STONE FROM MIGARY CASTLE KILCHOAN, ARNAMURCHAN, SCOTLAND SITE OF THE ORIGIN OF THE MACIAINS. The two-by-two foot stepping stones in front of the university snack bar are painted in a red and green pattern, reportedly as a facsimile of McCain's family coat of arms, And in 1963, "The Pride," USM's marching band, added the "Scottish Highlanders" unit to its group. "The organization was initially a thirty-piece bagpipe and drum corps attired in authentic Scottish costumes featuring the plaid of the McCain clan."[6]

MCCAIN'S VIEWS ON SCHOLARSHIP:
"IT'S NOT WORTH BOTHERING ABOUT"

"You can imagine how I felt," a USM English professor said angrily. "The day after I emphasized the seriousness of plagiarism to my freshmen classes, it turns out the president of the school has copied a paper verbatim." General McCain is not your average freshman term-paper plagiarizer. He has a solid academic record: Ph.D. in history from Duke University, director (for eighteen years) of the Mississippi State Department of Archives and History, and founder of the *Journal of Mississippi History*.[7]

What exactly had General McCain done? According to Mrs. Frances Melton Racine, he took virtually verbatim a large portion of her 1966 master's thesis and tried to pass it off as his own. The work in question, published in the November 1967 issue of the *Journal of Mississippi History*, is entitled "The Administration of David Holmes, Governor of Mississippi Territory, 1809-1820." McCain's article contains only one footnote in which he cites sources. There, the General states that he "relied heavily" on two master's theses: William Horton's thesis at the University of Colorado in 1935 and Mrs. Racine's 1966 Emory University thesis.[8] McCain added that he "consulted" twenty-two other sources which he also listed. Where he utilized any of them, if indeed he did consult them, is not evident, since there is not a single sentence in McCain's article which cannot be directly attributed to either the Racine or Horton thesis. Mrs. Racine initially wrote a detailed letter on 9 May 1968, to Dr. John E. Gonzales, editor of the *Journal of Mississippi History,* (and occupant of the William D. McCain chair of history at USM), setting out her complaint against use of her thesis in the McCain article without proper attribution. She stated:

> Even a cursory comparison of my thesis with Mr. McCain's article reveals that he has done more than "relied heavily" on it. He has, in fact, reproduced essential portions of it without my permission and without the permission of any authorized person at Emory University. In organization, interpretation, and narration, Mr. McCain's article is identical to my thesis. His article contains sixty-five (65) paragraphs. Sixty (60) of these vary only slightly, if at all, from what I wrote in my thesis. Often the language of my thesis is used verbatim: and Mr. McCain has made no pretense of using quotation marks or acknowledgments in footnotes.

Mrs. Racine went on to place side-by-side examples of sentences and paragraphs from her thesis and those in the McCain article showing they were identical with only an occasional word or comma changed. To illustrate, three of the paragraphs juxtaposed by Mrs. Racine were the following:

McCain's Article	Racine's Original Thesis
"He was empowered to decide questions of order, to recognize speakers on the floor, and to appoint committees. He voted only when the yeas and nays on an issue were demanded. Most of the work on the convention was done in the committee of the whole."	He was empowered to decide questions of order, to recognize speakers on the floor, and to appoint committees. He voted only when the yeas and nays on an issue were demanded. Most of the work of the convention was done in committees of the whole.
"The majority of the people of the Baton Rouge area want-	The majority of the people of the Baton Rouge area great-

ed to be annexed to the United States, but they did not want to go through the territorial stage to reach statehood. They wanted to be annexed as a state..."	ly desired to be annexed to the United States, but they did not want to go through the territorial stage to reach statehood. They wanted to be annexed by treaty as a state...
"The War Department, acting upon the authority of an act passed in a secret session of Congress on February 12, 1813, directed General Wilkinson to proceed against Mobile."	...the War Department, acting upon the authority of an act passed in a secret session of Congress on 12 February 1813 authorized General Wilkinson to proceed against the town of Mobile.[9]

A full year of fruitless exchanges between Mrs. Racine and Dr. Gonzales followed. (Dr. Gonzales excused the duplication by defending the McCain piece as a "summary article"—a scholarly classification apparently originating with Dr. Gonzales.) Finally, Mrs. Racine turned to the American Association of University Professors (AAUP) and the American Historical Association (AHA) for relief.[10] The AHA created a special committee of professional historians to inquire into the matter. In the judgment of the committee, "Dr. McCain's article represents a violation of approved scholarly usage with respect to another author's literary property." It added that General McCain's action "has significantly diminished the scholarly return in the form of publication which Mrs. Racine might reasonably have expected." The committee concluded that it "cannot agree with the editor and editorial board of the *Journal of Mississippi History* that the single reference to Mrs. Racine's thesis embedded in a long footnote was adequate or proper recognition for such extensive use of her material."[11]

Despite the seriousness of the charges against him—and his failure to offer rebuttal—General McCain rode out the storm. The majority of the USM faculty had been coerced into silence, and the concept of plagiarism was probably a bit too academic to arouse the interest of the Board of Trustees. Asked by the New Orleans *Times-Picayune* for a comment on the AHA committee finding, McCain said, "It's not worth bothering about. I don't have any time to follow that...[12]

MCCAIN'S POLITICAL PHILOSOPHY: "THE TIME IS NEAR WHEN THERE WILL BE LITTLE TO CHOOSE FROM BETWEEN OUR SYSTEM AND COMMUNISM"

General McCain's political views offer additional insight into his stunning personality. The General has a totally conspiratorial view of history. When trouble breaks out, McCain blames outside enemies and psychological misfits. In an incredible speech of welcome to the freshmen in September 1970, General McCain alleged that the radicals in America are part of an international conspiracy directed and financed from "a building just outside the airport in Prague."[13] And in December 1971, McCain told Hattiesburg Kiwanians

> I have found that when there is trouble with students, there are usually some faculty members in the background. There is a nationwide effort to destroy the leadership in this country, including that of the educational system. When they destroy the leadership, they will destroy the country.[14]

General McCain is a frequent contributor to *The Citizen,* a monthly journal of the segregationist White Citizens' Council. The November 1962 issue of *The Citizen* contained an article by McCain entitled "History Is Being Made in Mississippi Now!"

> The events which have taken place in recent weeks in relationship to the efforts of a negro to enter the University of Mississippi constitute the greatest test of constitutional authority in the United States since 1865...On Sunday, September 30, 1962, the Attorney General of the United States, callously and without regard for the officials of the University of Mississippi, forced the negro into the campus of the institution...The shocking conduct of the representatives and officials of the United States government displayed well the characteristics of a police state at its worst.

And on the political condition of the United States, the General wrote: "The fact seems evident that the United States is traveling down the road to socialism and the time is near when there will be little to choose from between our system and communism."[15] A year later, on 7 February 1964, General McCain told the Jackson Lions Club that the United States is slowly but surely surrendering "our freedoms to the United Nations. Large numbers of primitive nations of Africa have been admitted on a footing equal with us.

The great mystery of history is why the Negro peoples of Africa constitute the only branch of the human race which has never developed a high-level civilization of its own nor learned one from its neighbors." The General predicted that "the time will come when liberal planners in Washington who are bent on world government are able to have the armed forces of the United States turned over to the United Nations."

Moving to domestic policies, General McCain stated that thirty years ago the Democratic leaders lost control of their party and were superseded by a revolutionary group determined to use the "depression as an excuse to change our form of government." He said that every segment of the federal government was infiltrated by "liberals, socialists, communists, planners, do-gooders, one-worlders, bleeding hearts, and others... determined to destroy the powers of the states and the liberties of the people. They believed that a new system was necessary to control our political, economic, social and intellectual life, for the people, after all, were not competent to look after themselves." As a result, the General concluded, "It is likely that we will become owned, managed and spineless creatures of a paternalistic government centralized in Washington."[16]

Taking his politics seriously, in late 1961 General McCain, two FBI agents, and Mrs. Sara McCorkle, the director of the youth activities division of the segregationist White Citizens' Council, founded the Patriotic American Youth (PAY), an anti-Communist organization for Mississippi high school students. PAY annually sponsors a summer forum in which hundreds of high school students sit through five days of indoctrination sessions. The 1972 Forum held at USM on July 17-21 was ominously entitled "Our Heritage 1776-19??" The featured speakers were: Dr. Fred Schwartz founder and president of the Christian Anti-Communist Crusade; W. Cleon Skousen, editorial director of *Law and Order,* a police magazine, and author of *The Naked Communist;* John Noble, author of *I was a Slave in Russia* and *I Found God in Soviet Russia;* and Dr. Medford Evans, editor of the monthly journal of both the White Citizens' Council and the John Birch Society. Thirteen others, including General McCain, also spoke. Miraculously, McCain said recently: "I despise one end of the [political] spectrum as much as the other."[17]

MCCAIN'S RAPPORT WITH STUDENTS: "WE ARE GOING TO START SUING PEOPLE"

General McCain visited Mississippi Southern College as USM was called then, on 23 May 1955 while "making up his mind" whether to accept the Board of Trustees' offer of the college's presidency. After the crowd of more than 1000 Southern students was warmed up by the 313th Army Reserve unit band, the General said: "If you don't like the way I look or the way I talk, now's the time to say so—now's the time to run me off."[18] They didn't, and thus occurred another of history's momentous "lost opportunities."

General McCain makes no pretense of understanding today's college students and their problems. He told a group of 300 high school students on 17 July 1972:

> Two or three years ago when things were more trouble-some on college and university campuses, I had several of the hippie-type here to pay me a visit. And one of the things they said to me was, "You don't love us." And I had no answer for that: I didn't...This thing of young people saying that they don't know who they are, they want to find themselves, they can't identify themselves. And they told me those things; they've been telling me those things here, and I can't understand...And when people come to me wanting to find themselves, I don't know what they're talking about.[19]

At a luncheon for the Political Science Department on 28 September 1971, McCain was asked his opinion concerning student requests for representation on university committees. The General replied typically: "The demands are only a passing fad. There is nothing to worry about; no concessions will be granted."[20]

Concerning student conduct on campus, McCain expressed himself well in his 1967 spring progress report: the "image" of the university takes precedence over subversive abstractions like "student rights." The General said:

> We continue to have trouble with our weak and emaciated males. They still have to cling to the females as they walk on the campus or tenderly hang to other portions of the female anatomy. Animals carry on their affairs in public. Human beings are supposed to be trained by their parents

to conduct themselves properly in public. Some of the students seem to have no knowledge whatever of decent public conduct. I have made numerous statements on this subject...Do not try to tell me that I cannot change your morals. I knew that before you were born. I am, at least, asking that we conduct ourselves in public so as to give the people who pass our way a good image of this University.

We seem now to live in a world where men want to wear their hair down to their shoulders and women want to wear their skirts up to their rumps. I shall not comment on the skirts. Whatever any of you think about long hair on men, beards, and general disreputable appearance, we still do not like tramps and beatniks in our midst. We think that it is best for the University of Southern Mississippi and for the students if we all dress with reasonable propriety, and shave and bathe regularly, and visit the barber at decent intervals. Smelly and trampish students do the image of the University no good.

Then McCain ironically scolded the students for not being more friendly to him:

As I go about the campus, I have great difficulty in getting students to speak to me. I occasionally stop one who refuses to exchange greetings and ask for his name and station in life...One of these days a student who refused to speak to me is going to appear in my office for help when in trouble with the office of the Dean of Student Affairs. I will then have the opportunity to remind him of his previous discourtesy.[21]

McCain has encountered differences of opinion with the official representative of student sentiment on campus, the Student Senate. Following rumors of financial mismanagement in the operations of the university bookstore, the USM Student Senate on 1 February 1971, passed a resolution asking the Mississippi state legislature to formally investigate the allegations.[22] General McCain's response was predictable—a lawsuit threat. "We are going to start suing people—students who tear down the reputation of people in this community. We can cause a great deal of trouble and expense to their families." Describing the resolution as "malicious," McCain said that the action was taken by "people who have been causing trouble ever since they have been here." He personally added, "If my character is besmirched by any one individual, I am hauling him into court."[23]

On 13 March 1972, General McCain addressed the Student Senate for the first time in two years. (The last time McCain addressed the Senate, the group considered a resolution demanding his resignation as University president.) McCain began by saying:

> I wanted to boast this month to people around here. I have worked a long time in this world and this month I reach complete financial independence, to the extent that I can tell everybody to go to hell. And I'm proud to tell everybody about that.

The General concluded with this tour de farce:

> I think it was last spring that something arose in the senate about investigation—calling the legislative investigating committee to come and see how the money was being handled here. I tried to tell everybody who'd listen that the auditors are looking over my shoulder all the time. Here is the audit of USM...Now, if you ever read an auditor's report, the auditors never say you're honest; they only talk about when they find you dishonest. So, this doesn't say we're honest; it just says they didn't find anybody dishonest here in the past...I'm certain that there are dishonest things that go on here as in any big corporation. At least in this audit they didn't find anything dishonest.[24]

Chapter Three

THE KILLING OF CLYDE KENNARD

I have no doubt that Clyde Kennard's life and martyrdom are among the most significant events of our age.
— *Jacques Maritain,*
Catholic philosopher at Princeton's
Institute of Advanced Studies.

Before describing in detail the educational machinations at the University of Southern Mississippi, it is essential to place the institution in its proper political perspective. For in a hyperorthodox social order there is generally an elaborate political superstructure which controls most socializing agencies, and certainly one as vital as education. To illustrate Mississippi's monolithic political system of a decade ago, this chapter recounts the tragic story of Clyde Kennard. Kennard, a black, attempted to enroll at USM in September 1959; he died on 4 July 1963. The connection between these two events was more than coincidental; indeed, it was nothing less than a heinous conspiracy.

The Kennary tragedy is the perfect example of the hopelessness of being completely at the mercy of hostile and malicious forces, which is so characteristic of the Exit 13 syndrome. Moreover, the story perhaps better than any other encounter of the period—documented "the totalitarian society of Mississippi [which] impose[d] on all its people an obedience to an official othodoxy almost identical with the pro-slavery philosophy..."[1] This interlocking system was all-inclusive, embracing the centers of authority from the justice of the peace to the governor—including even the office of the university president. Referring to the Kennard affair, James Meredith incisively observed: "I would not question the individual integrity per se, of, say, the president of Mississippi Southern, but it would make no difference whether he was trustworthy or not, because under the system of 'White Supremacy' it is not the individual that counts, only the system. The system always prevails."[2]

APPLYING TO COLLEGE: "SHADY DEALINGS WERE DISCOVERED."

A native of Hattiesburg, Clyde Kennard served ten years as a paratrooper in Germany and in Korea.[3] He saved his money, and when he returned home he bought some land near Hattiesburg which he turned over to his mother and stepfather. Meanwhile, Kennard attended the University of Chicago meritoriously for three years. However, in 1955 his stepfather died and he had to come home to take over the farm and to take care of his mother. Kennard wanted to finish college, and the University of Southern Mississippi, then called Mississippi Southern College (MSC), was a fifteen-minute drive from his farm. Accordingly, over a period of three years he discussed the possibility of enrolling at MSC with President William D. McCain.[4] Because Kennard had already earned college credits in Chicago, and because he lived near MSC, a school supported completely by state tax funds, he felt justified in trying to enroll there.

Kennard submitted his application in the fall of 1959. The State Sovereignty Commission approached several of Kennard's friends to have them persuade him to withdraw his application. But on 15 September 1959, Kennard drove to MSC to meet with President McCain for a formal interview. Kennard took no special notice of a local civil rights leader's warning that McCain was in contact with the White Citizens' Council or of McCain's phone call that morning to find out just when he expected to be on campus. The interview with McCain was witnessed by the chief investigator for the Sovereignty Commission.

After the interview, Kennard returned to his locked car, which was parked in front of the Administrative Building, and that's when Old Dixieland lowered the boom. The most respected enforcer of the law known to Americans, the High Constable, arrested Kennard on charges of reckless driving. Kennard gave the constables his car keys. They took him in a car to the Hattiesburg police station and another policeman drove Kennard's car. And when this policeman walked into the station, he carried a sack of five bottles of whiskey which he claimed he found in Kennard's car. So Kennard was additionally charged with possession of liquor, then illegal in "dry" Mississippi.

Of course, Kennard's application to MSC was rejected. According to the official university statement, Kennard was denied admission because of "deficiencies and irregularities in his application papers." President McCain said that the MSC security police investigated Kennard's past and "shady dealings were discovered." McCain is alleged to have said that he could do more to "develop honesty, culture, and individual integrity as president of Mississippi Southern than he can in a silly martyrdom for one Negro."[5]

POSSESSING MOONSHINE: "THE STATE PROVED CLEARLY THE GUILT OF THE DEFENDANT."

On 28 September 1959, Kennard was tried before a Forrest County Justice of the Peace. The constables who arrested Kennard said they had received a "tip" that a load of whiskey was headed their way.[6] According to the constables, they had seen a speeding car on the highway, followed it, then lost it, picked it up again at MSC, and then waited for its driver to return. Under cross-examination, the constables said they could not understand how they got close enough to Kennard to read his license tag—they said they did—without being able to catch up with him. When it was pointed out that Kennard didn't drink, one of the constables pointedly remarked, "Most bootleggers don't." After hearing the testimony of the constables, the JP said he had never known a case "where the state proved more clearly the guilt of the defendant."[7]

In Mississippi it is customary for the defense to withhold its evidence and witnesses at the JP level when it intends to appeal to a higher court. Kennard's attorney followed this course. He posted a

$1500 appeal bond and said the matter would be taken to Forrest County Circuit Court. However, an appeal of Kennard's conviction was never heard. Because of misleading information given Kennard by the JP and the Forrest County district attorney, and to Kennard's attorney by the Forrest County jailor with whom bond was posted, the defense was not present at the setting of the docket for the appeal. Further appeals to have the original appeal heard were twice denied by Mississippi courts.

STEALING CHICKEN FEED: "THE PENALTY WOULD NORMALLY HAVE BEEN 90 DAYS AT MOST."

Although Kennard's application to MSC had been rejected, he could always try again. The Honorable Governor James P. Coleman reportedly had said that "if Clyde did reapply, they'd be no way of holding him out because his record was sufficient. There'd be no alternative but to close the college."[8] But surely hard-core Mississippi patriots could save the state from a potential Armageddon. In Mississippi there is a law which prohibits a felon from being admitted to a state school. If only Kennard would commit a felony like burglary for instance, the Mississippi establishment reasoned, any future attempt on his part to enroll at MSC could be legally denied.[9]

By a kind of coincidence that often works in Exit 13, it happened that on Saturday morning, 25 September 1960, the Forrest County Cooperative warehouse was burglarized of twenty-five dollars worth of chicken feed. Kennard was arrested as an accessory the same morning. A nineteen-year old black, Johnny Lee Roberts, who was employed by the co-op as a helper on the trucks, admitted to actually stealing the feed. Roberts said that he sold the feed to Kennard, and that Kennard bought it knowing it was stolen.[10]

On 21 November 1960, the farcical trial was held. The Forrest County Circuit Court found Roberts guilty of having stolen the feed and gave him a suspended sentence. (He did not even lose his job!) The all-white jury found Kennard guilty of having bought the feed. Judge Stanton A. Hall gave him the maximum sentence of seven years at hard labor. Everyone, of course, knew who Kennard was and what he had tried to do the previous year.

The tangible evidence in the case would have convicted Kennard of possession of stolen goods. But even assuming that Kennard was guilty of being an accessory in the theft, "the penalty for such a crime would normally have been 90 days at most."[11] The Jackson *State Times* commented that one year for each $3.57 stolen seemed rather severe; twenty-five dollars seemed to be petty larceny rather than burglary. The *State Times* was soon defunct.

In one of the more bizarre sidelights to the Kennard trial, Medgar Evers, who was then Mississippi field representative of the NAACP, was convicted in December 1960, of contempt of court for an *out-of-court* criticism of the Kennard conviction. Forrest County Circuit Judge Stanton A. Hall fined Evers $100 and sentenced him to days 30 days in jail. In a statement issued in Jackson after the trial, Evers had called Kennard's conviction "the greatest mockery to judicial justice...in a courtroom of segregationists, apparently resolved to put Kennard legally away."[12]

DYING IN PRISON: "THIS ISN'T AMERICA. THIS IS DACHAU AND AUSCHWITZ."

The remainder of Clyde Kennard's life was truly wretched. It is best told by Kennard's close personal friend, John Howard Griffin, author of *Black Like Me*. In a July 1964 interview, Griffin said:

He was put in a prison and at first was treated well. Soon he developed intestinal cancer and was put in the hospital at Jackson. But it happened that this was at the time James Meredith made his first tentative move to enter the University of Mississippi. Clyde Kennard and James Meredith had no connection whatsoever, but through a strange kind of vengeance Clyde Kennard was taken out of the hospital and put on the hardest work gang at the penitentiary— the sunup to sundown gang. Though his cancer developed rapidly, this extraordinary man spent his Sundays writing thirty or forty letters for inmates who could not read or write, and he began to set up classes to teach reading and writing. But he rapidly became too ill. He wrote his sister, a registered nurse in Chicago, that he was beginning to hemorrhage. She reached the doctor at Jackson who immediately ordered Clyde Kennard back into the hospital. The doctor's prognosis was that Clyde had less than a twenty percent chance of surviving under optimum conditions.

The warden refused to let him go back to the hospital.

As he became very weak he began to realize they were deliberately allowing him to die. He would be carried out in the mornings, and he would work until he would collapse, and he would be carried back. And when he began to collapse before noon, they would carry him back, put him in his bed, and if he did not get up and walk to the mess hall, he would go without food because they did not allow food to be brought to him.

Finally, a group of us, Martin Luther King, Dick Gregory, and others, discussed this and we began to put pressure on Governor Ross Barnett. We vitually said that if Clyde Kennard died in prison it would be murder because he would not have been allowed treatment.[13]

Almost immediately he was released, and we found out these last events. His mother and sister had gone to see him and bring him food, They found him bleeding badly, starving, and weighing less than 100 pounds. The next morning when the prisoners came to carry him out to work, they said they could carry him out but that they would have to leave him on the ground, because he would not work any longer. He hemorrhaged badly that night.

They saw that it was useless to carry him out and they called a guard. A guard came and carried him in a car to the prison doctor. The guard's only words to Clyde were, "Damn you, if you mess up this car, I'll kick you out." The guard left Clyde in the waiting room. After two or three steps Clyde's legs gave way, and this great man, this enormously gifted man, this American soldier and scholar ended up crawling on his belly to the doctor's room. And the doctor said, "We know what's happened. You can't pull this kind of thing. I know that smart-alec sister of yours brought you some food and she probably put some pills in it which made you sick so you wouldn't have to go on the work gang." Clyde asked the doctor to examine him and see if this were possible. The doctor did, and he saw that Clyde Kennard was very close to death. Presumably he notified Governor Barnett, who immediately gave an indefinite pardon so he wouldn't have Clyde's body on his hands.

Clyde Kennard was brought to Chicago for an eight-hour operation and briefly there was hope for temporary recovery. I went on and got as far as Cincinnati, where I received a call asking me to come to see him. The doctor said he had given up hope, and that he could not keep him alive if he did not have the will to live. I replied that this did not sound like Clyde, and the doctor told me that Clyde had been allowed visitors and someone had told him that a few days previously vandals had moved onto his place at night and had burned down some of the buildings he had built. This seemed to be the final blow for him.

I returned to Chicago. We got the post-operative tests that showed that we were too late and Clyde would be dead in a few weeks. I went in to see him. He was a tiny little dwarf. He lay with a sheet pulled on up over his face so no one could see the grimace of pain on that face. Only his hands stuck out. He was the who consoled us. And he said something that almost killed me. He said, "Mr. Griffin, I'd be glad it happened if only it would show this country where racism finally leads. But the people aren't going to know it, are they?" But I said, "They'll know it, if I have to tell it in every lecture."

Then this man who had suffered such agony for three years said: "Be sure and tell them what happened to me isn't as bad as what happened to the guard, because this system has turned him into a beast, and it will turn his children into beasts."

This man died with this kind of magnanimity, sending out this kind of message. When he died I asked his mother, "How can we stand it?" This isn't America. This is Dachau and Auschwitz. This was a man who had great things to contribute, and because he wanted to finish his education in an area where he had every right, where his tax dollar supported the school, he was thrown to the mad dogs and ended up a martyr.[14]

There is one last bit of grim symbolism to the Kennard story. Clyde Kennard died on 4 July 1963, exactly one hundred years to the day after the fall of Vicksburg, the turning point in the Civil War. On 27 October 1971, I asked a gathering of over 350 students at the University of Southern Mississippi if they had ever heard of Clyde Kennard. Only one student had—a transfer student from the University of Chicago.

Chapter Four

THE BOARD OF TRUSTEES: ACCOUNTABLE ONLY TO GOD

The mind of a bigot is like the pupil of an eye. The more light you pour into it, the more it contracts.
—*Oliver Wendell Holmes*

It should be reemphasized that the state's eight public institutions of higher learning are not autonomous; rather, they are controlled by an intransigent and nearly monolithic political structure. By way of illustration, the chancellor of the University of Mississippi (Ole Miss) said in 1961 that steps to prevent desegregation of Mississippi's white senior colleges "will not be made at the university," but they will be mapped "in Jackson" by the governor, legislature, and the board of trustees.[1] In a similar vein, USM President William D. McCain pointed out that as an employee of the board of trustees, he had only two choices in the Clyde Kennard case: to follow their decision or to resign.[2]

Higher education in Mississippi is controlled by thirteen aging retrogressives, otherwise known as the board of trustees of State Institutions of Higher Learning. Therefore, this chapter studies the policies of this group during the past two decades, to test the persistence of Mississippi's "closed society" in which dissenters from the orthodox view of white supremacy are silenced. The two areas of specific concentration are the board's racial politics and its posture concerning academic freedom (freedom of inquiry and expression).

28

THE 1930 IMBROGLIO: "IT WAS THE MOST NOTORIOUS AND DISGRACEFUL ACT IN THE HISTORY OF AMERICAN EDUCATION."

Before reviewing the politics of the board of trustees in the 1960s and 1970s, it is enlightening to flash back to the actions of the board in 1930, which established the standards of intellectual liberty and academic freedom for future boards to emulate. On 13 June 1930, Mississippi Governor Theodore G. Bilbo (himself born on 13 October 1877) swaggered out of a meeting of the board of trustees to greet the waiting reporters. "Boys," said he, with a ring of pride in his voice, "We've just hung up a new record. We've bounced three college presidents and made three new ones in the record time of two hours. And that's just the beginning of what's going to happen."[3] This was Bilbo's inimitable way of proclaiming that the spoils system henceforth was to be the rule in the appointments of all state and college officials, from the presidents to the grass cutters. It was a declaration of war upon the immunity of education from political influence and corruption, a war which cost 179 officials and faculty members of the 5 state colleges their positions.[4] The only institution to escape slaughter was Alcorn Agricultural and Mechanical College for Negroes. The reason for this was obvious: there were no aspirants for jobs at that institution.[5]

The people of the state and indeed the nation were shocked beyond measure. The editor of the Jackson *Daily News* wrote that the faculty was not merely revised. "It was ravished. Criminally, assaulted without reason, justification, or excuse."[6] Chancellor James H. Kirkland of Vanderbilt University exclaimed, "It was the most notorious and disgraceful act in the history of American Education." The newly elected college presidents were kept waiting in an outside office while the board of trustees ripped out the old faculties and named the successors. When the changes had been made, lists were handed to the new presidents.[2] Upon receiving the blacklist of victims, Hugh Critz, the president of Mississippi A&M College, was so stunned by its magnitude that he said to reporters: "Many of them are my friends and others are higher trained in their technical professions and I do not see how they are going to be replaced. I am shocked and paralyzed. Indeed, gentlemen, it has sent me through the Garden of Gethsemane."[9]

Moreover, none of the beneficiaries of the board's generosity had any assurance of security. Their jobs could be lopped off at any minute "at the pleasure of the Board." They were not even assured of two weeks' notice; they could be fired like "common laborers." So they were advised in this illuminating notice to the heads of all departments:

> Ordered, that the heads of all institutions give notice to each member of the faculty and all their employees: that they are all subject to the pleasure of this board and to immediate discharges by the heads of these institutions for any cause whatsoever.[10]

The Bilbo-packed board of trustees rewarded a number of the governor's legislative supporters with college positions. The new vice chancellor at Ole Miss, who also held the office of dean of Men and head of the Department of Philosophy and Psychology, had been a state senator and Bilbo floor leader.[11] The dean of the Ole Miss School of Law, who held Ph.D. and L.L.B. degrees, was demoted to a professorship and replaced by a Democratic national committeeman and political friend of Bilbo. One law professor who was author of *The Code of Mississippi*, which had been used in the courts since 1906, was dropped from the faculty and replaced by someone who had never won a degree but who managed the campaign for Governor Bilbo's candidate for Lieutenant-Governor. Some of Bilbo's friends were not given teaching positions but they won jobs nevertheless. A "Young Guard" administration floor leader in the legislature became Ole Miss night watchman. Several senators were given assignments as proctors. One legislator drew the honorable position of "captain of grass cutters."[12]

Reverberations of horror and official denunciation followed. The American Medical Association, the American Association of Law Schools, the American Association of University Professors, the American Association of University Women, and most importantly, the Southern Association of College and Secondary Schools all suspended the Mississippi colleges. One of the trustees proposed a "solution" to the problem which now faced the state. Launching a tirade against the "tyranny" of the Southern Association of Colleges and Secondary Schools and crying, "The doctrine of state rights is not dead," he called upon the schools of Mississippi to defy the sentence of suspension, form their own accrediting association, and summon other states to secede from the Southern Association and form a new one.[13] If at first you don't secede...

THE CLENNON KING CASE: "ANY NIGGER WHO TRIES TO ENTER OLE MISS MUST BE CRAZY."

Wilson F. Minor, a highly perceptive columnist for the New Orleans *Times-Picayune,* characterized the Mississippi Board of Trustees in April 1972, as "the Damocles sword which for a decade has been over the head of higher education because of the segregationist, intransigent philosophy."[14] The following three sections of this chapter substantiate Minor's statement.

Probably the single most destructive conflict produced by the Board of Trustees' defiance of federal court desegregation orders was the riot on 20 September 1962, which accompanied the admission of James Meredith into Ole Miss. Meredith got into the university all right, with a little help from his friends (30,000 U.S. troops and 500 federal marshalls). However, the purely physical price was 2 killed, 30 wounded by gunfire, and over 300 struck by flying bricks and bottles.[15]

The Board of Trustees at first simply had prohibited any action on Meredith's admission request. But the height of absurdity occurred later when the Board abrogated its own constitutional responsibility by naming Governor Ross Barnett acting registrar at Ole Miss in order to block Meredith.[16] The Southern Association of College and Secondary Schools placed Mississippi's institutions on "extraordinary status" because of political interference.[17]

While nearly everyone knows of the James Meredith saga the forgotten man in Mississippi's desegregation history is Clennon King. A black Reverend and history professor at all-black Alcorn A&M College in Mississippi, King actually was an employee of the Board of Trustees in the late 1950s. Already holding a master's degree from Western Reserve, and having done work toward a Ph.D at Ohio State and the University of Chicago, King desired to further his doctoral studies at Ole Miss. Accordingly, on 5 June 1958, he attempted to enroll there. The board showed its displeasure by having him hauled off to an insane asylum.

Mississippi Governor James P. Coleman had set up an elaborate arrangement of highway patrolmen to follow King from the moment he boarded a bus in Gulfport until he arrived at Ole Miss,

400 miles later.[18] When King arrived on campus the Ole Miss registrar told him that his application couldn't be processed until after the last day of resistration. King said that when he sought to leave the registrar's office he was forced out another entrance by highway patrolmen. Student witnesses on the campus said King was carried to a waiting station wagon and sped away.[19]

King was placed in a cell on the top floor of the Highway Patrol headquarters building in Jackson. After being held incommunicado for twenty hours, he was examined by two doctors following a statement by Governor Coleman that King "went beserk" during his attempt to register at Ole Miss. The physicians examined King before the Chancery Court and recommended that he be committed to the state mental hospital at Whitfield for examination. He was ordered committed, but not before the chancellor ejected King's black attorney from the courtroom, charging the lawyer with "interfering with the examination of Clennon King while under the influence of alcohol or goofballs."[20]

King was hauled off to the state mental hospital on June 6.[21] After holding him at Whitfield for thirteen days, "the doctors demonstrated their lack of understanding by ruling him sane."[22] Sane or not, King had demonstrated the impracticality of assuming that a black could gain admission at Ole Miss without going to court. According to Governor Coleman, any black who would attempt to enter the all-white institution was by definition "a lunatic."[23] Mississipians followed the governor's lead with the more direct comment, "Any nigger who tries to enter Ole Miss must be crazy."[24] The day after his release from Whitfield, King fled to his native Albany, Georgia, "for his own safety."[25]

Reverend King made news more recently as a result of another quixotic crusade—his celebrated unsuccessful attempt to join Jimmy Carter's segregated Baptist Church in Plains, Georgia on Halloween Day, 1976.

PARTICIPATING IN INTERCOLLEGIATE ATHLETICS: "THE GREATEST CHALLENGE TO OUR WAY OF LIFE SINCE RECONSTRUCTION."

The board of trustees was determined to maintain racial segregation even if a few token blacks had to be admitted into the state's colleges. On 28 August 1964, the board prohibited all blacks not enrolled as students or working as employees from entering public buildings on the campuses of the white institutions. The board's order deputized white employees of the Ole Miss cafeteria with the power of arresting black "intruders." This policy was enforced on 9 September 1964, when parents of two black students at Ole Miss were denied permission to eat in the university cafeteria.[26]

Intercollegiate athletic events created even more ominous threats to Mississippi's Revised Standard Version of the Constitution. A crisis erupted in the fall of 1964 when there was great fear of an "invasion" by black students from Memphis State University at the Ole Miss football game. One member of the board of trustees insisted that all Memphis State blacks be arrested at the Oxford, Mississippi, city limits.[27]

But the most chilling threats to "old magnolia" obviously would occur when Mississippi athletes ventured out-of-state. Rising to the occasion, the board in 1956 ruled against colleges participating in racially integrated athletic events. During three seasons Mississippi State won the Southeastern Conference basketball championship, but had to reject a bid to the NCAA tournament. Finally, in the spring of 1963, Mississippi faced what one member of the board of trustees called "the greatest challenge to our way of life since Reconstruction." Mississippi State had won another SEC basketball title and the new university president said it might actually participate in the NCAA tournament this time.[28]

SEGREGATED HIGHER EDUCATION IN 1974: "THE COSTLIEST BATTLE."

After a decade of federal lawsuits and discreditation threats, what is the current status of desegregation in Mississippi colleges? Nothing short of shocking! The "opposite-race" enrollment figures which the U.S. Department of Health, Education, and Welfare reported for 1973-74 in Mississippi colleges revealed, for instance, that 11 years after James Meredith entered Ole Miss the university was still 96.7 percent white, and only 1 out of the 395 faculty members on the Oxford campus was black. The HEW figures also showed that there were only eight black faculty members on the five "white" campuses. Rather remarkably, blacks comprised 99.8 percent of the student body at Mississippi's three "traditionally black" colleges.[29]

While the board of trustees apparently thought that a few black football players running around the field wearing Ole Miss uniforms put everything in perfect order on the score of desegregation, HEW had other ideas. On several occasions HEW rejected the board of trustees' rather feeble attempts to submit a desegregation plan. Finally, on 21 June 1974, HEW announced acceptance of college desegregation plans in eight states but said it was referring the case of a ninth state—Mississippi—to the Justice Department for legal action.[30] This set the stage for what columnist Wilson F. Minor called "the last great battle in the dismantling of Mississippi's long-time segregated way of educating its young people, and possibly the costliest battle in terms of money, in the state's higher education system." What was at stake was $40 to $50 million a year in essential federal funds for Mississippi higher education. Nevertheless, the board of trustees claimed that it considered itself in compliance with the 1964 Civil Rights Act and reverted to some of its Barnett-era logic, saying that it could not "understand" what federal authorities wanted.[31]

THE SPEAKER BAN CONTROVERSY: "THIS IS NOT THE DITCH I CHOOSE TO DIE IN."

In addition to its intransigent racial bias, the board of trustees has demonstrated a penchant for undermining academic freedom, as manifested in its so-called "speaker ban." "Dissent has been suspect in Dixie since talk of abolition first made slaves—and master—nervous."[32] Thus wrote Ken Vinson in June 1968, and for that and similar statements he made in an article entitled "Trustees of the Closed Society," Vinson was banished from his position as professor at the Ole Miss Law School.[33] Firing professors and refusing to admit undesirable students was easy enough, but by the mid-fifties the Board had still another problem on its hands: how to block "black outside speakers and other liberal rifraff from Mississippi campuses."[34]

The idea that civil liberties are part of some kind of communist trick became apparent to the Board of Trustees in 1955, when a professed pacifist spoke at Mississippi Southern College. The Hattiesburg *American* branded his work as "dangerous talk"[35] and thereby began a reaction which resulted in the board adopting a "speaker screening" resolution. This edict required the heads of colleges to investigate and approve every speaker invited to the campus and to file a statement of approval with the board. Although the regulation specified no criteria for approval or review, it was not hard to know what it meant.[36]

During the spring of 1956, the Reverend Alvin Kershaw, an Episcopal minister of Oxford, Ohio, was scheduled to appear as a Religious Emphasis Week speaker at Ole Miss. But the invitation was withdrawn when it became known that Kershaw had announced over nationwide television that he planned to give part of his winnings on a TV quiz show to the NAACP. The Ole Miss chancellor placated his faculty on this issue by saying, "This is not the ditch I choose to die in."[37] Religious Emphasis Week was thereafter permanently abolished. A few years later, Professor Joseph J. Mathews, the 1964 president of the Southern Historical Association, was paid his full fee for *not* delivering a history lecture after the shocking disclosure that his wife had written in the *Saturday Evening Post* of her experiences teaching black students in Atlanta.[38] Then Al Capp was declared ineligible to speak at Ole Miss because of rumors that he had used dirty words at Texas Christian University.[39]

Some folks, for instance college students, just need looking after. Accordingly, during the sixties, the board of trustees barred integrationists such as Senators Hubert Humphrey and Paul Douglas from state campuses. Martin Luther King and Bishop James Pike were banned. William Sloane Coffin was not permitted to speak on the Vietnam War. A Quaker minister from Japan, visiting Oxford, spoke on U.S. war policies in Southeast Asia—and the University of Mississippi got a court order enjoining such dangerous talk.[40]

In the spring of 1966, a censor motion before the Board failed to carry and Senator Robert Kennedy was allowed in the coliseum at Ole Miss. In his talk Kennedy recounted, counteroffer by counteroffer, the lengthy hot-line negotiations between Governor Ross Barnett and the Kennedys which had preceded the Oxford riots. How many U.S. marshals did Governor Barnett want on "stage" to "force" James Meredith past the standing-tall governor? Were the marshals to draw guns or would merely putting hands on holsters satisfy? Obviously, Kennedy's talk signaled that there was too much free speech at Ole Miss![41]

In October 1966, Mississippi State University President William Giles refused a YMCA petition for five guest speakers. Senator Edward Kennedy was snubbed because Giles thought "it would appear rather poor for MSU to sponsor the younger brother of Robert Kennedy since the latter appeared at Ole Miss last spring." Aaron Henry was rejected because, according to President Giles, "his appearance on our campus could cause considerable damage in relationships within the Negro community."[42] Henry was the state NAACP president!

Henry eventually spoke on the Starkville campus—but not until a band of MSU students threatened to file a First Amendment suit in federal court. President Giles, afraid of bad publicity, took his NAACP problem to the board of trustees. Visibly shaken, the guardians of Mississippi's Magnolia Curtain backed off from the lawsuit and allowed the enemy into MSU this once. However, on the same day that Henry spoke at MSU—17 November 1966—the board passed the "Aaron Henry speaker ban," a regulation which said:

> [Not to be invited are] speakers who will do violence to the academic atmosphere of the respective institutions; and persons in disrepute in the area from whence they come, and those charged with crimes or other moral wrongs shall not be invited...[43]

In the summer of 1967 the chairman of the Ole Miss Department of Political Science invited Aaron Henry to speak to a class in a civics institute conducted for high school teachers. Acting on orders from the sharp-eyed trustees, the Ole Miss chancellor fired "Professor" Henry in a letter reminding Henry that he had once been accused of a moral wrong. The Justice of the Peace of Bolivar County, Mississippi, had convicted Henry of disturbing the peace.[44]

CHARLES EVERS ON A MISSISSIPPI CAMPUS: "A BOLL WEEVIL SIX FEET LONG!"

At last, the board of trustees was in command again, with ever watchful college presidents screening all invited speakers and with absolute veto authority reserved for the board. However, there was one hitch: suppose that the board was informed only *after* the speaker was approved and invited. This loophole proved to be the Board's undoing.

In October 1968, Mississippi State President Giles approved Charles Evers, then state NAACP field secretary, as a campus speaker. After the invitation to Evers was issued, Giles reported this fact to the board of trustees. The Old South patricians held a hasty meeting and ordered Giles to "request" that the students withdraw the invitation to Evers. The students refused to so the board simply prohibited Evers from speaking. The MSU Young Democrats sued in federal district court. After hearing this case, William G. Keady, Chief U.S. Judge for Mississippi's Northern District, stated on 21 October 1968, that the board of trustees' actions had been "arbitrary and irrational...a disservice to the state of Mississippi, and damaging to the independence of college administrators." Finding that there had been "various if not curious application of the regulation," Keady turned the entire matter over to the Fifth Circuit Court of Appeals to rule on the constitutionality of the board's policy.[45]

The three-judge federal court on 14 January 1969, found the board's speaker policy unconstitutional on its face. Judge James P. Coleman declared, "These regulations can never be enforced on any of these state supported campuses." The board was given sixty days to write a more specific list of rules governing speakers that was not unconstitutionally vague."[46]

The board of trustees submitted its new policy to the judgment of the courts in March 1969. Unlike the old speaker ban policy which was very unclear and very illegal, the board's new one was very clear and very illegal. In fact, the new policy was so specific as to be potentially more crippling than ever. The new regulations— thirteen in number—banned any speakers who *might* incite riots or whose presence *might* cause a riot. Banned also were announced candidates for public office, speakers who come from off-campus for a religious meeting, and anyone who had been convicted of a felony or crime of moral turpitude.[47]

Not surprisingly, in December 1969, the federal court held all thirteen regulations unconstitutional. Since the board showed no apparent inclination to write a policy that satisfied the radical dictates of the U.S. Constitution, the court itself wrote a policy. Subsequently, on 9 March 1970, sixteen months and twenty-one days after he was originally invited by the Young Democrats, Charles Evers finally spoke at Mississippi State University.[48] No riots occurred.

BOARD PRESIDENT M.M. ROBERTS: "I HOPE CHARLES EVERS SMELLED LIKE NEGROES USUALLY DO."

While the board of trustees controls higher education in Mississippi, the Board itself was dominated from 1960 to 1972 by its president, M.M. Roberts, a Hattiesburg attorney and USM alumnus who was 76 years old at the time he stepped down from the board.[49] Indeed, Roberts was chiefly responsible for blazing the downward path of higher education in Mississippi.

Roberts' career as a student at the University of Southern Mississippi spanned exactly fifty years. He entered USM (then called Mississippi Normal College) in the fall of 1914, just two years after it opened, and received a diploma in 1918. Roberts earned a law degree in 1926 from Ole Miss, where he was a classmate of Governor Ross Barnett. It may be surprising that Mississippi's board of trustees accepted a student board member long before most other states, but trustee Roberts did attend USM in the early 60s, receiving a Ph.D. in educational administration at the age of sixty-eight in 1964.

Throughout his life, Roberts has been a highly successful practicing attorney in Hattiesburg. Although much of the twentieth century is alien to him, he recognized the virtue of old-fashioned hard work. A lawyer friend of Roberts' passed through Hattiesburg early one morning and asked a janitor when Roberts might be in the office. "You look down that street there at exactly seven o'clock and you'll see Mr. Roberts coming, running." Lawyers who oppose Roberts in the courtroom say the M.M. stands for Many Motions.[50] According to one Ole Miss law professor, Roberts goes to the jury and builds a case out of, as one Mississippi lawyer put it, "Bias, passion and prejudice." The formula appears to have worked very well for him.[51]

Roberts came to politics late in life; that is, he wasn't appointed to the board of trustees until 1960, when Governor Ross Barnett packed the board with rigid segregationists. Trustee Roberts confirmed Barnett's trust when he voted in August 1963, to withhold James Meredith's diploma, even though Meredith had completed all requirements for graduation from Ole Miss.[52] Later, in December 1969, Roberts told a group of USM professors that he guessed he was "when you get right down to it," a racist. "I have no apologies" said Roberts, adding that he was brought up to believe in God, Mississippi, and the principles of the Old South. These principles led Roberts and others to offer $20,000 to Ole Miss law professor Mike Trister—fired by Ole Miss because of his civil rights activities—if Trister would drop his academic freedom complaint. Trister refused the money.[53]

The board of trustees frequently had depended upon Roberts' legal talents. In fact, on 19 April 1972, the president of the board boasted that "We have relied on him over the years to keep us out of jail. It's been very close several times."[54] In 1970, in recognition of (among other things) Roberts' contributions as president of the board, the American Association of University Professors censured the rest of the university for its academic repression.

But it was with regard to the speaker ban controversy that Roberts proved unable to thwart the judicial blows to the "Magnolia Curtain." Following Robert Kennedy's appearance at Ole Miss in the spring of 1966, a very embarrassed Roberts explained, "My prayer is that the one-teacher school will return."[57] Roberts then personally drafted the "Aaron Henry speaker ban." When Charles Evers challenged the board of trustees' speaker policy, trustee Roberts naturally served as the board's defense attorney. But for all his histrionics, Roberts "proved his own worst enemy...in a performance which left skeptical even presiding Judge J.P. Coleman...a former Governor of Mississippi."[56] Roberts contended that speeches by Evers "do violence to the attitude of the fathers and mothers who send their children to school." The board president's most convincing argument was that his birthday was on the day of the proposed Evers speech, and that if Evers were allowed to speak, he, Roberts, would not have a happy birthday.[57] The board's regulations were invalidated after opening arguments.

Shaken to his magnolia core, Roberts was determined to have the last word. On 10 March 1970, Roberts wrote a widely circulated letter to his co-trustees, lamenting the federal court injunction barring board interference with Charles Evers' speech at Mississippi State University the night before. The board president explained Roberts' rules of campus order:

> I have a feeling of despair. Somehow, I wish it were so that we could clean house for those who do not understand Mississippi and its ways of life, but I guess this is expecting too much of our Board. If I had my way, we would have one rule about speakers and that is that no one would be permitted on any campus of any school in this State except those who

appear for classroom teaching. If I had my way, we would stop using funds collected from students for the operation of student newspapers. My information is that a sophomore Negro has a prominent place on the student newspaper staff at Mississippi State. Somehow, I cannot believe that Mississippi State is no longer a cow college. It is controlled by the influx of foreign ideologies, maybe city slickers.

Roberts' concluded his letter with this extraordinary passage:

One of the interesting things was that this President of the Young Democrats testified that they were going to have an unusual luncheon for Charles Evers before he spoke at 7:30 last night. I know they enjoyed it. I hope he smelled like Negroes usually do.[58]

In December 1969, Roberts addressed a meeting of the American Association of University Professors at USM. His speech, which could best be labeled, "Racism: Love It or Leave"—was reported in such nationally important periodicals as the *New York Times* and *Newsweek*.[59] With typical candor, Roberts said:

I have been on the Board for nine and a half years now, and some of them haven't been so pleasant. The first real task I had for myself was to try to decide what to do with [James] Meredith going to the University of Mississippi, and I said "no, he won't go." I felt like he would go over my dead body. But as I've gone along through the years and looked back I've said to myself really that I am a racist. Everytime I read a definition I say, "Well, that's me." I have no apologies for it, though. It's me.

Roberts then stated that there was no possibility of large numbers of fulltime black faculty members being hired in the near future:

I hope none of you are stirring for that kind of thing. I think if you want to be a stupid idiot just stir for that kind of thing. That's a thing that's destructive, and one who thinks it seriously in his heart ought to get out of here and get out of this institution, because you don't belong in our society if you think that is necessary—a thing we've got to do.

Roberts told the scholars that next to Jim Crow he had the greatest admiration for Governor Theodore Bilbo:

He's the one who got us off accreditation, and I got tired of hearing that. Somebody said, "If we don't do this we'll lose our accreditation," and I always said, "To hell with it," you know, because what do we have? Do we have education for accreditation, or do we have it to educate boys and girls?

The board president ended his speech by urging professors to

say kindly things about your fellows, about your institutions, and about the administrative heads, and be very kindly disposed in a Christian manner...It really ought to be a rule on the campus of every institution that if one wants to talk about the other, they ought to leave. If they don't like their environment, they ought to leave, and that applies to presidents, vice presidents, and all the rest.[60]

Clearly, President Roberts was fighting a rear guard effort against the twentieth century. Even at Ole Miss the Maginot Line against time was crumbling. Ole Miss' Young Republican Club, Student Senate and Omicron Delta Kappa chapter joined the school's Intrafraternity Council and Mortar Board (the latter two groups by unanimous vote) in calling for Roberts' resignation from the board of trustees.[61] In even more spectacular fashion, on 11 December 1969, the USM Progressive Student Association passed the following resolution:

Be it therefore resolved by the University of Southern Mississippi Progressive Student Association: That Dr. Roberts, not being in agreement with the majority sentiments in the United States, accept our offer of two hundred eighty one dollars and one cent to help purchase him a one-way airplane ticket to the Union of South Africa...[62]

Roberts did not accept the students' plane ticket offer. But when his twelve year term on the board of trustees expired in 1972, Roberts did accept the board's offer to continue serving as their lawyer. Thus, somewhat ironically, the self-confessed racist was given the job of drawing up plans for the desegregation of colleges— plans which were totally and flatly rejected by HEW. Roberts' cryptic reply to this rejection, "We are in troubled times,"[63] holds true not only for the board of trustees that Roberts represents, but also for all higher education.

Referring to the board of trustees' reaffirmation, in August

1974, of its traditional policy of closing its meetings to the public, the Mississippi Coast Crime Commission said that the board was, in effect, saying, "We are accountable to no one—not the governor, not the legislature, and certainly not the people."[64] Accountable only to God!

As a final irony, the board of trustees in March 1975 voted to name the new 36,000-seat football stadium at the University of Southern Mississippi in honor of M.M. Roberts—a stadium, where black athletes are now among the key performers.

THE BOARD PRESIDENT DEFENDS THE UNIVERSITY PRESIDENT: "WHAT HE SAID WAS NOT THAT UNUSUAL."

Perhaps M.M. Roberts' most outstanding achievement on behalf of higher education in Mississippi occurred in a recent series of bizarre courtroom episodes that might best be labeled "Perry Mason in Wonderland." In April 1978, Raymond Mannoni, dean of the USM School of Fine Arts, was indicted by the Forrest County Grand Jury for allegedly embezzling $400 in band company money. After testifying on Mannoni's behalf on 23 August 1978, USM President McCain was cited for contempt of court for the use of profanity in the courtroom. For his defense attorney, McCain turned to the dean of Hattiesburg's lawyers, his longtime friend, M.M. Roberts.

Roberts clearly had a difficult case. In fact, on 8 September 1978, President McCain was convicted of the contempt of court charges, fined $500 and given a thirty-day suspended sentence. Before sentencing McCain, the Forrest County Circuit judge said that in 1956 when President McCain presented him with a citizenship award during USM graduation exercises, that he never dreamed he would be presiding over contempt proceedings against McCain in 1978. But, the judge added, "No individual is above or below the process of this court or the system."[65]

Specifically, the district attorney's petition to the circuit court charged President McCain with directing "profane, vulgar, and indecent language toward Forrest County Prosecutor George Phillips." According to the petition, upon being excused from the witness stand following his testimony in the Mannoni trial, McCain "proceeded to the rear of the courtroom and then and there...stated in a hostile and threatening manner...'that damn son-of-a-bitch' " and directed other foul language toward Phillips. Other reports of the incident alleged that McCain also stated, "If I see him [Phillips] on the street, I'll beat his damn brains out."[66]

Although a number of persons had been subpoened to testify for the September 8 hearing on the charges against McCain, the president's attorneys presented no defense for their client. However, head defense attorney, M.M. Roberts, did address the court, asserting that *because McCain was a retired army general, "what he said was not that unusual."* Following the guilty verdict for his client, Roberts remarked, "I'm not going to be run over."[67]

Roberts, the patriarch of Hattiesburg jurisprudence for half a century, was indeed prophetic. On September 13, just five days after he had verbally sentenced McCain for the contempt of court charge, the Forrest County circuit court judge filed a written order in which he ruled that he had lacked the authority to convict McCain from the bench, in effect setting aside the proceedings against the USM president. On October 23, the judge scheduled a new trial to give McCain the opportunity to present his defense and cross-examine the state's witnesses. In addition, the judge acceded to the request of McCain's attorney that his client be tried before a panel of his peers.[68]

Not surprisingly, on November 14, the McCain contempt of court trial ended in a *mistrial.* The jury reported that after four hours of deliberation, it was hopelessly deadlocked at eight to four, but it did not report what the majority opinion was.[69] Almost one year later, in August 1979, the charge of contempt of court against President McCain was nol-prossed when the Forrest County district attorney made an unopposed motion not to prosecute the case. Another client of M.M. Roberts had not been "run over."

Chapter Five

STUDENT LIFE THROUGH THE LOOKING GLASS

The student is a passive recipient of university services, that's all he is. Rather like a welfare recipient.
—Charles Wilson
Vice Chancellor, UCLA

Having established the political environment within which Mississippi colleges function, let's return to the University of Southern Mississippi to begin a concentrated study of its "career oriented" education. While this chapter provides a general survey of student life at USM, the following section is a detailed case study of the largest department in the school's College of Liberal Arts— the Department of Political Science.

A TOUR OF THE SOUTHERN CAMPUS

The buildings on the USM campus reflect the authoritarian personality of the university's ruling structure. They seem to have been built to serve as monuments to administrators obsessed with their own power, with little regard to the fact that buildings are supposed to serve students' educational needs. In fact, the last three major buildings constructed on the USM campus have been named by the Mississippi College Board of Trustees in honor of a USM dean, the USM president, and the College Board's own head. Specifically, these buildings are: the Raymond Mannoni Fine Arts Performing Center (1972), named after the dean of the USM School of Fine Arts since 1960; the William D. McCain Graduate Library (1975), in deference to the USM president since 1955; and the M.M. Roberts Stadium (1975), honoring the longtime member and president of the State College Board.

Pretend you are a new student arriving at USM for the first time—obviously very anxious to see the campus. White-columned, red-bricked, broad-walked and ivied, and with lily pond and kissing bridge, the campus impresses you by its calm and charm. But behind this conventional facade, a treasure of mysteries awaits you.

The tour begins at the USM baseball diamond where you notice the four-foot-high chain link fence around the perimeter of the outfield. The jagged edge of the fence is turned upward so that as an outfielder reaches over the fence to catch a fly ball, he may make the "out" but he will get his arm ripped in the process. To view a baseball game, one sits on the single set of wooden stands located on the third base line. However, the third base dugout was built directly in front of the stands so that the fans, except for those seated in the top few rows, cannot see the field over the dugout.

Structural idiosyncrasies seem to be endemic to USM buildings. In speaking of the new USM swimming pool, General McCain said on 13 March 1972:

> I got the money about six years ago. We have had a tremendous amount of trouble getting that thing designed and built. The architect I guess didn't know about how to design a swimming pool. I could have gone to Auburn University and learned to be an architect and design a swimming pool far quicker than they have. We have not been able to get that thing accepted.[1]

The showcase on the Southern campus is the new $1.5 million Mannoni Fine Arts Performing Center which opened in early 1972. The facility is described as "one of the most complex engineering construction projects ever undertaken in the state ...the most singularly intricate and adequate building for the job for which it was intended."[2] There was one minor problem, however. The balcony was so constructed that one seated in any of its 218 seats could not see the front half of the stage. From the front row balcony seats one could not see the stage at all. Perhaps this explains why balcony tickets sold for less than one-third the price of those for main floor seats.[3]

THE LIBRARY: A NICE BUILDING, BUT...

Undoubtedly the most important building on a university campus is the library. The USM library is a nice, modern two-story bulding, completely fire-proof and air-conditioned. But weird things transpire there. In 1970 the library contained exactly half the number of books required in a fully accredited university of USM's size.[4] The head librarian points out, "The library lags behind the academic program, and funds have not been adequate to close the gap."[5] Indeed, there is some irony in the fact that a student with an M.A. degree in library science from Southern cannot qualify as director of the Hattiesburg Public Library because Southern's library science program is not accredited by the American Library Association.[6]

Why the shortage? Well, as I said, weird things transpire over there. Even though it cannot support a self-respecting graduate program, the library contains what reportedly is the largest collection of *children's books* in the world.[7] But don't make plans to go over and see the collection; it is locked up and is opened only under special permission.

The library has books, but perhaps not the books students need. For instance, the university has a graduate degree program in Business Administration but the library has no copy of the index to the *Wall Street Journal*. Popular weeklies such as *Time* and *Newsweek* are in the library—but issues since 1961 are on microfilm only! However, the library has twenty-one original copies of Ernest Sevier Cox' *White America*, a nearly extinct 1923 ultraracist book published by the White American Society.[8]

Perhaps the library's most distinctive characteristic is its interlibrary loan service. The *USM Faculty Handbook* contains the paradoxical provision that "faculty and graduate students are expected to select dissertation topics that will not require heavy borrowing from other libraries."[9] That's like telling someone they can swim as long as they don't get wet. But those who run the library obviously are serious about this policy.

For one entire year, Ken Kerr, a graduate student in political science, attempted unsuccessfully to get a book, *Theory and Methods of Scaling* from the USM library. Library officials told Ken on his monthly visit that the book was checked out to a professor and that there was no way they could retrieve it. On 19 September 1972, Ken tried to order a copy of the book through the interlibrary loan service. The circulation librarian said, "As long as we've got the book listed in the card catalogue, even if it is checked out and we can't get it for you, you can't order it through the interlibrary loan."[10]

In a similar vein, Ed Fleming, another political science graduate student, attempted to order some issues of *The Times* (of London) from the Tulane University library through interlibrary loan. The USM librarian would not order them because, although Ed cited the exact day and year of the issues he desired, he didn't indicate the *volume number*. Ed went through the entire USM hierarchy: finally, the dean of the university commanded the librarian to order the newspapers. Ed's good fortune ended when Tulane sent more issues than he had requested. Because of the discrepancy in the order the USM librarian naturally refused to give Ed any of the newspapers, until he threatened to report her again.[11] Incidentally, issues of *The Times* do not have volume numbers.

THE FACULTY: THE PETER PRINCIPLE PERSONIFIED

A physical plant is only window dressing and even library resources are not decisive in determining the quality of education college students receive. The essence of a university is its faculty. We will begin our examination of the USM faculty by surveying the highest ranking faculty, the chairperson.

The USM administration demands complete obedience from all of its subordinates. Unwilling to tolerate even an iota of disagreement, the administration recruits "middle managers" who have been socialized to be totally obsequious. Accordingly, the prerequisites for administrative positions at Southern, including department heads, are a high rank in the military and/or USM degree. President McCain is a general as is his administrative assistant. Dean of Men Radar Grantham and Campus Security Chief Willie Oubre both received their degrees from USM. The dean of USM's School of Health, Physical Education, and Recreation, served twenty-seven years in the army and received his B.A. and Ph.D degrees from USM in history.[12]

Turning to department chairmen, Roger Johnson, Jr., a USM alumnus, is the chairman of the Department of Foreign Languages. He also is the son of General McCain's administrative assistant, "Colonel" Roger Johnson, Sr. The chairman of the Department of Anthropology, Philosophy, and Comparative Religion spent seventeen years in Asia as a British army officer. The political science department apparently had been under fire for a lack of "balance." It had an air force colonel and a navy rear admiral as professors, but no one representing the army. Hence in 1971 the department snatched the chief of the army's Criminal Investigation and Security Division to head its new Law Enforcement Studies program. And, lest we forget, the chairman of the geography department is an air force colonel with twenty-one years of active duty. In early 1972, this professor informed his classes that General Curtis Le May (the fire-bomber of Dresden who served as George Wallace's vice-presidential running mate in 1968), wasn't really a "hawk." As proof, the professor told of the time when "Curtis and I" placed red flags on a map of the Soviet Union at the appropriate spots where bombs could be dropped to annihilate the country. During the exercise, he told the class, General Le May exclaimed, "My God, I hope it doesn't come to this."[13]

In a 1971 issue of *USM Perspective,* a faculty newsletter published by the USM Office of Public Information, the university conceded that a low ratio of provincialism and inbreeding was a sign of a strong faculty:

> Educators agree generally that the scholar-professor should obtain degrees from various institutions to ensure his and his student's exposure to different philosophies and to validate academic competence. USM administrators are of the opinion that inbreeding and provincialism can lead to academic narrowness and retardation.

The same article indicated that 140 professors at USM, (exactly one-third the entire faculty), held USM degrees[14]—probably one of the highest number of inbred professors at any university in the United States.

THE QUALITY OF EDUCATION: "THE UNIVERSITY
HAS ITS SHARE OF DREADFUL TEACHERS."

The *raison d'etre* of the American college, the basis of its survival and current importance, is education. But as Christopher Jencks and David Riesman observe in their study, *The Academic Revolution,* certification may be replacing education as a college's primary function: "A 'college' that does not offer any instruction-...can still find a market for its degrees, and substantial number of these diploma mills do in fact exist."[15] USM stands as vivid testimony to this statement.

General McCain told the Southern freshman orientation assembly on 6 September 1971: "You should understand that you can get as good an education at this university in the fields offered as you can in any college or university in the United States."[16] The catch phrase at vocationally oriented USM, of course, is "in the fields offered." ROTC students flock to Southern because participation in ROTC exempts them from the requirement that students have a minor as well as a major subject.[17] For the "jocks" Southern's Department of Athletic Administration and Coaching is the first department in the country with the word "coaching" in its title.[18] Southern also offers a bachelor's degree in hotel and restaurant administration. But very little philosophy is taught at USM. Indeed, four of the five professors in the philosophy department were fired during the 1972-73 school year.

USM offers students such a wide choice of majors that there is substantial reason to believe—as Mississippi Governor William Waller's 1974 select committee on higher education apparently did—that the university has become a "degree fctory." Strangely enough, Southern is giving Ph.D.'s in seventy different subjects, more than some of the "finest" eastern universities offer. USM is also turning out masters' degrees in 127 separate fields. That is nearly twice the number of masters' degrees offered at Ole Miss or Mississippi State University. Among questions raised by the governor's select committee was why should USM offer a whopping 263 different baccalaureate degrees, while Ole Miss, with approximately the same number of students, only offers 57?[19]

Instruction in the USM classroom sometimes is as bizarre as the course offerings. "General Psychology," a course taught during the summer quarter of 1972, was organized in the following manner: On Mondays the class viewed a movie, and every Friday was taken up with an exam. Wednesday was "lecture" day, and for this occasion a slide projector flashed a hand-written lecture on the side wall of the class. The professor read the lecture off the wall very slowly, as the class took it down verbatim. The professor almost never uttered a word more or less than was projected on the wall. If, for example, the professor read, "It is off..." and the word "off" was at the bottom of the wall, there was silence until the next page was inserted into the slide projector. The professor discouraged questions from the class.[20]

The USM administration recognizes its problems. The Dean of the College of Liberal Arts told his faculty on 9 May 1972: "In a university that has its share of dreadful teachers, we have ours and some intellectual dilettantes as well."[21] In an apparent effort to upgrade the quality of instruction at Southern, the Student Government Association in 1969 began publishing *The Keyhole,* a teacher-course evaluation booklet. Praised by the administration, *The Keyhole* reportedly was consulted in assessing salaries of faculty members.[22] The faculty soon became so irate at *The Keyhole* as to discredit it. In its two years of operation, the survey was conducted by professors, making it subject to distortion. In March 1972 the SGA president said: "We're going to have to scrap the old *Keyhole* stuff that we put out last quarter because we have a belief that many instructors read it, censored it, and also threatened some of their students with repercussions."[23] In fact, *The Keyhole* has not been published since 1970. There seems to be no way to prevent professors from stuffing the ballot box. In one case, a professor handed in five separate evaluations of his course which were in the exact same handwriting and even contained identical language. They gave near perfect ratings, too.[24]

THE UNIVERSITY COMMONS AND UNIVERSITY CLINIC: MASOCHISTIC MEALS AND MEDICAL CARE.

Between listening to lectures all day and working all night in the library, students look forward to mealtime. This activity is neatly arranged for them at Southern. All persons living on campus must purchase a three-meal-a-day meal ticket and eat in the University Commons, a dining hall. The result is often a stop at the University Clinic, an infirmary. The USM Clinic has two doctors. According to the Director of Student Health Services, "The University of Alabama has eight doctors and a budget of nine times USM's for medical services. However, USM's Clinic sees more patients."[25] But then not every university caters to as many hard-core masochists as Southern.

Consider the following statement by Southern student Sharon Anderson in the fall of 1971:

I got sick after last Tuesday's evening meal and went over to the clinic.

A friend came with me and told the nurse I thought I might have food poisoning because of my symptoms and they weren't like any virus that was in town because I had experienced two types of intestinal viruses.

The nurse was quoted as saying, "Don't let me hear you accuse the Commons of food poisoning. A virus is going around at Hattiesburg High School and it really makes me mad to hear something like that." I was given a shot and sent back to my room, since there was no room in the clinic.

After four hours of being violently ill, I called my personal physician and he admitted me past midnight in the Forrest County General Hospital. The only meals I had eaten in two days were from the Commons and after three days at the hospital and numerous tests plus a drip and shots every three hours, they determined I had food poisoning from (not Wednesday's roast beef) but Tuesday's salad and chocolate pie.

I'm glad I didn't stay in my room as the nurses suggested, as did most of the others who were sick with the "virus." I knew better because of two past experiences with the clinic: a broken leg they had x-rayed and told me it was a sprained ankle and I had whirlpool treatments twice a day and walked on it for a week before another doctor took more x-rays and told me it was broken.

And once I waited four hours until almost 2 a.m. for five stitches in my thumb because they wouldn't contact another doctor and the university doctor was in Memphis at a Freshmen football game.

I went to see Mr. Smalling, our Financial Secretary, to get a refund back on my meal ticket or what was left in the quarter and he refused to give it to me with my doctor's excuse I had in my hand. He acted very perturbed and told me I'd have to have a letter on letterhead and an attached diet to follow.

I even tried to see President McCain, but was told he was out of town [visiting Europe] until November 8. Every time I pass the Commons and Clinic I get ill thinking of the unnecessary pain I have endured because of the service to the students.[26]

ENTERTAINMENT ON CAMPUS: "I DON'T FEEL THAT THIS UNIVERSITY SHOULD SPONSOR PEOPLE OF THIS CALIBER."

Between visits to the Health Clinic, Southern students can partake of the entertainment on campus. All fulltime students pay a three-dollar fee every quarter which goes to the University Activities Council (UAC). For this amount of approximately $100,000 per year, students get free movies and concerts, which is all very well in theory, but...

When things get really dull around campus, students can always play the guessing game called "Name the UAC Movie of the Week." The UAC must have every movie it selects approved by the Director of Student Activities William Kirkpatrick, before it is ordered. Kirkpatrick says, "I try to get what the students want, but the UAC has to maintain decency and discretion in its selection of movies."[27] A member of the UAC executive council says that Kirkpatrick advised him to order substitute movies in the cases of *Goodbye Columbus* and *Repulsion* because Kirkpatrick did not approve of these movies.[28] A screening of *Abbott and Costello Meet Frankenstein* was permitted instead.

Concerts didn't fare much better than movies. The Allman Brothers Band concert scheduled for 23 March 1971 was cancelled because on March 21, five of the rock band's members were arrested in Grove Hill, Alabama on charges of possession of illegal drugs. The band's manager then notified Southern officials that the band was ready to play, but Kirkpatrick cancelled the concert anyway, saying: "We cancelled the concert...I don't feel that this University should sponsor people of this caliber to come to the campus and perform. We're extremely lucky that this hasn't happened with us before with rock groups."[29]

Alabama is well-known for very speedy justice but some students doubted that a group of five men could possibly be arrested, arraigned, tried, convicted, and sentenced—all in one day! In fact, the Allman Brothers Band was *not* convicted of the possession charges.[30]

In an apparent effort to control the smoking of marijuana at concerts, the administration in April 1973, prohibited all smoking in the entire seating area of the 9000-seat Reed Green Coliseum. Campus Security Chief Oubre said: "If smoking was allowed to continue it would mean that every time a cigarette was lit, we would have to go check to see whether it was tobacco or marijuana...I don't think they will die from lack of nicotine. The music will kill them first,"[31] added Director of Student Activities Kirkpatrick.

Chapter Six

THE POLITICAL SCIENCE DEPARTMENT: A FACULTY OR A FUNNY FARM?

Things are seldom what they seem,
Skim milk masquerades as cream
—H.M.S. Pinafore

In order to illustrate the quality of instruction at the University of Southern Mississippi, I will describe in detail that section to which I myself belonged, the Department of Political Science. I have every reason to believe that this department is representative of Southern's brand of education. Indeed, the story of how political science grew from a fledgling department with a dozen or so majors to the largest department in USM's College of Liberal Arts (with 528 majors during the fall quarter of 1972)[1] is a truly heartwarming one.

In 1972, the 10-person professional ranks in political science included a rear admiral, an air force colonel, the former chief of the army's Criminal Investigations and Security Division, a former chairman whose terminal degree is in education (not political science), a native Greek, a native Ukranian, and one of the country's foremost breeders and handlers of American foxhounds. The department's secretary is Greather Octavia Heathcock. The department leadership includes:

William H. Hatcher: Department chairman since 1967; six of the department's seven professors hired between 1967 and 1971 were fired; known by former colleagues as "Hatchet."

Colonel Orley B. Caudhill: Department "Assistant chairman"; served 27 years in Air Force; believes that the kids at Woodstock should have been maced by helicopter and arrested for smoking marijuana. ("We must use as much force as necessary.")

THE SOUTHERN QUARTERLY: "THE POLITICAL RESTRICTIONS IMPOSED BY THE PRESIDENT HAVE [BROUGHT] THE UNITED STATES TO THE VERGE OF ANARCHY"

The Southern Quarterly, a "scholarly journal of studies in the Humanities and Social Sciences by the Faculty of the University of Southern Mississippi," is almost totally dominated by the Political Science Department. Chairman Hatcher, the *Quarterly's* editor, is responsible for assembling the journal's staff, Accordingly, in the summer of 1971 Hatcher appointed G., a political science graduate student, to replace the *Quarterly's* regular student editor who was on vacation. (The student editor's job is to correct grammar and spelling in articles submitted for publication.) The following is a sample of G.'s writing, taken from a term paper he presented to me:

> The "separation of powers" and "checks and balances" schemes find themselves lacking for a place to reside...From this comes the purpose of the following study and its goal is to show that the discovery of missiles in Cuba in 1962 reveals the importance of Executive policy making...In fact, the President primarily was the one to alert the public thereby seeking its approval and not their elected representatives-...While Franklin Roosevelt was notorious for his use of Executive initiative. From the years 1933 to 1961 the President's initiative has remained predominant. This being the case possibly in one sense because of the position taken by past Presidents in "crisis" situations...This reveals the necessity for unification should war have resulted; at which time the Constitution would have reflected its greatness, and most importantly, its demand for obeyance.[2]

G. later occupied the department's American Government and Politics slot which I once held.[3]

The *Quarterly,* like any other journal, is only as good as its material. Editor Hatcher wrote the following letter to all USM department chairmen on 25 June 1971:

> The *Southern Quarterly* is in desperate need of manuscripts for the October, 1971, number. Thus far we have NONE to process. Will you please comb your department for likely articles and send them or have them sent to me at Box 78. The deadline is July 20, 1971.[4]

When articles are "located," Editor Hatcher invariably selects the best ones for publication. For the *Quarterly's* October 1970 issue, Hatcher accepted an article by his department colleague Colonel Caudill, entitled "The Americans, the World and the Future." Some excerpts follow:

> The Vietnam war has been "unwinnable" for several and specific reasons, most of which are not very complimentary of American conduct as a great people of a great nation....The tremendous concern of American leaders that "civilians" not be injured and "civilian" facilities not be damaged dictated that vital targets not be struck, or if struck, the "damage limitation" be so precise that the very effort was almost self-defeating. The political restrictions imposed by the President ...have undermined American diplomacy around the world, strengthened our enemies, weakened our alliances and in the long run have helped the enemy to hold out while bringing the United States to the verge of anarchy...With respect to Senator [Eugene] McCarthy, one is tempted to question either his policies, or his state of mental health, or both...One studying [William Fulbright's] actions can only conclude that he has reached a state of "intellectual senility" which precludes much further constructive service to his state or nation.[5]

Colonel Caudill's article received a rave review from at least one of the country's educational leaders. On 4 February 1971, Hatcher wrote to state board of trustees President M.M. Roberts:

> Dr. Orley B. Caudill...showed me your recent letter and your kind remarks about his article in *The Southern Quarterly.* I agree with your evaluation of his article...It is most gratifying to know that someone is aware of our more constructive efforts here at the University of Southern Mississippi. Sometimes I think that only our mistakes make the news.[6]

DEPARTMENT MEETINGS: "IF THEY DIDN'T SMOKE SO MANY JOINTS THE NIGHT BEFORE..."

Discussions at political science departmental meetings ranged from inane to absurd. Indeed, the only reason these contrived monthly meetings were held at all was for the administration to communicate orders efficiently through its spokesperson, the department head, to the assembled faculty members. Since the faculty had only marginal impact in determining significant decisions, such as the hiring of new teachers for the department, its sole collective prerogative was to deal with internal housekeeping matters. In this context, it is not surprising that the discussions invariably degenerated into pettiness and nonsense.

A typical political science department meeting occurred on 2 September 1971. The meeting began with a reference to President McCain's "free" luncheon earlier in the day, which Chairman Hatcher had demanded that we attend—the one which the president didn't attend and wasn't free. The first particular on the formal agenda was an order by Chairman Hatcher that our department members not use ditto machines housed in other departments. The discussion was abbreviated because Hatcher considered the issue too delicate to thrash out publicly. (Both culprits subsequently were fired.) The next item was the adoption of a new textbook for the introductory course. Hatcher told us that a new request for an up-to-date text containing the 1968 and 1970 election results was turned down by the dean of the university with these words. "Please tell the students who won the elections." Throughout the meeting, Chairman Hatcher referred to the departments newest member, Winfield Rose, as "Professor Rose." Winfield respectfully asked to be called by his first name, which Hatcher simply wouldn't do. Finally, Hatcher called him simply "Rose."

Several professors complained about the quality of student secretaries at the departmental meeting on 17 March 1971. One professor pointed that Debbie J. had done a particularly poor job, which might be due to her "obsession with the Miss Southern contest." One of the department's sexagenerians, with raised eyebrows, asked, "She's in the beauty contest? Isn't she black?"

Most of the departmental meeting on 23 September 1971 was spent discussing a proposal to change a two-quarter political theory course to a three-quarter offering. Rose objected to the term "political theory" for the course, and suggested the appellative "political philosophy." Doumas vehemently disagreed with Rose and stated. "We don't teach philosophy, which implies the pursuit of truth." A compromise was struck; the course was called "political thought," a name which Colonel Caudill suggested was "kind of thoughtful." Another profesor noted that the titles of two other existing courses included the phrase "political theory." Chairman Hatcher, ever helpful, said, "It doesn't hurt to keep the students guessing!" Still another professor argued that the proposed names of the three-quarter unit course were too long to fit into a student's transcript! After a heated battle concerning where the break-off points of the three courses should be, Chairman Hatcher Socratically suggested that "Political Science 405 ought to include whatever is left and whatever is right."

Next we discussed which students to recommend for a National Science Foundation summer research program. One professor suggested that Whittington was a good student, but "he'll need a hair cut by next summer." The last item on the chairman's agenda was the department's malfunctioning air conditioner.[7] Hatcher made the problem perfectly clear to us: "The air conditioner broke down two days ago which explains the problem that day. Since then, the discomfort has been due to the fact that professors simply have not closed the windows that they opened the day the air conditioning broke down." Hatcher concluded his presentation by explaining that he placed a sign in all the classrooms on the second day of the crisis requesting that professors close the windows: "If we would just keep the G.D. windows closed things will work out."

One professor then asked, "If, in a crowded classroom, the students are sweating, what do I do?" Admiral Virden replied, "If they didn't smoke so many joints the night before..."

ADMINISTERING COMPREHENSIVE EXAMS: "I THINK YOU SHOULD PASS HIM."

The objectivity of the political science department perhaps is best displayed in its administration of comprehensive examinations. Jerry E. was scheduled to take his Ph.D. exams in October 1971 but requested that they be postponed. Jerry's excuse was that he couldn't do adequate work during the vernal equinox or the autumnal equinox. According to Jerry, a manic-depressive like himself is depressed during the vernal equinox as he slows down for the upcoming warm weather and is manic during the autumnal equinox period, when he speeds up in preparation for the cold weather. The department agreed to postpone Jerry's exams.[8]

During the winter quarter of 1971, Bill A., another graduate student, took his Ph.D. exams. Following the oral portion of the exams, Bill's committee met to decide his fate. Professor K., Bill's committee chairman, first called for Chairman Hatcher's vote. Hatcher whispered, "I pass." What could be clearer? Just as at the national party convention, Hatcher had abstained to assess the general mood of the group. Nevertheless, K. recorded Hatcher's remarks as a *passing vote* for Bill. Colonel Caudill was next to vote. Although he already had expressed the opinion that Bill had performed very poorly in the exams, the Colonel abstained—apparently unwilling to vote against the candidate until someone else did. Admiral Virden then voted to pass Bill. Doumas registered the first "fail" vote. Suddenly, Colonel Caudill, who originally had asked for a "couple of minutes" to decide, voted "fail." The two remaining members of the committee voted to pass Bill. Admiral Virden then dramatically asked to have his vote changed from "pass" to "fail."

The "official" tally was three passing votes and two failing votes. (Admiral Virden was not an official member of the committee; I have no idea why he was asked to vote.) At that point, K. accused Doumas of voting against Bill as "punishment" because Bill had almost finished writing his dissertation and even had a teaching position for the following year.[9] K. said: "To be honest, I've sat here and I believe that Bill got at least 75% of your questions correct. I think you should pass him." Doumas respectfully resigned from the committee.

In late 1972 Bill handed Professor K. a "final" copy of his dissertation. Although no rough draft had ever been presented to the members of Bill's dissertation committee, K. gave this final copy to Doumas during the break between fall and winter quarters and demanded its approval within two days. Doumas found 105 errors and therefore would not approve the dissertation in its present form. Bill had to correct his errors and pay another $300 to have the manuscript retyped. Bill's mother complained to the dean of the graduate school, who then called Chairman Hatcher to task because his department didn't have a standardized policy to guide its graduate students in this matter.

The comprehensive exams for both the Master's and Ph.D. degrees also illustrate the general quality of both learning and teaching at USM. The examination of one M.S. candidate in the spring of 1973 is especially noteworthy. He reportedly answered one of his questions by reviewing a recent television news special program. During his oral exam he asserted that the Declaration of Independence did not contain a theory of revolution and that treaties do not have to be ratified by the U.S. Senate. In the fall of 1973 this student began teaching U.S. government and politics at a junior college in Florida.

AWARDING FELLOWSHIPS: "ISN'T MURPHY THE GUY WHO COMES INTO THE OFFICE LOOKING DOPEY?"

The professionalism of the political science department also is revealed in its awarding of fellowships. At the faculty meeting on 17 March 1971, we were to select the outstanding graduating senior majoring in political science. Secretary Greather Octavia Heathcock handed out an alphabetical list of seniors with a 2.75 or better grade point average (GPA). Acting upon Chairman Hatcher's orders, Colonel Caudill reduced the list to the top ten and handed out a sheet of additional information on these students. However, Thomas R., whose 3.64 was the third highest GPA on the original list, was conspicuously missing from Caudill's list. As we were just about to choose the winner of an annual subscription to the *National Observer* magazine, I asked Hatcher why Thomas' name was expurgated. The chairman openly admitted that he personally eliminated Thomas, whom he considered to be "irresponsible," "a troublemaker," and a "long-haired radical."

The department met again in April 1971 to distribute its $27,000 for graduate fellowships. At this meeting one professor expressed strong objections to Tim Murphy, an applicant for a fellowship renewal, noting that Murphy had "long hair." Dropping his shoulders in an imitation of Murphy, another professor rhetorically asked, "Isn't Murphy the guy who comes into the office looking dopey?" Murphy's case was deferred until the next meeting two days later because of lack of time. At this meeting, the same professor who had voiced strenuous objections to Murphy two days before actually spoke in Murphy's behalf. This professor noted that he had supervised Murphy's student teaching and praised Murphy's "pleasing personality, congeniality with people, and classroom performance." With the prestigious endorsement of this former department chairman, Murphy, despite his long hair, was awarded a fellowship. Of course, Murphy had never student-taught in his life: apparently this professor became confused during the two days between meetings on the Murphy case, finally mistaking someone else for Murphy.

While the political science department ultimately awarded a fellowship to a longhair—even if through caprice—it refused at this same meeting to even consider granting a fellowship to Hugo Johnson, an ultraconservative campus political leader. Hugo was president of the American Independent Youth, the campus arm of George Wallace's American Independent Party. The official publication of Hugo's association, entitled *US,* contained innumerable gems of political wisdom like the following:

> Last quarter the colored boy on the *Student Printz* suggested that the word "Negro" be stricken from the English Language because certain White folk couldn't pronounce it according to Webster. If, in turn, we dropped all the words which most "Blacks" cannot correctly pronounce, our language would deteriorate to nothing but grunts and groans![10]

Hugo composed original witticisms under the heading of "Quick Pricks" for each issue of *US,* such as these:

> —The Kennedy brothers are the best argument yet for family planning.
> —When a Peace Freak says he wants to donate blood to the Viet Cong, I agree and urge that he give his all.
> —Another leftist Peace Freak was walking down the street when he saw a sign saying "Wet Cement," and he did.
> —At least the Klan keeps its sheets clean.[11]

Copies of *US* were run off on the political science department's mimeograph machine.

Clearly, the department did not reject Hugo's fellowship application because of his political views. It turned out that Hugo had recently approached Dean of the University Charles Moorman to request that "conservative" political views be adequately represented on the campus student newspaper. Dean Moorman characteristically rejoined, "Is this a threat? I don't respond well to threats!" Moorman immediately ordered Chairman Hatcher to reject Hugo's fellowship bid. So, despite Hugo's excellent academic record—far better than many political science graduate students who received fellowships—his application was unceremoniously turned down.

THE DEPARTMENT'S GRADUATE STUDENTS: "ALL LONGHAIRS OUGHT TO BE LINED UP AGAINST THE WALL AND SHOT."

According to "A Guide to Graduate Study in Political Science 1972," a publication of the American Political Science Association, 111 universities in the United States had Ph.D. programs in political science in that year. The highest "minimum score generally expected" on the Graduate Record Examination for admission to a program was 1400 at the University of Connecticut. Only three schools accepted a score of less than 1000, the second lowest being Ole Miss at 900. Southern's requirement for graduate studies in political science was 750, by far the lowest in the country.[12]

However, the department at USM eagerly makes exceptions for graduate students who cannot meet its rigorous criteria. For instance, Charles B. took the Graduate Record Exam (GRE) in March 1965 and scored a 330 in the verbal section and a 290 in the quantitative portion for a 620 total. Charles was admitted to the USM graduate school as a political science major in the summer of 1966. He took the GRE again in April 1967, apparently to improve his score, and this time he made a 270 in the verbal portion and a 300 in the quantitative test for a still lower 570 total. (The examinee is given 200 points in each section of the GRE even if he or she misses all the questions: thus, Charles compiled only 170 points out of a possible 1200.) On 8 August 1971, Chairman Hatcher wrote to the graduate school dean, "This is to report that Charles B. has successfully completed his oral and written portions of his comprehensive examinations for the Ph.D. degree."[13]

With a surplus of money for fellowships, the political science department is able to recruit outstanding graduate students. One of our fellowship holders, Harold P. was born in 1912 and attended eight colleges before coming to USM. Harold, who had served as headmaster at "segregation" and military academies, is past president of several major rifle and pistol associations and fencing clubs, and also is a past post commander of the VFW. When I walked into my first class at USM in the fall of 1970, Harold, seated in the front row, asked his neighbor, "Is he Jewish?" During the same quarter, Harold spotted fellow graduate student Q. in the restroom. Harold shook Q. against the wall and shouted, "You longhaired pinko, get your hair cut!" Q. replied, "Get off me. I was fighting in the Mekong Delta protesting this country in 1963. I didn't see you there, brother."[14] During the winter quarter of 1970, Harold told Ken Kerr, another graduate student, "All longhairs ought to be lined up against the wall and shot." When Ken suggested that this position was "too extreme," Harold retorted, "I can tell that you are Jewish because of your liberal attitude."[15] Later I showed Harold a copy of an American Civil Liberties Union bulletin and as he read down the names on the executive board he exclaimed, "Jew...Jew...Jew..." In his term paper in my course on political parties, Harold made the following statements:

> The Prohibition Party's symbol is the camel. That seems to be a most appropriate beast for the camel can go a long time between drinks...The Farmer-Labor Party tried for the presidency...for the last time, in 1932 with Jacob Coxey, as its candidate. He was known for having led a group of unemployed men to Washington where he was arrested for walking on the grass. How times have changed![16]

Harold subsequently received a Ph.D. from the political science department.

Expressing his confidence in the cast of characters presented above, Chairman Hatcher wrote on 12 January 1973: "We have a flourishing graduate program in Political Science with an outstanding faculty."[17]

Chapter Seven

ACADEMIC FREEDOM: THE FACULTY AS NIGGER

If I were founding a university I would found first a smoking room; then when I had a litle more money in hand I would found a dormitory; then after that or more probably with it, a decent reading room and a library. After that, if I still had more money that I couldn't use, I would hire a professor and get some textbooks.

—*Stephen Leacock*

Sidney Hook, an emeritus philosophy professor and leading spokesperson for the education Establishment, states well the doctrine of academic freedom:

The qualified teacher...has the right honestly to reach, and hold, and proclaim any conclusion in the field of his competence. In other words, academic freedom carries with it the *right to heresy* as well as the right to restate and defend the traditional views. This takes in considerable ground. If a teacher in honest pursuit of an inquiry or argument comes to a conclusion that appears fascist or communist or racist or what-not in the eyes of others, once he has been certified as professionally competent by his peers, then those who believe in academic freedom must defend his right to be wrong—if they consider him wrong—whatever their orthodoxy might be.[1]

64

This chapter and the following one demonstrate that despite the lofty principles of academic freedom proclaimed by university administrators, *academic oppression* has been the fate of professors who criticize the status quo.. Faculty members who challenge specific university policies invariably face recrimination. While the discussion here is limited to an analysis of academic freedom at the University of Southern Mississippi, it will be suggested later that all universities in the United States function, in one way or another, like USM.

Certainly the Southern Deanery understands the concept of academic freedom. Consider:

> Charles W. Moorman: As Dean of the University since 1969, he is second in command to General McCain: as an undergraduate at Kenyon College he roomed with actor Paul Newman; reportedly has a very keen sense of humor as evidenced by the following quotations: "I don't know what students rights are";[2] "Professors are no different than plumbers, leaders of business, etc.";[3] his syllabus for a course in the twentieth century British novel one quarter read: "One word of Advice: If You're Taking Another Course, Drop It."

> Claude E. Fike: Dean of the College of Liberal Arts since 1961; said in January 1969, "The only natural right a student has is being a student."[4]

SOUTHERN'S "CAREER UNIVERSITY": FROM LIBERAL ARTIST TO TECHNICIAN

In the late 1960s and early 1970s, the Carnegie Commission on Higher Education recommended that, with the exception of a few elite universities, U.S. colleges should make vocational and technical education their fundamental institutional objective. According to the Commission, the "career university" concept would accomplish two significant goals: divert students clamoring for access to college away from more selective institutions, and offer a convenient means of training the increased numbers of technicians needed in both the private and public sectors of the economy.

Always in the avant garde of educational reform which serves the interest of the business community, the University of Southern Mississippi began in 1971 to implement the kind of vocational training program advocated by the Carnegie Commission. Since the USM faculty has virtually no participation in the university's academic decision making process, the most momentous educational decision in decades at Southern, too, was presented to the faculty as a *fait accompli*. Consulting Tarot cards, perhaps, but definitely not the profesors, Dean Moorman called on the Southern faculty to turn its energies toward creating a "Career University." On 3 September 1971, he explained:

> Out of that long drive to Jackson, somewhere appropriately enough around Sister Glendora's fortune telling parlor, there came the phrase "Career University." For this is what we have been moving toward, a total commitment to "career" training. Look at the evidence: more attention to career-oriented programs and less to academically-oriented majors and minors...Such a philosophy, of course, has ramifications far beyond its immediate effects. A Career University, for example, has little use for Liberal Arts or the Pure Sciences as such, as parts of programs, yes, but as ends in themselves, no...We will no longer be able to require the taking of a foreign language simply because such study is considered disciplinary or is culturally rewarding...It will be charged, of course, that I am attempting to turn a university into a vocational school. Right. So I am. The reason is that I went to one.[5]

Southern's commitment to the career university necessitated many other administrative decisions without faculty consultation. Speaking to a full faculty assembly on 9 May 1972, Dean Moorman announced that, with the advent of the fall quarter, Southern would move toward a three-year baccalaureate degree program by granting semester hours of academic credit while continuing to operate within the framework of calender terms of three months, or quarters. Moorman called the unilateral action

> the most revolutionary step ever taken in the history of this University and one which may be one of the most significant moves in public higher education in this country...The new program caps our progress toward becoming the nation's most fervently career-oriented university.[6]

The reason the faculty wasn't consulted probably was that, under the new system, professors must teach approximately 10 percent more class-contact hours at the same salary schedules. To avert possible faculty discontent, General McCain jumped up and exclaimed that he "stole $40,000 from the budget," and was giving each fulltime professor $100 compensation for the additional work load. Thereupon, John Gonzales, the "William D. McCain Professor of History," asked the faculty to applaud General McCain for giving the faculty "a salary raise." A thunderous ovation followed. Dean Moorman then asked if there were any other business and the chairman of the Department of Library Science asked, "How can this new 'semester-quarter' system be adopted without faculty consultation?" General McCain instantaneously adjourned the meeting. He and Dean Moorman walked off the stage, leaving the professor's question unanswered. As the faculty filed out of the meeting, one professor said, "Who was that crazy Chinese obstructionist?"

In preparation for the major forthcoming curriculum changes and again without faculty consultation, Southern adopted a new five-day-a-week class schedule for the winter quarter of 1970. (Previously, there had been no classes on Wednesday.) The new schedule included one-hour-and-forty-minute classes on Tuesday and Thursday. Dean Moorman admitted that "we have a number of teachers who say they can't lecture that long." Moorman's administrative assistant expressed the same attitude: "The one thing that bothers me is whether or not the students are having the material presented in a way so as to keep them invigorated. The worst thing has been the problem of boredom in the 100-minute classes." Despite universal dissatisfaction, the new schedule continues. But as Dean Moorman notes, "Tuesday night is no longer party and sex night."[8]

THE TEXTBOOK LENDING SERVICE: "TO MY KNOWLEDGE IT IS THE ONLY ONE IN EXISTENCE."

From 27 April 1970, when I accepted the job offer to teach at USM, until 1 September 1970, when I arrived on campus to begin work, no one from the university told me which courses I would be teaching. During my first day on campus I fortuitously stumbled on a class schedule and thereby found that information. Later that day, while browsing through the shelves of the university bookstore, I chanced upon the books to be used in *my* courses. This was my first acquaintance with Southern's "textbook lending service."

Inherent in the concept of academic freedom is the right of the professor to chose his or her own textbook; however, it doesn't exactly work that way at Southern. Jessie Gore, USM's bookstore manager for the past twenty-five years, says: "To my knowledge, our Textbook Lending Service, established in 1964, is the only one in existence."[8] That is a gross understatement. Southern students don't purchase their textbooks; the bookstore "lends" them one "free" book per course which the students must return at the end of the quarter. The university publicly proclaims that it benevolently provides students with free texbooks, that the lending service is motivated entirely by altruism. According to bookstore manager Gore: "After a survey indicated that some students failed courses because they could not afford to buy textbooks, Dr. McCain asked that the lending service be established."[9] However, this simply is not true. Dean Moorman explicitly states:

> Mr. Gore estimated in 1965 (and still does so) that the average-printed textbook in the average-enrolled course "pays for itself" in terms of the amount of *student fees designated for textbook operations* (which, of course, varies) in about three years. [Author's emphasis.][10]

Thus, the first catch in this deal is that the "free" rental service was initiated only after a competing student co-operative bookstore undersold the USM store, threatening to put the latter out of business. The textbook lending service was a last-ditch effort to maintain monopolistic control over providing students' textbooks.

Another myth perpetuated by the administration is that the textbook service enhances the quality of education for USM students. Mr. Gore says that the system assures that all students will have the books "they need."[11] However, a professor is a prisoner of the one book which the system provides to students for at least three years—so that the book "pays for itself." Obviously, this rule can *prevent* students from having the textbooks "they need."

This procedure for changing a textbook, according to the *USM Faculty Handbook,* is:

> When changes are to be made in textbooks, the instructor desiring the change will make a request through his department chairman who, if in agreement, will contact his dean for approval. He will then check with the Bookstore to ascertain when such change can become effective.[12]

Let's see how this labyrinthine process works in practice. Chairman Hatcher sent the following letter to the university bookstore on 27 May 1970:

> The Department of Political Science is recommending two texts for P.S. 101 beginning in the Fall Quarter, 1970-71. In this, we have Dean Moorman's permission. It will be "an either or" kind of proposition—that is we will order a certain number of Burns & Peltason (new edition—not the one being used now) and a certain number of Irish & Prothro—according to the professor's wishes.[13]

On 28 May 1970, bookstore Manager Gore wrote Dean Moorman, "This can be the beginning of the end for the textbook service."[14] Four days later Dean Moorman sent this reply to Chairman Hatcher:

> I am returning your memo to Mr. Gore along with his comment. He feels, and having discussed the matter with him I am inclined to agree, that the use of two textbooks on a shifting basis from quarter to quarter will mean that the bookstore inevitably will have to overstock in both books and should the practice of ordering separate textbooks for multi-section courses become general on the campus the book service could indeed be in jeopardy. I should like you therefore to reconsider your choice of text and to settle on the one text for Political Science 101. May I suggest also that you seriously consider retaining the sixth edition of Burns and Peltason since we do have a rather heavy investment in this text.[15]

Dean Moorman freely admits that the textbook service is an "anathema to a number of faculty, who regard its very existence, whatever its advantages to their students, as a violation of their academic freedom." Some faculty members naturally have asked their students to purchase extra texts because the bookstore provides the student with only one textbook per course. However, Dean Moorman has refused this underhanded attempt to circumvent Big Brother. According to Moorman:

> The main problem currently confronting the Bookstore lies with the increasing faculty abuse of the use of supplementary texts, those purchased by the student...I have therefore asked the department chairman to refuse to permit title

changes even in supplementary texts until the Bookstore
can clear its backlog. I do so not to limit academic freedom,
but to help the Bookstore, which as an auxilliary University
enterprise must support itself.[16]

Dean Moorman's zeal in protecting the bookstore's interests
sometimes even goes beyond the bookstore's own guidelines.
Chairman Hatcher wrote to Dean Moorman on 12 October 1971:
"Please note and consider favorably the following: P.S. 525—Note
the change in which four older texts were deleted and one new text
is added." Dean Moorman wrote on Hatcher's request. "What on
earth do we do with them?" And to Dean Fike, Moorman said,
"Please consult with Hatcher—He's taking orders from professors."[17] What Dean Moorman apparently had overlooked is that
"P.S. 525" is a graduate course and the textbook lending service
does not apply to graduate students who must purchase their own
books.

THE COLLEGE OF LIBERAL ARTS FACULTY:
REPRESSION WITH A VENGEANCE

Claude Fike, the dean of the College of Liberal Arts, apparently
has a hypercritical, perhaps even hostile attitude toward his own
faculty. Speaking to a full assembly of the Liberal Arts faculty on 9
May 1972, Dean Fike said:

In my judgment we were clearly in the forefront of this
university a few years ago. Today we stand in dire peril of
being stranded in the eddies and the backwash of a dynamic,
changing university. There is an old Chinese proverb that
says when the dragon is stranded in shallow waters it is
easily teased by a swarm of shrimp. We are viewed by other
segments of the University as the laziest, fattest, smuggest,
vainest and most wasteful of the colleges or schools. Moreover it is my embarrassment to note that whenever and
wherever trouble erupts there is generally one of our faculty
members in the midst of it. Never from the other schools,
only from ours. It seems, for instance, a contradiction of logic
that a male member of our group should be leading and
haranguing the current Women's Lib movement on campus.
[A not too oblique reference to the author.] Indifferent teaching, indifferent scholarship and a hostile frame of reference
have inspired many pragmatic legislators to view the liberal

arts as having become invalid-sick, if not indeed already invalid-dead. As a result the cruel and dispassionate accounting axe is falling. And we have deserved much of what we are getting.[18]

Indeed, liberal arts itself is an anachronism in a "career university."

The administration's solution to the slothfulness and indifferent scholarship of the Liberal Arts faculty was immediately forthcoming. The political science department was notified in the fall quarter of 1972 that it must get prior permission from Dean Fike each time any faculty member wants to be in any building on campus after 10 p.m. This applied to holding a night class overtime (classes end at 10 p.m.), working late in one's private office, or even returning to the office to pick up a book after the pumpkin hour. Someone suggested that the janitorial crew, who work all night, could simply let faculty members into their offices. (Presumably, professors could identify themselves with their faculty ID cards.) The reply from administration, of course, was, "Maintenance can't read."

Professor Sidney Hook states that "in most institutions to observe the teaching of one's colleagues is an unforgivable breach of decorum."[19] However, monitoring of classes apparently is consistent with Dean Fike's version of academic freedom. At the Dean's request, the Liberal Arts Curriculum Committee on 1 September 1971 adopted the following policy: "In the future it will be necessary for chairmen to be more discriminating and discerning in recommendations for salary increases and for promotions in rank. Chairmen are requested to begin visiting classrooms in order to form more valid judgments of faculty members."[20] Eight months later Dean Fike told the Liberal Arts faculty: "I have, within the past few weeks, visited unannounced the classrooms of the chairmen. I have urged that they visit the classrooms of their faculty."[21]

One faculty prerogative which has never been questioned anywhere is the right to assign students their grades. Except at Southern! I received the following memorandum from Dean Fike on 9 February 1971, nine days before the end of the winter quarter: "I take this means to notify you that I have given permission for Mr. H. to drop P.S. 406 with a grade of 'WG' withdraw with a passing grade and to add the course on an audit basis."[22] H. had not asked me for permission to drop the course, nor had Dean Fike conferred with me concerning H.'s grade. In other words, Dean Fike simply took the liberty of assigning a passing grade to a student in my class when, incidentally, the student was not passing the course.

THE PHILOSOPHY DEPARTMENT:
A MODEL OF ACADEMIC FREEDOM.

In his annual report on 3 September 1971, Dean Moorman left no doubt that in a career university the growth of the university is more important than the growth of the students. Moorman said: "We must continually upgrade our faculty...by replacing faculty members who for whatever reason do not contribute to the growth of the University."[23] Subsequently, the administration launched an undeclared war on the philosophy department.

Through the 1970-71 academic year, USM had a department of Religion and Philosophy. However, in September 1971, the administration transferred the "religion" of Religion and Philosophy to the new Department of Anthropology, to form the Department of Anthropology and Comparative Religous Studies. Nine months later, the doddering Department of Philosophy was officially dissolved as a separate entity. Philosophy was merged with the Department of Anthropology and Comparative Religious Studies, which was renamed the Department of Anthropology, Philosophy and Religion. Someone suggested that the department be named "Comparative Religion, Anthropology and Philosophy," which forms the appropriate acronym CRAP.

The "administrative reorientation" only masked the problems which plagued the philosophy department. Truly, the department was a model of Southern's version of academic freedom—instructors fired, courses eliminated, textbooks changed, and classrooms monitored. Cedric Evans, hired as chairman of the philosophy department starting in September 1971, was removed within a year but not before Dean Fike personally monitored his class on 19 April 1972. Evans adopted the textbook *Philosophy; A Modern Encounter* for the introductory course at the start of the winter quarter of 1972, but the book didn't survive a year—the "three-year rule" of the texbook lending service notwithstanding. Some have suggested that the text was purged because it reportedly contained a picture of police clubbing students.[24] Sanford Wood, a member of the beleaguered philosophy department, told the student newspaper

[Department Chairman] Dr. Pearson has told me and others in the department that philosophy must conform to the conservative image of the University. One thing he did to bring this about was changing the textbook. Dr. Pearson chose the textbook himself after the other philosophy instructors had chosen another. Also he has eliminated courses that were popular with the students also in opposition to the philosophy intructors. Dr. Pearson even intimated that class room teaching would be monitored so he can be sure that what is said in class conforms with University policy. The apparent purpose of his move is to censor the philosophy department.[25]

The death knell for philosophy was announced in the dramatic headlines of 1 February 1973 issue of the student newspaper: "MORE FIRINGS MADE IN PHILOSOPHY DEPT., FOUR OF FIVE CONTRACTS NOT RENEWED."[26] Only one professor was left—and he had tenure and couldn't be fired. Dean Moorman staunchly defended the termination of the philosophy department: "In that department there was too much emphasis on discussion of things in the abstract, unconnected with formal training in philosophy."[27] Someone naively suggested that philosophy *is* the discussion of "things in the abstract."

The USM administration conducted an exhaustive search to replace the fired professors who allegedly did not concentrate enough on "formal training in philosophy." Selected as the new man from CRAP" was Robert E. Kuttner, holder of a doctorate in biochemistry and a specialist in brain chemistry. Kuttner came to Southern directly from a stint as research assistant to William Shockley. Shockley is a Stanford physicist who not only claims that blacks are genetically inferior to whites but campaigns for a federally funded bonus to blacks with low IQs who accept voluntary sterilization. Kuttner, who teaches cultural anthropology at USM, presented his "academic philosophy" to the 17th Annual Leadership Conference of the White Citizens' Councils of America on 2 September 1972. He said:

There are people in the South who think that we Northerners don't understand the Negro. Well, there were always Northerners who understood the Negro and there's more everyday! Now, don't misunderstand me about the black man. I'm not prejudiced; I'm experienced...
Now, what's my reaction to this famous phrase, "Do

you want your sister or your daughter to marry a black man?"...What ever made the Southerner believe that the ghetto black man had intentions as respectable as marriage for his daughter or his sister? Come up to the ghetto and take a look for yourself...That business of marriage. These girls never walked down the aisle dressed in white Sunday morning. I'll give you the raw facts. They're walking in the ghetto on Saturday night wearing their hot pants and their wigs and their boots. These girls got no wedding bands on their fingers. They've got needle scars on their arms, up and down the veins. And they don't try to catch the bridal bouquet; they're dodging the vice squad. There's no marriage license on file in the court house but a long police record on file in the hall of justice for prostitution and drug abuse. That's integration! Now, is there a moral in this? I can put it in a nutshell: If you keep busing your daughters into the ghetto, one of these days they're not going to come back...

For every interracial marriage there are four or five or six pimp-prostitute relationships. These are the ones the Southerner never talks about. He's worried about intermarriage. Here's another raw fact. The principle economic resource of the black ghetto male is the white girl! He can't afford a sixty or an eighty dollar a day drug habit without a white girl and integration makes it easier to get one...Can you beat up the old white pensioner for his social security check? Once a month you can but that's not enough for one good drug high. The only way you can afford a drug habit is to get a white girl to work for you...

The girl is going to be on a drug habit too because when the stardust is gone from her eyes she's going to go back to her mother. These girls will wake up and take the brown baby home to mother. You make sure she's got a good drug habit and that takes care of her...

Come into the ghetto. Medical services free. Trouble from the police? Free legal advice, free legal services. Kids? Grandmother's raising them and welfare is paying for them. Housing? For women there's a project. There aren't too many men who live there but when the checks arrive they come up. They won't live in the projects; they can do better. If you're a black dude you don't live in the project. If you park your Cadillac in the ghetto parking lot someone will steal your tires!...

Now, this kind of integration is not the only way to lose your daughter. I've met people who've been integrated without even sitting next to a black student. What you have to learn is there is a *remote control, long range type of integration.* I call it "invisible integration!" You can have a nice home in the liberal suburbs, country club, tennis court. You live in a split level ranch home. Daddy is prosperous. Mother told you everything you have to know. You go to an elite high school that sends seventy percent of its graduates to college. And you think you're safe? No, you see, you've got friends that go to integrated schools. Your girlfriend from that other high school dates a black boy. Your basketball team drinks wine with their team. And daddy's a liberal and daddy says all the problems in the ghetto are due to oppression, due to whites stepping on blacks, due to lack of opportunity. And you feel sympathetic; you want to be a social worker. And the nearest Negro is four blocks away and he's a dentist. You don't know anything about the Negro but you've been hooked; you've been integrated! This is invisible integration which you have to guard against.[28]

At long last there will be no more discussions of "things in the abstract" in the USM philosopy department.

Chapter Eight

FACULTY FIRINGS:
THE PERMANENT PURGE

*It's easy to find the credentials and training. But we want also a
teacher who won't have culture shock in Hattiesburg and be a
headache to the department.*

—*John Skates*
Chairperson, Department of History
University of Southern Mississippi

*I believe that sometimes, from time to time, the master must
without fail go through the ranks of the Party with a broom in
his hands.* [1]

—*Joseph Stalin,*
Thirteenth Party Congress

The above quotations perfectly describe the situation which
the USM faculty faces. For professors with opinions not identical
with those of the adminstrative hierarchy, the past has been a
nightmare of threats, economic reprisals, and outright firings.
There are, for faculty members, no methods of obtaining redress or
protection from the whims and animosities of the regime. In short,
the administration simply does not tolerate an honest difference of
opinion on professional, political, or administrative matters.

By way of introduction, let's take a look at total faculty turnover at USM for 1970 to 1973. In sum, in these years, a total of 211
Southern faculty members left for one reason or another.[2] Admit-

tedly, all of these people were not fired. Some simply retired and others, no doubt, went on to greener pastures without ever having gotten into trouble with the administration. On the other hand, some were very pointedly fired.[3] This chapter tells the story of some of them.

FREEDOM OF EXPRESSION: "PLEASE LET
SLEEPING MONKEYS LIE."

The concept of the university as a bastion of free expression is absolutely unheard of at Southern. Referring to the textbook rental service initiated in the fall of 1966, General McCain said:

> The ringleaders in the faculty who plotted against this inno-
> vation are no longer with us...If I do not watch myself care-
> fully, I will get the idea into my mind that all students and
> faculty members are like the ones who cause trouble...Some
> of these professors lecture against my methods in class;
> perhaps they will not be present on campus next fall.[4]

In a public speech to the Jackson Lions Club on 7 February 1964, the General said:

> There has been a lot of trouble with college professors on the
> matter of integration and segregation. We don't have that
> trouble at Southern. Each year I tell our instructors they are
> employed to teach...I will handle all other problems.[5]

Compliance with administrative policies at Southern would be simplified even further if there were no professors or students at all!

Dean of Men Rader Grantham is also well-known for his stand on free speech. He attained notoriety several years ago by confiscat-ing all copies of the student newspaper which con-tained the story of Southern's first black applicant since Clyde Kennard. In the spring of 1969, Dean Grantham sent an open letter to the faculty of the College of Arts and Sciences scolding them for "airing the University's 'dirty laundry' in meetings, in the newspapers and on TV..." Grantham continued: "I ask you to make an attempt to conduct your activities in a matter which befits your positions of esteem in this community more so than the manner pursued in recent days." Predictably, Dean Grantham's letter incensed many of its recipients. Typical was the response of an English professor who concluded a biting rebuttal with this comment: "I respectfully submit that for a faculty member to receive a letter of chastisement from a Dean of Men is quite like receiving a letter from the Guardian of Building and Grounds."[6]

It can be dangerous at Southern even to ask someone else's opinion. Consider the case of Ashley Morgan, chairman of the Department of Science Education in 1968. Morgan, in his position as regional director of the National Science Teachers Association, wrote to Mississippi Attorney General Joe Patterson for an opinion on the state's anti-evolution laws. The NSTA had participated as *amicus curiae* in the Arkansas "monkey law" case, when the law was declared unconstitutional by the U.S. Supreme Court. Morgan wanted to know if a similar suit would be necessary in Mississippi, the last state with a monkey law on its books (or backs).

He did not hear from Patterson; instead Morgan received a letter from Claude Fike, dean of the College of Arts and Sciences, who told him bluntly:

> You have...no right to address [Patterson] as a private individual on a matter of public policy with implications that affect public institutions. President McCain alone can speak for this institution on institutional matters. You should have gone through the President. This has caused embarrassment to him and to me.
>
> Will you kindly in the future refrain from letters that implicate the University or at least discuss them with someone before "sounding off." The particular issue you raised is somewhat redundant and irrelevent in light of the fact that there has been complete academic freedom to teach whatever a teacher feels must be taught in the name of academic truth.
>
> In the future, please let "sleeping monkeys lie."

Morgan took the suggestion and asked General McCain to obtain the requested opinion; his letter drew no response.[7] Morgan got the message and subsequently resigned without having to go through the messy ritual of overt firing.[8]

FREEDOM OF ASSOCIATION: "WE DON'T ASK WHAT ORGANIZATIONS PEOPLE ARE MEMBERS OF, DO WE?"

In 1960, the U.S. Supreme Court ruled unconstitutional an Arkansas law which required that every teacher file annually an affidavit listing every organization to which he or she had belonged or regularly contributed within the preceding five years.[9] Nevertheless, for a period of six years the Mississippi College Board of Trustees continued to enforce a statute with provisions identical to those declared unconstitutional. It was 1966 before a plaintiff with enough courage was found to challenge the statute in a federal court. The inevitable permanent injunction, of course, was the result.[10]

Still today it is suicidal for a USM professor to be associated with an unpopular organization, such as the American Civil Liberties Union. When W.D. Norwood, Jr. was interviewed by General McCain in the spring of 1969 for the chair of the English Department, he asked McCain, "What's going to happen the first time I hire a man here who's a member of the ACLU?" McCain rhetorically asked his secretary, "We don't ask what organization people are members of, do we?" She answered, "No, Sir, there's no place on the application blank for it." The General turned to Norwood and concluded, "Well, there's your answer!"[11]

Despite the rosy picture painted by General McCain, ACLU members at Southern have suffered a wretched fate. On 8 July 1970, an informational meeting was held to discuss the nature of the ACLU. A "visitor" from the administration, namely the director of Student Activities, strolled back and forth outside the room recording the names of the five professors attending the meeting.[12] Four of these have subsequently been fired and the fifth resigned before he could be fired. In fact, every faculty advisor to the student chapter of the ACLU has been fired, except one who resigned under pressure. Sanford Wood, the organization's advisor for 1972-73, received notice of his termination six weeks after he became the group's advisor.[13]

Simply the mention of the ACLU strikes fear in the hearts of administration officials. You'd think they had seen the ghost of Clyde Kennard! On 18 January 1971 Dean Fike interviewed Fred Bergerson for a position in the Political Science Department. Bergerson said that he was a liberal Democrat interested in politics, and that he was a member of the ACLU. At the mention of the ACLU, Dean Fike's jaw dropped, he clenched his teeth, doubled his fist, and went almost livid with rage; he couldn't terminate the interview quickly enough. As Bergerson exited, the Dean exclaimed, "Another one!"[14]

Every advisor to the liberal Progressive Student Association (PSA) has been fired. In May 1971, the PSA found itself again without an advisor. It approached B., a conservative tenured full professor, who agreed to be the group's advisor simply to keep PSA alive. The administration hardly could object to Professor B.'s conservative political views which clearly resembled its own. For example, at a "Peace by Victory" rally on 14 May 1970, Professor B. referred to the absence of most of the key participants in the past week's antiwar rally this way: "I can see we are being boycotted. Not only can I see it; I can smell it. For once, the air is fresh and clean."[15]

Nevertheless, the administration exhorted B. "as a colleague and a friend" not to assume the position of PSA advisor. The subtle hints had their effect and B. immediately reneged on his promise to serve. But for his libertarian gesture of initially offering to serve as the group's advisor, this professor, who had just been named the "Outstanding Faculty Member" in the entire university, received not a penny's increase in salary for the following year. (Even *I* got a $500 raise in my terminal contract for 1971-72.) Of course, the PSA kept receiving ultimatums from the administration saying that "It ought to locate an advisor as soon as possible."

Although the university's faculty handbook states on page thirteen that "the University of Southern Mississippi has an active chapter of the American Association of University Professors," [16] the organization has not met since 17 September 1970, when it protested the firing of its president, Julia Davis, and Robert Pierle, the faculty advisor to the PSA. At that meeting, the AAUP chapter passed a resolution requesting a hearing for Davis and Pierle, which the administration summarily turned down.[17] Intimidated by a fear of reprisals to its members, the group never reconvened after that fateful gathering. Alluding to this meeting, Charles Moorman, dean of the university, boasted in a 3 September 1971 address to a full faculty assembly: "Dean Gunn managed to fire six instructors with less commotion than Dean Fike aroused in doing away with two."[18]

Association with a right wing organization has been squelched as sternly as association with what at USM passes for a left wing group. In the fall of 1968 William Scarborough, faculty advisor to the American Independent Youth Chapter, spoke to its members in support of the George Wallace candidacy. For this he received a reprimand from Dean Fike, who contended that Scarborough's talk had "left the impression that the administration is endorsing [Wallace's] candidacy." Scarborough replied:

> The issue is not political. It's a question of how much control the administration should have over the activities of the faculty. They can get away with running the other ones off, by labeling them as left-wingers and communists. But I'm as conservative as anybody around, and I plan to stay.[19]

THE FIKE-SCARBOROUGH ETHICS HEARING: "WE DON'T PUT PRESSURE ON PEOPLE. GOOD LORD, I WISH WE COULD."

This William Scarborough is a truly remarkable man; in fact, he is one of the genuine heroes of Exit 13. A Phi Beta Kappa graduate from the University of North Carolina, Scarborough holds a masters degree from Cornell and a Ph. D. in history from UNC. Among the several published books he has written is the definitive work on plantation management in the Old South. A tenured professor of history at USM, Scarborough consistently receives excellent ratings from the students in the faculty evaluation handbook.

Scarborough operates from a tiny, green, concrete-block cubicle in the deepest recesses of the history department. On the door is a Sons of the Confederate Veterans decal (My great-great uncle or was killed in Pickett's Charge at Gettysburg," he'll tell you.) and on the wall is a full-size rebel flag and a color picture of George Wallace with a personal inscription. One would expect that Scarborough would be an administration favorite. After all, he has been a member of the White Citizens' Council since 1962, and General McCain has published articles in the Council's official journal. Beyond doubt, the heart of Scarborough's politics is his white supremacy attitude:

> I like a lot of them as individuals...it's as a group that I hate them... I'm a segregationist, no apologies, no denials..."Segregationist" or "white supremacist," yes, definitely. "Racist" I don't like; it is a loaded word. I base my attitudes on common sense and the evidence of history...I think Carleton Coons, who is a professor of physical anthropology at the University of Pennsylvania, has the best theory. He attributes the Negro's shortcomings to "cultural lag"—the hundreds of thousands of years later that the Negro developed into homo sapiens.

Scarborough says that he opens his Old South course with the warning: "We lost in 1865, but we'll win in 1970...we'll run out of time just after Chancellorsville."[20]

It was not Scarborough's political views but rather his personal code of justice and fair play which ultimately got him in trouble with the Southern administration. Scarborough publicly dissented, in the spring of 1969, from the arbitrary demotion of the chairman of the history department, who had given twenty-one years of service to USM. Because honest dissent is unheard of at Southern, Scarborough had to be purged.

To give a veneer of legitimacy to their case against Scarborough, General McCain and Dean Fike formed an Advisory Council in April 1969, composed of one faculty member from each of the seventeen departments in the College of Arts and Sciences. The Council performed one task before disbanding: it considered charges by Dean Fike that Scarborough was guilty of "contumacious and unethical conduct detrimental to the University." It was necessary to prove Scarborough guilty of such heinous charges because the administration had committed the ultimate folly of granting Scarborough tenure for his excellent scholarship and sound political views. Little had it realized that white supremacists cannot be trusted in all matters.

Following a lengthy hearing, the advisory council issued its report on 14 July 1969. It concluded that evidence to support Dean Fike's charges "was insufficient and inconclusive" and therefore the Council completely exonerated Scarborough of the charges. Things seldom work out as expected in Exit 13. To the consternation of Dean Fike and his forces, Scarborough *countercharged* that Dean Fike "has vindictively and capriciously manipulated recommendations concerning salary and rank of members of the history department in retribution for political and academic activities which happen to run counter to his beliefs." In its report, the council upheld Scarborough's allegations: "The Council finds that there is evidence to support this charge and consequently concludes that the charge of unethical conduct in the manipulation of recommendations regarding salary and rank is substantiated." The council pointed out in particular the following instances:

1.   Dr. John Phillip Posey has alleged that his recommended salary for the academic year 1968-69 was cut to punish him for his affiliation with the Loyal Democrats of Mississippi.

Dean Fike admitted that he personally reduced Dr. Posey's recommended salary by $1000 as a result of his [Posey's] activities as a member of the Loyalist Democratic Party. While there have been suggestions that Dean Fike was under pressure to reduce Dr. Posey's salary recommendation, the Dean has repeatedly assumed personal responsibility for the action. It is the view of this Council that all faculty members have the right to full participation in established political processes, even when it may be temporarily unpopular to so participate. It is quite clear that the reduction of Dr. Posey's recommended salary constituted punishment for his having exercised this political right. Such punishment is clearly an unethical infringement upon academic freedom.[21]
2. The Council is not in a position to judge the professional qualifications of members of the history department, but evidence exists to indicate that factors other than professional merit were used in determining the amount of salary increases to be recommended and that at least three members of the History Department suffered a reduction in their salary recommendations as a result of their responsible dissent.[22]

Scarborough further charged that Dean Fike "has blatantly and openly intimidated and threatened faculty members who have responsibly and lawfully dissented from his policies and/or sought to institute salutory changes in the University." On this point, the council report concluded: "The evidence supports the charge of unethical and unprofessional conduct in the intimidation of lawfully and responsibly dissenting faculty members. The council has reached this decision on the basis of a substantial body of evidence." In particular, the council pointed out the following instances:

1. Dean Fike, evidently in anger, answered Dr. John Phillip Posey's possible call for an A.A.U.P. investigation by stating that he [the Dean] would contact Dr. Posey's future employer and tell such that Dr. Posey was a "troublemaker." Professor Kenneth G. McCarty has alleged that Dean Fike informed him that his dissent from the administration's decisions was "jeopardizing your [McCarty's] position at this University" and that perhaps "you'd be better off if you found another job." Mr. McCarty considered this intimidation. No evidence to refute this testimony was presented.
2. The Council finds that Dean Fike contacted various members of the faculty in order to intimidate those who had promoted, signed, or considered signing a petition supporting the creation of a faculty senate.[23]

Thus ended Southern's version of the Army-McCarthy hearings. A council created expressly to find a history professor guilty of contumacious behavior and unethical conduct had exonerated him and, instead, adjudged the Dean of the College of Liberal Arts and Sciences guilty of unethical and unprofessional conduct. Although Professor Scarborough kept his job (Dean Moorman ironically boasts that "In the history of this university we have never failed to renew the contract of a faculty member on tenure."),[24] he receives only token salary raises—far below his colleagues.[25] And in this strange world where heroes and villains reverse roles with a vengeance, seven of the seventeen members of the advisory council either resigned or were fired in the year following the council's report. As usual, Dean Moorman had the last word:

> We don't put pressure on people. Good Lord, I wish we could...Nobody is terminated around here because his politics for example disagrees with my politics or the President's or anybody elses. Now, you understand that we believe very firmly around here in what is called academic freedom.[26]

TWO CARDINAL SINS: A BEARD AND A BABY

To this point I have dealt merely with the administration's consternation concerning the expression of unpopular opinions. The administration also gets very uptight about things like the hair on a man's face and a married woman having a baby.

Although Samson had flowing locks, Lincoln wore a beard, and even Uncle Sam sports a goatee, male teachers who seek to follow this hirsute tradition are commonly faced with official disapproval and discipline. Consider the case of X., a Military Science professor. In March 1971, the USM Military Science department recommended X. for an Army Commendation Medal (ARCOM). Immediately following the ROTC commissioning exercise on 23 May 1971, in the presence of the chairman of the Military Science Department and X.'s wife, X.'s endorser said words to this effect: "X., come on by the office, we have something to pin on you." The endorser repeated this statement, clearly implying that the ARCOM had been approved.

The next day X. officially signed out from the ROTC Detachment and departed for a leave of absence. Meanwhile, X.'s rater wrote a "superior" Officer Efficiency Report on him, covering the period from 1 August 1970 to 7 June 1971. X. arrived back on campus and on June 15 reported to his endorser, expecting the ARCOM and a good efficiency report. Instead, he received no award and a suprisingly adverse report which contained contradictory, inconsistent, and derogatory remarks.

The mystery of the "Great ARCOM Robbery" may never be unraveled, but one substantial clue is available. X. grew a *beard* during his official leave of absence from May 24 to June 12, and shaved it off before returning on June 10. At no time in these nineteen days was X. in uniform. However, X. enrolled in classes as a graduate student at Southern on June 7 and his beard undoubtedly was observed by members of the ROTC Detachment. Justice delayed may be justice denied, but at Southern one settles for small favors. Following an extensive investigation of X.'s case by the army, his adverse Officer Efficiency Report was rescinded.[27]

Another episode concerns I., a married professor of music who had taught at USM since 1968. In the winter of 1971 she committed the unpardonable *faux pas* of becoming pregnant. In late March 1972, the dean of I.'s college told her that she was being fired at the end of the current spring quarter, explicitly because she was having a baby. I. taught out the remainder of the quarter. Her baby was born on June 7, nineteen days after the spring quarter ended. I. wasn't ordered to take a temporary leave of absence in order to have her baby. Rather she was, in effect, fired as a punishment for having a baby.[28]

FIRINGS IN THE PHILOSOPHY DEPARTMENT: FOR "PERSONAL REASONS."

Department chairs who refuse to be "yes men" for the administration are arbitrarily fired. Cedric Evans, a Englishman, was hired as chair of the philosophy department as of September 1971. All went well for a while—about one week. The College of Liberal Arts Curriculum Committee met in early September to consider the application of Becky J., a campus student leader in disfavor with the administration, for readmission to Southern.[29] One professor moved that Becky be accepted. A long silence ensued. Just as the motion was about to die for lack of a second, Evans supported it. The motion passed! After the meeting, the chair of the department of Anthropology and Comparative Religious Studies, himself an

Englishman, told Evans that it was inappropriate for a "foreigner" to "rock the boat."

Evans' next "mistake" was to recommend that tenure be granted to G., a philosophy professor who was completing his sixth year at USM, and who formerly was chair of the philosophy department. Dean Moorman rejected Evans' recommendation, extemporizing a new policy that a chair's recommendation need not be followed if the chair had served for less than one year. This "policy" was implemented retroactively and G. was not awarded tenure. A few months later G. was fired.

The greatest insult occurred on 19 April 1972 when Dean Fike monitored Evans' philosophy class. For the entire session, Fike sat in the back of the room, and his presence may have gone unnoticed if he had not rudely conversed with a Vietnam veteran—obviously about Evans—loudly enough to be heard in the front of the room. At the conclusion of the class, Dean Fike filed out of the room, pausing only to say to Evans in an extremely sarcastic voice, "Very lively discussion!"

In May 1972 Dean Fike informed Evans that he was fired as chair of the philosophy department. The Dean assured Evans that he would be promoted from associate professor to full professor in order to "cushion" his inevitable reduction in salary. The promotion never materialized. However, Evans' salary for 1972-73 was $6000 *less* than he made the previous year. One of Evans' courses, "Ideology and Utopia," was dropped from the new curriculum. Finally, in September 1972, Evans received notice that he was being fired outright, effective 1 June 1973. The stated reason was "administrative reorganization." At the same time, Sanford Wood, another philosophy professor, who just happened to have become faculty advisor to the ACLU six weeks earlier, also received an identical letter of termination.[30]

In January 1973 two other philosophy professors were notified of their dismissals for "personal reasons."[31] Both were associate professors who had given five and seven years of service respectively to Southern. This left only one philosophy professor, a "Distinguished University Professor" (there have only been three professors so honored in the history of the university) with tenure. The administration tried unsuccessfully to demote him to university chaplain.[32]

Perhaps the administration should be merciful to the Southern student by completely abolishing all philosophy courses. This would make little difference, since it can always tell future students that anthropology is just another word for philosophy.

FIRINGS IN THE ENGLISH DEPARTMENT: "EVERYTHING IS PEACE AND LOVE AND HEARTY GOOD FELLOWSHIP BUT SORRY YOU GOTTA GO"

In the spring of 1969 Dean Moorman called W.D. Norwood, Jr., chair of the English department at San Angelo State University in Texas, and said, "We want you to come down here and look around and see if you would think about being our chairman." Norwood replied, "Lord, have you ever read *Black Like Me?* The worst scene of all took place in Hattiesburg!" Norwood was flown to Hattiesburg for an interview when the azaleas were in bloom in the spring. Like everyone, he was immediately enchanted by the beauty of the environs, was persuaded that Mississippi was becoming part of the "New South," and therefore accepted the position as chair of Southern's English department effective 1 July 1969.

Norwood became suspicious of things his very first day on the job. During his spring interview, Norwood had called the English department into a meeting and told department members: "I want you to understand that I'm not Dean Moorman (who had been the department's chair for ten years) and if I'm going to run the department, it's going to have to be run my way. I don't see everything the way he does. For example, I don't think his freshman program is worth a damn." Norwood had an agreement with Deans Moorman and Fike that, following his address, the English department was to vote as to whether or not it wanted him as chair. Although Norwood had been assured that such a vote was held, he discovered that the "election" consisted of Deans Moorman and Fike consulting with three senior members of the department who said, "Yeah, well, fine." After all, that was customarily the way the English department had always held elections.[33]

Norwood got along very well with the administration his first year, even receiving Dean Moorman's lavish praise in the annual Dean's report in late 1969.[34] But the summer of '70 proved to be Norwood's undoing. Dean Moorman disapproved of the presence of Norwood and four other faculty members ("the five pinko professors") at an informational meeting to discuss the ACLU on 8 July 1970.[35] Next came the matter of Norwood's dress. During that fateful summer, he wore sports shirts and slacks because of the unbearable heat. One of Norwood's colleagues reported that Dean Moorman was very upset with Norwood's casual clothing which Moorman interpreted as indicating an anti-Establishment attitude. Moorman told Norwood: "You are the chairman of the biggest department here and the businessmen in town would consider this to be just not properly dignified." Norwood started wearing coats and ties again, but by then it was too late; the Dean's concern had shifted to Norwood's luncheon companions. Norwood had always eaten lunch with whomever happened to be in the English department office at noon. That particular quarter it happened to be Richard Johnson and Robert Pierle, two professors who were in ill-favor with the administration. Norwood refused to capitulate on his eating habits.

The key factor in Norwood's firing came in September of 1970. Dean Fike called Norwood into his office and told him that he and Dean Moorman had decided to give a terminal contract to Robert Pierle, an English professor. (Pierle's crimes against the regime were grievous: he had not only attended the infamous ACLU informational meeting and was faculty advisor to the Progressive Student Association, but he had even served on the advisory council which condemned Dean Fike in the Scarborough affair.) Dean Fike told Norwood that as Pierle's chair, he would like for Norwood to *recommend* the termination of Pierle. In fact, the matter was put to Norwood in precisely these terms: "You've got to make up your mind whether you're going to go down with the ship or take the life boats." In short, Norwood was told explicitly that he himself would be fired if he didn't personally recommend Pierle's firing.[36]

Norwood understood perfectly well why the deans wanted him to recommend the firing: that way, if the AAUP investigated the affair, it would look like the firing was based upon ineffective teaching, but if Norwood didn't concur, it would look like a political firing. Pierle, himself, advised Norwood to go along with the administration because he could be of more value to the university by playing the game than by trying to take a stand on a losing issue. However, Norwood firmly believed that Pierle was an excellent professor and that his own role as chair was to recommend what he thought was in the best interest of the English department and the university. Furthermore, Norwood concluded that if he recommended Pierle's dismissal he would sacrifice his own self-respect and the respect of his colleagues in the department. Therefore, while Norwood wrote the letter terminating Pierle, he refused to recommend the firing. As Norwood told Dean Fike: "All right, sir, I've decided. I'll just have to go down with the ship if that's the way it is."

Norwood was not removed as department chair until 24 May 1971—eight months later—but he might as well have been because, in effect, he was not the chair. General McCain boasted on 13 March 1972: "Ever since I arrived here, each department chairman has been responsible for recruiting his own faculty."[37] Things didn't work that way in the English department during Norwood's second year as chair. The case of Z. is instructive.

Z. had received her masters' degree from USM and presently was teaching at Florida State. She wanted a teaching position in the English department at Southern in order to be near her mother, who was ill and lived in Laurel, Mississippi. Dean Fike apparently promised Z. a job at USM and then referred her to Norwood, expecting him to formally recommend her. Exercizing his independent judgment regarding the current personnel needs of the English department, Norwood refused to recommend Z. because the department already had three professors in Renaissance literature, Z.'s area of specialization. Nevertheless, Norwood began getting suggestions from the administration that he ought to hire Z. Finally, Dean Fike unilaterally *invited Z. to join the English department.*[38]

Several of the professors who Norwood recruited to teach in the English department while he was chair were fired almost as soon as they arrived on the Southern campus. In fact, Richard Johnson, a full professor hired by Norwood in the summer of 1970 to direct the Center for Writers, got in trouble his very *first day* at USM when he wore a peace button in his coat lapel to registration. Johnson also attended the notorious ACLU informational meeting and even served as the group's first faculty advisor. He resigned before he could be fired.

Robert Cochran, another Norwood recruit, was fired in June 1972. Marice Brown, acting chair of the English department at that time, asked to see Cochran about the matter of his dress—he did not wear a tie to work—and suggested that he see the wisdom of bringing his attire into line with the style favored by the USM administration. Cochran replied that he had no intention of modeling his personal appearance after that of Colonel Sanders. He perceived the whole gambit as a simple harrassment and provocation, and replied that no such subterfuge was needed. They had fired people before and surely knew how it was done.

The next day Cochran wore a tuxedo to class. In a matter of days he received the inevitable letter of termination, effective at the end of the following academic year (May 1972). Cochran resigned immediately—effective August 1971—with these words: "My year in this University, and more especially, the recent auto-da-fe within the English Department, have made it clear that our radically different notions of university education make it in our mutual interest to accomplish our separation as speedily as possible."[39] Cochran reflected on these events in a letter to me:

> Following this exchange of letters I *had no conferences* with Fike, Moorman, McCain, or any other administrative figures. I packed my bags and got out. Your experience at USM surely taught you that such overt confrontations are avoided at all cost—everything is peace and love and hearty good fellowship but sorry you gotta go—this being a cardinal tenet of the "Southern gentleman" syndrome. Moorman and Fike, hating everything I ever represented or loved, were always, nonetheless (and this remains one of the most bizarre of experiences offered by the USM funny farm), near perfect models of that bloated and overacted courtesy that passes for decorum among certain Southerners best described as refugees from *Gone With the Wind.* All we ever did was smile at each other![40]

When Norwood himself got the inevitable ax on 24 May 1971, he was called into Dean Moorman's office. In the presence of Dean Fike, Moorman said, "Bill, you told us one time that if we were ever dissatisfied with you as chairman, you would resign. Well, that's our feeling." Norwood replied, "All right, that's what I said." Norwood compliantly signed a letter of resignation as English department chair. Dean Moorman said specifically, "Now, you understand that this doesn't affect your position as a professor," and then walked out of the room.

Marice Brown, a USM alumna, was appointed the English department acting chair. About a month later, Brown called Norwood into her office and asked him what his plans were. She concluded: "Well, you see, if you stay here, that will give us two dismissed chairmen. Somehow or other we've got to heal the wounds of the department, and I'd like to either have a letter of resignation from you or I'll have to send you a terminal contract."[41] Norwood replied, "You send me a terminal contract. I'd just as soon keep the thing reasonably clear on the record. I already signed one resignation." On 8 July 1971, Norwood was fired. No written explanation or statement of reasons for Norwood's termination was given by the university, nor was any opportunity for a hearing afforded.

When Norwood was first interviewed for the post at Southern, it was agreed that if he ever were relieved of the chairship or if he resigned the position and went back to classroom teaching only, his salary would remain at the same level as when he was chair. This verbal agreement was an explicit condition of his employment. Nevertheless, the terminal contract which Norwood received for 1971-72 contained a $2500 cut in salary from what he had received as department chair.[42]

WOOD V. UNIVERSITY OF SOUTHERN MISSISSIPPI: AN ATMOSPHERE OF TERROR

The eerie sight of a nearly vacant courtroom set the stage for the denouement of the Norwood firing. Deposed philosophy professor Sanford Wood and W.D. Norwood jointly sued the University of Southern Mississippi, alleging that their firings were in violation of constitutionally protected expression and association. In order to strengthen their case, the two professors attempted to demonstrate in the court that the USM administration has habitually intimidated any faculty member who lawfully dissents from its policies. But ironically this same deadening intimidation victimized the plaintiffs in the trial, which took place in federal district court in Hattiesburg on 16 July 1974. The atmosphere of terror at USM deterred countless potential witnesses from telling the court their horror stories. Only one non-tenured professor, Gordon Weaver, the current ACLU faculty advisor, came forward to rebut administration testimony. Another English professor did come into the courtroom one morning for about five minutes, but felt the walls closing on him. Not surprisingly, the administration won a directed verdict of "not guilty."

Chapter Nine

THE ADMINISTRATION: TRUTH, JUSTICE...AND THE SOUTHERN WAY

Catch 22 says that they have the right to do anything we can't stop them from doing.

— *Joseph Heller*

This chapter title brings to mind the prologue of television's "Superman" series which ended: "Superman...disguised as Clark Kent...fights the never-ending battle for truth, justice, and the American way." Superman had an uphill fight on his hands, but for mortals at the University of Southern Mississippi, it is a downright futile struggle.

The administrative agencies with which Southern students have their greatest contact are the campus security, which arrests them, and the Office of the Dean of Students, which sentences them. What the Constitution of the United States giveth, the Southern administration taketh away.

The heads of staff:

Willie V. Oubre: Director of Campus Security; M.S. degree from USM; first displayed his mettle in the law enforcement field when, as Deputy Sheriff, he arrested Clyde Kennard in the chicken feed caper.[1]

Rader Grantham: Dean of Men; M.S. degree from USM with a major in physical education.

CAMPUS SECURITY CHECKS OUT A CAR:
"THERE'S NOT ENOUGH DEW ON IT."

Sometimes campus security merely imitates the Keystone Cops. One November night in 1971, J.C. Gardner, a Southern student, parked his car in the parking lot of the Hillcrest dormitory at 11:30 and drove off with Hugo Johnson to a house party. At 4:30 the next morning Hugo drove J.C. back to the Hillcrest dorm. As J.C. was walking through the parking lot towards his car, two USM campus security officers approached. The conversation went like this:

    Officers: What are you doing here?
        J.C.: I'm going to get in my car.
    Officers: How long has your car been here?
        J.C.: Since 11:30
    Officers: Where's your car?
        J.C.: Over there, that red Corvette
    Officers: How long did you say it's been here?
        J.C.: Since 11:30.
    Officers: This car hasn't been here since 11:30; there's not
               dew on it.

Not satisfied with J.C.'s explanation of his whereabouts for the evening, the policeman made him spend the next one hour and forty-five minutes riding around with them while they checked out his story. Of course, the officers readily conceded that as a *male* USM student, J.C. had a right to be anywhere on campus at any time.[2]

SETTLING A DISPUTE: "WELL, I'M
GOING TO MAKE YOU FUNNY."

J.C. was lucky—not all confrontations with the campus security end as harmoniously as his. On the evening of 11 February 1973, Willie C., a black USM student, and his friend were watching TV in the lobby of the student union building. Randy, the student employee working at the nearby information desk, held the front door open so that he could listen for the telephone while he talked to a friend outside the building. Willie politely requested that Randy close the door because it created a very cold draft. Randy refused, saying, "The door's going to stay open; that's the way it's going to be." When Willie threatened to call the campus security to arbitrate the matter, Randy obligingly called the security office himself.

Officer Richard H. arrived immediately. Willie explained his case and Officer H. concluded, "Randy's in charge here and what he says goes. Randy has responsibility to run things the way he pleases. I'm just telling you how it is." Willie tried to talk but the patrolman interrupted, "You just sit down and shut up." Willie never raised his voice or cursed, but he did smile. Officer H. was visibly upset. Willie explained, "I'm not trying to be funny." Officer H. replied, "Well, I'm going to make you funny," and with that the policeman slugged Willie, knocking his eyeglasses across the floor. Then the officer put his walkie-talkie down, apparently expecting Willie to fight back. But Willie merely said that he was going to call the campus security office. Officer H. replied, "I'll call for you." He did and then left.

A funny thing happened as Willie went to the campus security office to press charges against Officer H. He found *himself* arrested by the Hattiesburg police, who already had arrived at the campus security office. Officer H. pressed charges against Willie for interfering with the duties of an officer and disturbing the peace. Willie had to post a $200 property bail bond and await trial.[3]

ENFORCING PROHIBITION: "I DIDN'T HAVE A CHANCE TO PUT IT IN A CUP."

Mississippi law forbids the possession, sale, or consumption of alcoholic beverages on college campuses. But in the state that from time immemorial tolerated the cynical disregard of its prohibition law and blithely collected a black market tax on liquor during the Prohibition era,[4] how could one assume that respect for the law would exist at USM? Let's examine the Southern strategy for a double-double standard.

The first type of a double standard is between students and non-students possessing beer on campus. Both the New Orleans Saints pro football team and the National Guard, two groups who annually visit Southern during the summer for training, reportedly keep beer on campus, while campus security turns its back on the situation. When the Southern student newspaper reported in August 1973 that the Saints players, coaches, and newsmen were consuming liquor in Thad Vann Hall, USM campus police recoiled at the thought of cracking down. Chief Oubre said: "Beer in Vann Hall is illegal but we don't have any authority to stop them." He added: "We don't really want to push things but, you know, taking beer away from these New Orleans people is like taking a bottle away from a baby."[5]

On the other hand, campus security takes its law enforcement responsibility against Southern students very seriously. For instance, at the Louisiana Tech football game on 16 September 1972, five Southern students were arrested in the stands for drinking and twenty-five had their booze confiscated. After the game Chief Oubre said: "The security department will use whatever means are at its disposal to prevent this type of activity from reoccurring." True to his word, about twenty-five officers from the Hattiesburg police department and campus security enforced the state's beer law at the October 7 football game against West Texas State. The Southern stadium was nearly turned into a prison as guards were stationed above the crowd on top of the press box with flashlights. Chief Oubre proudly boasted: "We had men all over the stadium, some in plain clothes even."[6]

Another symbol of the double standard, which has popular usage at Southern, is the "cup"—as in "Dixie cup." Even though liquor is illegal on campus, social fraternities freely consume booze with the tacit approval of university officials. In the fall of 1972 the assistant dean of students told members of a social fraternity that alcohol may be consumed as long as it is in a cup. One student picked up by campus security for carrying a bottle of wine on campus defended himself by saying, "I didn't have a chance to put it in a cup."[7]

The dramatic showdown on this double standard occurred on Fraternity Row on Saturday night 16 December 1972. Fred Horne, the head resident of Scott Hall, and Joe Brashier, president of the Association of Men Students, executed a perfectly planned "bust" in which two informants who were friends of fraternity members were used. The undercover agents took pictures and sampled the punch of a fraternity party on campus. When Horne and Brashier asked campus security "to do your duty" by enforcing the state law on fraternities, the agent stammered and stuttered and said that he "couldn't do that." The reaction of the assistant dean of students was: "You are trying to be saviors." And lower, in a hushed voice, "and you might just be crucified."[8] Horne was fired as head resident of Scott Hall.

In April 1975 Hattiesburg District Attorney Rex Jones was presented with a petition signed by 1300 USM students (85 percent of all on-campus students who were not fraternity members) alleging selective enforcement of state alcohol laws; the D.A. immediately launched an investigation of the university. General McCain's response was: "Mr. Jones can do as he damn pleases."

DISCIPLINING STUDENTS: "YOU'RE GOING TO FIND YOURSELF DOWN THERE LOCKED UP."

While the handling of troublesome students haunts officials at many universities, "Southern has adequate provision for due process in handling student discipline." At least that's what the dean of student affairs says.[9] Let's observe this justice firsthand.

On 5 May 1972, Associate Dean of Students Rader Grantham called USM student Stephen Pike into his office. Dean Grantham violently objected to Pike's pressing charges at the campus security office against the dean of women for confiscating his ID card at the student senate meeting on 1 May 1972. The following is a transcript of this remarkable "hearing" in Dean Grantham's office, tape recorded with the Dean's permission:

Grantham: You are not going to interfere with an official of this university. You understand? You are not going to have an administrative official arrested.

Pike: As long as they're not interfering with my rights.

Grantham: No one has interfered with your rights, Pike.

Pike: Well, I was under the understanding since it was my ID, someone took it without a warrant, it's personal property.

Grantham: No, you see the identification card is for the purpose of identifying students, or else they'll be no purpose in having it.

Pike: I'm obligated to show it, but not necessarily to give it away.

Grantham: Was it taken and not returned?

Pike: It was refused to be returned when I asked for it. There was quite a lot of time that went on.

Grantham: But your identification card was returned to you.

Pike: Only after.

Grantham: *If you press charges again on this campus against an administrative official, you're going to be able to get all of your things together and move, because you're going to find yourself down there locked up.*

Pike: What I'm asking is: regardless of whether it's my right or not, I'm not allowed to press charges against anyone on this campus?

Grantham: Not in the performance of their duties.

Pike: Well, there's been some question whether it's the performance of their duties or violation of my rights.

Grantham: There is no question.

Pike: But don't you see that if I take it to court.

Grantham: You take it buddy. If you can get it up and go with it to court. O.K. Bye.

Pike: What I'm saying is that as a citizen of the United States I have a right to press charges.

Grantham: Go right ahead but get off this campus to do it. Get off the campus.

Pike: I don't understand. If I'm on campus it doesn't take away my rights as a citizen of the United States.

Grantham: No sir, but it doesn't take away her authority either.

Pike: I showed her my ID. She had plenty of time to take care of it. I asked for it back. She refused.

Grantham: You understand?

Pike: Yes, I understand.

Grantham: Because if it happens again, I'm promising you.

Pike: If the same thing happens again, I'll probably take it to court.

Grantham: Good. You can have fun...I'm saying that if he goes back to attempt to have a member of the administrative staff of this university arrested for performing their duties, you see, I'm going to have them do whatever necessary...I don't care who you go to; you can go to the FBI...

Pike: You mean just for pressing charges at all?

Grantham: You bet'cha. You bet'cha.

Pike: It seems to me that if I press charges it is up to the police to find out.

Grantham: You don't have to worry about a single thing. You see, I'm just telling you how it is. And you can like it or not like it; I really don't care. You understand?

Pike: What I'm asking is that shouldn't it be up to the security?

Grantham: It shouldn't be up to anybody. You see, it's up to her to do as she pleases in the performance of her duties and it's not up to you to question it at all, except you can come over here the next day and question it. But you're not going to interfere with it, do you understand me? If you interfere with it again, I'll promise you something.

Pike: What I was saying is that I wasn't interfering with her. All I did is go to Security and press charges. This is my right as a citizen of the United States. Now, if Security wants to interfere, that's their business. If the police want to interfere, that's their business. Then, *they're* interfering; not me.

Grantham: No, you're interfering.

Pile: All I'm doing is taking care of my own civil rights and that's my duty as an American citizen.

Grantham: You really had them violated. You really had them taken away.

Pike: Well, it's up to the court.

Grantham: You've ridiculed this lady unjustly without any reason at all; you've been critical of her.

Pike: I had backing and if you want to take it to court I have witnesses.

Grantham: You've got backing? You can get your backing and, you know, I don't care what you do with it.

Pike: If you think I've ridiculed her unjustly you can take it to court. I've got witnesses to back me up.

Grantham: What would I do taking it to court?

Pike: Well, if you feel your rights have been violated, you have the right to go to court.

Grantham: I don't want to go to court. Do you understand? I'm telling you, we're not going to court. If you want to got to court, get yourself up and go; see, I don't care. If you want to go to court, you go; that's your own business. You can take it any-time you want to, but next time—I'll make you an honest, sincere and faithful promise—next time you interfere with that lady, you're going to have a problem that you're going to have to deal with.

Pike: Thank you. Is that all?

Grantham: That's all.[10]

"BLACKLISTED" STUDENTS AND A FIRED DEAN: HE REFUSED TO REFUSE.

According to the *USM Bulletin*, any student placed on academic suspension has an automatic right to appeal her or his suspension after one quarter.[11] That's what the *Bulletin* says, but...At the beginning of the spring quarter of 1971, a group of Southern students who had been placed on academic suspension the previous quarter attempted to appeal their suspensions. Their requests were turned down, with no reasons at all—academic or otherwise—given for the rejections. The suspended students had one thing in common: several of them had been associated with the *Foundation Press,* a now defunct Hattiesburg "underground" newspaper.

Various Southern administrators sincerely denied the existence of any sort of "blacklist." However, just a few hours after the denials, such a list was located and "liberated" from the Southern Registrar's Office.[12] When the concerned students showed a copy of the blacklist to several administrators, the reaction was indifference. The one exception was the reaction of the dean whose job it was to inform blacklisted students that they would be refused admission. This dean admitted that the administration used "systematic discrimination" against students it didn't want. In one instance, this dean balked at dismissing a student who was on the blacklist. He was fired as dean and his post was abolished. He had refused to refuse.[13]

THE "SOUTHERN FOUR": "THE PLAINTIFFS WERE NOT ACCORDED PROCEDURAL DUE PROCESS."

Despite the administration's boasting about its enlightened disciplinary procedures, it was under its leadership that four USM students were tried, found guilty, and expelled by a judicial process in which the defendants were denied the right to legal counsel, the right to call witnesses for their defense, and the right to cross-examine witnesses brought against them.

On 18 May 1970 these four students were notified that they were to appear before the Men's Disciplinary Committee. Eight days later, they were informed that the committee was placing them on indefinite suspension and that they could apply for readmission only after a period of one year. The suspensions were for alleged possession (not distribution) of leaflets on May 18 which mistakenly informed students that classes would be suspended on that same day in a memorial for two youths slain at Jackson State College. The defendants denied having any knowledge of the presence of the notices in the vehicle in which they were riding.[14]

The suspended students filed for an injunction in federal court, asking that they be reinstated. They maintained that their constitutional rights were violated in the disciplinary proceedings against them. On 15 June 1970 U.S. District Court Judge Walter L. Nixon, Jr. ordered that the students be reinstated to the university and that they be given a new hearing by the board of trustees. In the words of the court:

> After a full hearing on the Motion for Temporary Order, this Court found in a written Memorandum Opinion filed herein that plaintiffs were not accorded procedural due process by the proceedings conducted by the disciplinary Committee of the defendant University insomuch as they were not given the specific names of witnesses who would testify against them, with the exception of the name of the defendant Grantham; they were not furnished with copies of statements of witnesses who were to testify; they were not accorded the right to hear the witnesses against them testify before the Committee; and they were denied the right to have their attorney present to participate therein.[15]

A CAMPUS CHARTER FOR THE ACLU

It was as a result of the maltreatment given the "Southern Four," that many USM students felt it was necessary to have a legal agency on campus. So, during the summer of 1970 a group of students began the process of forming a campus chapter of the American Civil Liberties Union (which later had so much trouble getting and keeping a faculty advisor).

The hopes of the chapter organizers were temporarily dashed when the Student-Faculty Committee on Campus Organizations met behind closed doors and denied the chapter's application for a charter. In a letter dated 3 July 1970, the Committee offered no explanation as to why the application was denied other than "that was the decision of the committee."[16] When the students concerned asked the chair of the Committee about the decision, he gave no reason except that "it isn't in the best interest of the university."[17] Perhaps there is something subversive about the Bill of Rights the administration wished to protect the students from.

With fall quarter beginning, the frustrated founding members decided not to waste any more time in trying to convince the administration of the attributes of the ACLU. In late October 1970 the chapter filed suit in the federal district court for a preliminary injunction to compel the university to approve its charter.

After a year of litigation, a three-judge panel of the Fifth District Circuit Court of Appeals on 10 November 1971 unanimously ordered USM to grant the ACLU a charter for its campus chapter. The court stated:

> We concluded that...the Committee failed to adduce any valid reasons for banning the Chapter from the University campus...It has now been more than a year since the Chapter was denied the same place in the sun on the campus of the University of Southern Mississippi accorded to other student organizations—without any justification at all, so far as we are able to discern.[18]

General McCain omnisciently observed, "We have not made a formal statement when any other organization was chartered. It's just another organization. It makes no difference to me if it was chartered by the committee or by the courts."[19] But it did make a difference to the taxpayers of Mississippi—a difference of more than $12,000. This was the taxable cost resulting from the lawsuits filed by the ACLU to get itself recognized by university officials, which the federal court directed USM to pay.[20]

Strangely, the administration seemed to welcome the ACLU once it had been enjoined by the Court of Appeals. The Dean of the University said:

> I think you'll find that the ACLU will have very little to investigate or do...I think the ACLU is going to find...that all of this great furor, that when they begin to look around, we're not violating any folks' civil rights around here...It is my opinion that when the ACLU does come on the campus, they're going to find very little to object to.[21]

Yes, the ACLU seems to have found a home at Southern.

Chapter Ten

STUDENT'S RIGHTS: ACADEMIC MARTIAL LAW

ABROGATION OF THE BILL OF RIGHTS: FREEDOM OF THE PRESS.

At Southern, much of the constitutional law is treated as a pinkish plot. The First Amendment guarantees of freedom of speech and press and "right of the people peaceably to assemble" have been eliminated. Even the prohibition against "an establishment of religion" was flagrantly violated by the requirement (until 1970) that Southern students be members of and pay dues to the Student Christian Federation.

Southern's version of freedom of the press is exemplified by administration censorship of the campus newspaper, the *Student Printz*. One would expect that the administration would approve of the politics of this paper. After all, its editor is selected by the administration on the basis of "the journalistic philosophy" espoused by the applicants.[1] Yet despite the *Printz'* invariable support of the administration, the latter does not spare the paper its wrath. On 27 September 1971 dean of the university characterized the *Printz* as too liberal, too opinionated, and grossly irresponsible. According to the dean, the newspaper should publish nothing but facts; it should read like a history book with no opinions whatsoever.[2]

Perhaps the most absurd censorship episode concerned the 21 March 1972 issue of the *Student Printz*. A cartoon which said, "Love is Never Having to Say You're Hungry" was censored. In fact, five thousand copies of the cartoon were burned and the students received newspapers with blank spaces where the cartoon had been. The faculty advisor to the newspaper maintained that the cartoon referred to "oral genital sex."[3]

THE RIGHT OF PEACEABLE ASSEMBLY: "MAKE SURE YOU HAUL HIM OFF CAMPUS."

The 1972 student handbook, like its predecessors, stated that "any student parade, serenade, demonstration, rally, and/or other meeting or gathering for any purpose, conducted on the campus-...must be scheduled with the President...at least 48 hours in advance of the event."[4] Let's see how this regulation operates at Southern.

On 13 October 1969, the USM Student Senate added its support to the October 15 National Vietnam Moratorium Day by sponsoring a rally for that date.[5] Student leaders attempted to get permission from the Student Activities Committee (composed entirely of administrators) to hold the rally. However, all committee members, when approached, denied that they were members of the committee, so it was impossible to schedule the rally legally.[6] Indeed, on 15 October 1969, Southern had what may have been the only moratorium in the country broken up by a university administration. More than 200 students participated in a silent and dignified march across campus—the epitome of orderliness. The procession had been in progress for twenty minutes when two campus security officers and the Dean of Men, Rader Grantham, halted the marchers and told them that they would have to disperse, which they did.[7] All along, about fifty non-marchers sat in front of the university snack bar, heckling and cursing the peace marchers. One of them ripped a black banner bearing a peace symbol from the front of the building and burned it in the gutter. The student responsible then walked away unmolested while campus security officers looked on.[8]

Even when the administration permits students to assemble, its "benign neglect" effectively scuttles the gathering. Consider the 7 May 1970 antiwar rally sponsored by the liberal Progressive

Student Association. Throughout the speeches hecklers made so much noise that no one could hear. Campus security did nothing. When one officer overheard some hecklers threatening to beat up one of the demonstrators, the officer's reply reportedly was, "Make sure you haul him off campus if you are going to do it." As the rally was ending, about ten hecklers approached a woman who had some protest posters. They attempted to take a poster away from her so they could, as they said, "punch a hole in it." An officer who observed the incident reportedly told the woman "We don't want any trouble here."[9]

Approximately eight-five Southern students gathered around the fountain in front of the administration building at 4:00 p.m. on 15 May 1974, for an ACLU-sponsored (and administration approved) protest against alleged administration interference in student government activity. At the conclusion of the rally, some participants entered the still-open administration building from the south side, walked double-file about fifty feet, and immediately exited through the west entrance. As a result of this action, the ACLU was charged and found guilty of holding an "unscheduled march" and placed on "activity probation" for one year.[10] The university's response in this instance was only part of its campaign of repression against the ACLU which was nicely summarized in the plaintiff's legal brief in the case of *Wood v. University of Southern Mississippi* (1974):

> What the University was unable to do, i.e. refuse to recognize the ACLU Chapter, above board, it has sought to do surreptitiously by making it extremely difficult for the Chapter to exist at all through terminations of the employment of faculty advisors, intimidation of Chapter members, and restrictions on the activities of the Chapter as an organization.[11]

The most outrageous recent violation of the right of peaceable assembly concerned a couple who were simply sitting on the grass by the lake on the Southern campus when a campus security officer "came along and handed them a parking ticket."[12]

FREEDOM OF SPEECH: "OF COURSE, YOU KNOW WHAT THEY WOULD COME HERE FOR."

The strictness with which speaker regulations are applied in all Mississippi colleges is determined almost entirely by the individual college president. In 1970, authoritarian speaker control at Southern was unique among the state's universities. As General McCain himself said, "999 times out of a thousand" the board of trustees would go along with his decisions.[13]

In November of 1966, Dr. William L. Giles, president of Mississippi State University, gave state NAACP President Aaron Henry permission to speak on his campus. General McCain's response was that the case at Mississipi State had no implication regarding Southern's speaker policy. The general stated that "an outside group was responsible for the decision. They created this entire case simply to embarrass Dr. Giles," McCain said, adding that if any such groups attempted the same at USM, he would perhaps handle the situation differently. "If anyone tries to give me a hard time," said General McCain. "I will return the favor."[14]

Prominent individuals such as Hodding Carter, Pulitzer prize-winning publisher from Greenville, Mississippi, and Frank Smith, former Mississippi congressman, have been turned down by General McCain with a great deal of consistency. McCain told a delegation from the campus Newman Foundation, a Catholic youth group, that it had "no concept of responsibility," as evidenced by its efforts to have George Wallace, Richard Nixon, and Robert Kennedy approved as campus speakers. The first two he readily authorized, according to a statement signed by two club members, but "concerning Kennedy he was hesitant. Kennedy, he felt, might cause Southern to gain the disfavor of the state legislature and the board of trustees."[15]

On the other hand, from 1970 to 1972 a parade of comedians, musicians, and anyone else who didn't have anything "dangerous" to say appeared at Southern, including Bob Hope, the singing group Up With People, and two psychics named Kreskin and David N. Bubar. Indeed, a few political programs were scheduled: a talk by Enoch Powell, the ultraconservative member of the British Parliament; a week-long forum sponsored by the anti-Communist Patriotic American Youth; and Edward Hunter, a vehement anti-Communist speaker provided by the John Birch Society.[16]

Perhaps the most illustrious speaker at Southern in recent years was Major General Edwin A. Walker. For his radically right wing efforts to indoctrinate his troops in Germany, Walker had been relieved of his command in 1961 and admonished by the secretary of the army.[17] General Walker had then contributed to the

Ole Miss desegregation crisis in September 1962 by calling for "10,000 strong, from every state in the union" to "rally to the cause of freedom" by aiding Governor Ross Barnett's policy of intransigent interposition. According to some accounts, Walker actually led a charge against federal forces at Oxford, Mississippi.[18] At the 1965 convention of the Reverend Billy Hargis' Christian Crusade, General Walker, in speaking of the man who killed Lee Harvey Oswald, had urged his listeners not to forget "that Ruby's name was Rubenstein, and they can't change that no matter how often they refer to him as Ruby."[19]

The speaker rule is so arranged that General McCain has the absolute and final decision over who speaks or performs on campus. In October of 1967 the USM Young Democrats asked McCain, for the fourth time, for permission to invite Claude Ramsay, president of the Mississippi AFL-CIO, to address their organization. On October 20 the General told YD's president:

> I have no personal objections to Mr. Ramsay appearing on campus but there are two members of the Board of Trustees who have personal and not political objections to him. Therefore, I will not submit Mr. Ramsay's name to the board for formal approval because I don't want to get these members personally against me.[20]

At this point, the YD president mentioned that Ramsay had spoken at both Ole Miss and Mississippi State. General McCain replied that Chancellor Williams was no longer at Ole Miss because he angered the members of the board of trustees over problems arising from speakers and campus organizations, and that he, McCain, had no intention of having the same thing happen to him.[21] Earlier that year, McCain had told the student senate that "no former President of Southern has resigned on his own choosing and that he plans to be the first to do so."[22]

Soon after the Fifth Circuit of Appeals declared in 1970 that speakers could be banned from college campuses only if they constituted a "clear and present danger" to the orderly operation of the institution, Charles Evers addressed both the Ole Miss and Mississippi State student bodies.[23] Obviously General McCain had to capitulate when USM student senate President Bill Patterson, in October 1971, filled out the necessary forms for Evers to speak at Southern. Right? Well, not really. In the tradition of other Southern leaders, the general denied this black man entrance to his campus.

Perhaps McCain was again running for governor![24] When Patterson asked McCain why Evers could not speak on campus, McCain simply replied, "Because I've said so. There is no need to discuss it further."[25]

Although it was not always easy, General McCain managed to protect Southern's permanent "Class of 1984" from speakers who exhibited tendencies subversive to the Mississippi way. On 2 October 1969, Pat Guyton, president of the Pre-Law Club, filled out a request form, asking that permission to speak at USM be granted to either a representative of the Lawyer's Constitutional Defense Committee of Mississippi or the president and general counsel of the Mississippi ACLU. McCain refused to act on the request. Guyton asked the general if he had objection to the speakers, and McCain said, "Yes, you know what they will do." Guyton asked if McCain meant by that that he thought they would start trouble or incite a riot. General McCain's reply was, "Of course, you know what they would come here for."[26]

ADMINISTRATION CONTROL OF THE SGA: "I DON'T KNOW WHAT STUDENT RIGHTS ARE."

Each year a tiny portion of the Southern student body gathers to perform a tragicomic ritual—tragic in its lost meaning and comic in its futility. The ceremony is not a religious one: it is the USM Student Government Association elections.

> "Bells Clang
> Horns Toot
> Vote for Me
> I'm so Cute"

Even with irresistible slogans like this, very few Southern students care enough to vote in SGA elections. For example, only 14 percent of the students—dangerously close to 13 percent, I might add—turned out to elect SGA officers in January 1971.

But can one entirely blame the Southerners for their apathy? The SGA plainly is a puppet for the administration, wielding only as much power as the administration is willing to grant. All legislation passed by the SGA must be approved by the administration, which may ignore with impunity all SGA decisions. On 14 May 1974 President McCain declared "the actions of the Student Senate during the past two years unconstitutional and null and void."[27] A slightly amused dean of the university said in 1971: "In the end, the power has got to lie where the responsibility is. I don't know what student rights are." At the same time, one high-ranking administration functionary stated that the SGA could perform a worthy service by inducing students to "pick up beer cans and cigarette butts."[28]

The subservience of the SGA to the administration was well illustrated when the Student Senate abandoned its attempt to take action during the McCain plagiarism controversy in the spring of 1969. The 12 May 1969 meeting of the Student Senate was reported by the *Student Printz* as follows:

> The Senate Monday night faced the most controversial issue of their current session.
>
> The controversy arose when Sen. Bill Waller attempted to introduce a resolution stating that "unless there be a public explanation of the aforementioned charge [of plagiarism] by Dr. McCain, we the members of the student Senate, representation of the student body, request the immediate resignation of Dr. McCain as president of the University of Southern Mississippi."
>
> After Waller took the floor and presented his resolution the Senate erupted into chaos. Sen. Danny Mitchell seemingly expressed the opinion of the Senate on the issue when he moved that the entire discussion be stricken from the record and that the information be withheld from the mass media.
>
> With the exception of two senators the motion passed unanimously and Mitchell received an ovation for the motion. In fact, the applause was so loud that Sen. Waller could not continue his argument for the resolution.

The newspaper article concluded:

> Throughout the discussion of the resolution, Dr. McCain sat in the back of Senate room without comment.[29]

Occasionally, the administration acquiesces to breathtaking SGA innovations. During the winter quarter of 1970, the Student Senate president stated in regard to the SGA finally obtaining the banquet room of the University Commons for Senate meetings, "This is a good example of what can be done with responsible student leaders who work through the administration in a responsible manner."[30]

THE ABOLISHMENT OF THE STUDENT SENATE: "WE'VE GOT TO COME TO OUR SENSES AROUND HERE."

In reality, the farcical conduct of the SGA is due largely to its servile status. The final insult to the SGA's integrity occurred in the spring of 1974. Following a lengthy trial, the Student Senate on 8 May 1974 voted overwhelmingly, thirty-two to nine, to convict the impeached SGA president for violation of the separation of powers doctrine of the SGA constitution. It appeared that the SGA president was ousted, but things did not quite work out that way.

It seems that the SGA president was a close ally of the administration, and repeatedly vetoed bills passed by the Student Senate which the administration didn't approve of. The infamous "Tombstone Bill" was a case in point. In March 1974 the senate, with only one dissenting vote, passed a bill calling for the placement of a tombstone in remembrance of fired USM professors. As stated in the bill, the SGA would purchase a tombstone to be inscribed "Exit 13," bearing the names of faculty who lost their jobs through no choice of their own. (The bill was amended to allow for two tombstones if one was not sufficient.) The tombstone was to be placed in the shadow of the administration building at high noon of the next Friday the 13th after enactment. However, this near unanimous legislation was torpedoed by the SGA president.

Clearly, General McCain faced a genuine crisis; the head of his puppet regime was impeached and convicted. The general carefully mapped out his counteroffensive. He simply ignored the enemy's action and unilaterally reinstated his ally as SGA president, even though the SGA constitution which McCain signed did not grant him the authority to reinstate elected officers of a chartered campus organization. McCain went even further. As the spring quarter came to a close the general appointed a twenty member "Scope and Purposes Committee" "to look at the effectiveness of the University's student government and make recommendations for improvement."[31] We've got to come to our senses around here," said McCain in explaining his action.[32]

The formula which General McCain's committee used to "improve" the SGA was simple: it unilaterally scrapped the entire SGA constitution. The committee's "solution" to the recalcitrant Student Senate which had defiantly impeached and convicted the administration-backed SGA president was equally effective; the Senate was abolished! The Student Seante did not meet again in

1974 after May 13; the reinstated SGA president *constituted* the entire body of the SGA.

Chapter Eleven

MY RISE AND FALL: CODE WORD ALISON

You'll like it at Southern; we're friendly folk.
—William Hatcher
Chair, Department of Political Science
University of Southern Mississippi

In March 1970, I answered an advertisement which the USM political science department had placed in the American Political Science Association Personnel Service Newsletter. One month later I received the following letter from department chair William Hatcher:

> I have here your letter of March 5, inquiring about a position in Political Science at the University of Southern Missis-sippi. I have not as of yet received your graduate transcipt from Tulane University. Please have them sent as soon as possible for I would like to have you come shortly thereafter for an interview.

Chair Hatcher called me the very day my transcript arrived and arranged to interview me at the end of the week. He ended the conversation by saying, "You'll like it at Southern; we're friendly folk."

I journeyed from New Orleans to Hattiesburg on 17 April 1970. Apparently, the crucial question in the interview was, "What do you think of the political climate in Mississippi?" I, in turn, asked chair Hatcher about the department's graduate program. He became very embarrassed and said that he didn't want to discuss it. When I asked to see the library facilities, I thought I was going to be escorted back to the bus station.

Chair Hatcher called me three days later and offered me the job at Southern, which I accepted. Thereupon my department chair at Tulane University asked me with a straight face, "You're going to commute, aren't you?" From Hatcher's telephone call on April 20 until September 1, when I arrived at Southern to begin working, the only communication I received from the university was a copy of my contract to sign and return. Therefore, when I arrived on campus I had no idea of which courses I would be teaching.

Actually, things went very well for me at first—so well that chair Hatcher notified me on 29 November 1970 that he had volunteered me to teach summer school for the following year. I think the beginning of my downfall occurred on 27 April 1971, the date of the Ike and Tina Turner Revue at Southern. I expected to meet Alison, a friend of mine from New Orleans, at the concert. Accordingly, just before the concert began, I made the following stage announcement: "If Alison is here, we would like to see you. We're sitting over there," and naturally I pointed to the left. The next day the administration wanted to know: "What is Alison a code word for?"

Six weeks later, on 8 July 1971, chair Hatcher called me into his office and said, "I hate to do this. What I am about to do doesn't give me pleasure." Chair Hatcher told me that he would not recommend that my contract be renewed after the upcoming school year. In other words, I was being fired. He offered no explanation whatsoever except that "things just didn't work out." Hatcher said that he was most satisfied with my teaching and explicitly stated that the firing decision was based on "non-academic grounds." The chair offered to write me a glowing recommendation and even gave me a $500 raise in my terminal contract. In fact, he praised me so highly that I thought he was going to hire me right back.

I was the administration's *bete noire* my second and last year at Southern. No one would dare risk the wrath of the administration by serving as faculty advisor to either the liberal Progressive Student Association or the conservative American Independent Youth, so I assumed both positions. (I suppose that the administration reasoned that if it weren't for me, it would have been rid of both nefarious groups.) I had the distinction of being one of the very few USM professors ever to have an article rejected for publication by the *Southern Quarterly*. Due to the vagaries of bureaucratic machinations, I didn't receive the travel allotment that I was entitled to for attending the Southern Political Science Association convention in November 1971. Robert Smith and I were the only members of the ten-member political science department not invited to General McCain's 5 October 1971 luncheon honoring the Right Honorable Enoch Powell, a member of the British Parliament. Chair Hatcher said that we weren't invited because "I didn't want any embarrassing questions asked!"[1]

The administration's antipathy toward me affected even seemingly extraneous matters. Chair Hatcher promised the political science department's criminal justice professor in January 1972 that he would attempt to recruit a particular professor from the University of Michigan. After a month elapsed with no reply to Hatcher's letter, the chair called in department secretary Greather Octavia Heathcock to ask if she had written the letter as he had instructed. Greather replied, "He's not married!" That meant that Greather—apparently profiting from my example—didn't want to hire another unmarried professor, so she simply didn't write the letter to the Michigan professor.

Another revealing incident occurred at the start of the spring quarter of 1972. Bette Pugh, a USM student and a good friend of mine, applied for a job through the university's student work-study program. Because Bette previously had worked as a secretary for the political science department, the head of the work-study program again assigned her to our office. Bette reported to Greather, who immediately consulted privately with chair Hatcher. Bette was told that she should apply elsewhere because the department didn't have any money. Within a week, the political science department hired four new secretaries through the work-study program.

And so it went until May 1972, when chair Hatcher taped the following note on my office door: "Dr. Piliawsky—will you please vacate your office and turn over to me your keys by no later than 31 May 1972." The only candidate interviewed for my position was scrutinized more carefully than John Birchers looking over President Nixon's Supreme Court appointees.

It was after I actually *left* Southern that the administration really began to get paranoid about me. I came to USM occasionally to visit friends, and the administration searched in vain for a legal method to keep me off the campus. In January 1973, two more political science professors—both personal friends of mine—were fired. One was fired explicitly because he permitted me to make some remarks to one of his classes on 8 November 1972 concerning the previous day's national presidential election. It seems that this professor had neglected to get the required *free speech pass for me.* The other fired professor was given no reason whatsoever for his dismissal. In fact, chair Hatcher had his aide-de-camp, Colonel Caudill, at the Southern Political Science Association convention early in November 1972, recruiting for this professor's replacement —a full two months before the professor himself was notified of this termination. On his last day at Southern, 31 May 1973, this professor sent a letter containing the following quotation to chair Hatcher:

> You may eliminate all the suspicious men from your institutions of learning, you may establish any number of new colleges which will relieve you of sending your sons to free institutions. But as long as people study, and read, and think among you, the absurdity of your system will be discovered and there will always be found some courageous intelligence to protest against your hateful tyranny.[2]

I left a legacy of sorts at Southern. Just before I was exiled I made a farewell address to the Student Senate on 1 May 1972 in which I explained the Exit 13 syndrome. The Senate voted by acclamation to change the name of the USM campus snack bar from "The Hanger" to "Exit 13." In introducing the bill, Senator Wayne Boyd stated that if objections were raised, it would only be further indication that the so-called Exit 13 syndrome really did exist. Soon thereafer, the snack bar circulated a menu list which said: "EXIT 13 IS COMING TO YOUR DORM."

PART TWO

Chapter Twelve

IMPLICATIONS FOR EDUCATION

"Elite" institutions of all types—colleges and universities ...should not be homogenized in the name of egalitarianism ...They should be protected by policies on diffentiation of functions.

—*Carnegie Commission on Higher Education*

If we can no longer keep the floodgates closed at the admissions office, it at least seems wise to channel the general flow away from four-year colleges and toward two-year extensions of high school in the junior and community colleges.

—*Amitai Etzioni*

To tyrants, indeed, and bad rulers, the progress of knowledge among the mass of mankind is a just object of terror; it is fatal to them and their designs.

—*Peter Brougham*

Although the University of Southern Mississippi is probably somewhat unique among U.S. colleges and universities, it would be wrong to dismiss the stories and anecdotes of the previous chapters as aberrant. Specifically, the USM experience directly relates to the current crisis in purpose in U.S. higher education concerning the relative merits of a liberal arts curriculum and vocationally oriented training. While USM Dean Charles Moorman boasts that his institution is becoming "the nation's most fervently career-oriented university," Southern is merely in the forefront of a rapidly growing movement among this country's colleges.

T.S. Eliot once said, "To know what we want in education, we must know what we want in general, we must derive our theory of education from our philosophy of life."[1] The theory of education at USM derives from Dean Moorman's philosophy of life: "Literature and history, unlike money and possessions, will not bring students solace and wisdom in times of disaster."[2] But again, the point must be emphasized that Dean Moorman's ideas are now being echoed by leaders of the education establishment. In January 1975, no less a luminary than United States Education Commissioner Terrel H. Bell, now secretary of Education, said:

> I feel that the college that devotes itself totally and unequiv-ocally to the liberal arts today is just kidding itself. Today we in education must recognize that it is our duty to provide our students also with salable skills...To send young men and women into today's world armed only with Aristotle, Freud, and Hemingway is like sending a lamb into the lion's den ...Many would argue that a student need merely master the basics in the liberal arts and humanities to be well on the way to becoming educated. As I see it, this is far too narrow a view of education.[3]

Dean Moorman and Secretary Bell's impassioned advocacy of vocational training for U.S. colleges is no accident. Because colleges play such a crucial role in meeting the needs of capitalist employ-ers, all major educational changes in the U.S. cannot be left to happenstance; rather they are determined by the leaders of the establishment. Moorman and Bell, as representatives of the educa-tional and political institutions in society, merely implement the developmental path proposed by the capitalist elite.

In order to give an aura of legitimacy to its recommendations, the capitalist leaders generally rely upon what appear to be scho-larly, nonpartisan commissions to develop strategies to deal with societal problems. In the late 1960s, those in power perceived that U.S. universities were confronted with three major crises: internal dissention caused by student radicalism, a deepening financial squeeze, and above all, an unprecedentedly large number of black and other minority students demanding access to a college educa-tion. To evolve a strategy for the restructuring of higher education to meet the needs of stable capitalist expansion, the Carnegie Commission on Higher Education was created in 1967.[4]

The composition of the Carnegie Commission dramatically revealed the group's establishment bias. The fourteen original members of the commission were, with one exception, either industrialists or highly placed college administrators. All were white, there was but one woman, and no member was younger than forty-five. "More striking was the total identification of its members with those institutions of power in American society that have demonstrable stakes in the maintenance of the status quo."[5] The fourteen members of the Commission were directors of at least fourteen major corporations, including such giants as American Airlines, New York Life Insurance Company, and First National City Bank. Four commissioners were fulltime board chairs of companies such as Time, Inc. and Hunt Foods. Members included trustees from eight colleges, including Harvard, Yale, and Pennsylvania. Finally, among commissioners could be found directors of such institutions as the Council on Foreign Relations, the Institute for Defense Analysis, and the Rand Corporation.[6] Clearly, the Carnegie Commission on Higher Education had a vested interest in assuring that the rapid changes occurring in higher education would not threaten the existing economic arrangements in the U.S.

The Carnegie Commission's most far-reaching recommendation was for the creation of a two-tier structure of institutions of higher learning. In this design, two-year community colleges and most four-year colleges would provide *vocational education* for the greatly expanded number of students clamoring for access to college. The Commission hoped that this channeling process could be accomplished without undermining the status and function of a selective group of established institutions which would remain free to provide traditional liberal arts education to the privileged elite. The Commission stated its intent clearly:

> "Elite" institutions of all types—colleges and universities should be protected and encouraged as a source of scholarship and leadership training at the highest levels. They should not be homogenized in the name of egalitarianism. Such institutions, whether public or private, should be given special support for instruction and research, and for the ablest of graduate students; they should be protected by policies on differentiation of functions.

The Commission concluded by quoting Sir Eric Ashby:

> All civilized countries...depend upon a thin clear stream of
> excellence to provide new ideas, new techniques, and the
> statesmanlike treatment of complex social and political
> problems.[7]

What has been the consequences of the stratification and vocationalization of higher education recommended a decade ago by the
Carnegie Commission? The community college was assigned the
major burden of providing vocational training in an effort to track
working class students away from the elite universities. Research
on community college students has consistently shown that at
least three times as many entering community college students
want to complete four or more years of college than actually suc-
ceed in doing so. Less than half of community college entrants
receive even the two-year Associate of Arts degree.[8] A classic case
study of students at San Jose College found that only one student in
four transferred to a four-year institution.[9] Acting as a terminal
rather than a transfer institution, the community college has ful-
filled in exemplary fashion the Carnegie Commission's expectations of protecting the elite institutions from the unwanted hordes
of low income and minority students.

Professor Burton Clark's extensive studies of community colleges have focused on a social phenomenon he labels the "cooling
out" process—a set of procedures and circumstances that conspire
to frustrate the high hopes of many community college students. In
this process, most students not only fail to realize their educational
aspirations, but actually end up accepting the message that it is
more "realistic" to lower their aspirations.[10] In this sense, the
cooling out function reconciles students' culturally induced hopes
for mobility with their eventual destinations by having the students blame themselves for their failures. As such, the community
college system serves the myth of an equal opportunity structure in
the U.S. as well as the position of the privileged.[11]

The success of the Carnegie Commission's recommendation to
track working class students away from elite universities and into
the vocational training curricula of the community college is a *total
abrogation of the concept of equality of educational opportunity.* The
very word "diploma" (folded over paper) means a recommendation;[12] in our supposedly open society, a college diploma is a permanent badge of social class distinction. All college diplomas are

not equal; indeed, the value of a diploma to the graduate depends strictly on which college awards it. The business establishment, which determines the ground rules for social mobility in the U.S., has ordained that, for the most part, only higher education at elite universities is the legitimate road to economic wealth and social prestige. Therefore, to deny low income students access to elite universities is to permanently limit their opportunity for advancement up the occupational hierarchy.

What benefits accrue from the type of liberal arts education that is being withheld from working class students? First, it must be conceded (as will be discussed in the next two chapters) that the content of the liberal arts education offered even at the elite universities in the U.S. is decidedly racist, sexist, nationalist, and pro-capitalist in orientation. Nevertheless, a liberal arts education can teach a certain process of thinking, the art of logical analysis. David Truman, dean of Columbia University during the sixties and later president of Mt. Holyoke College puts it this way:

> A liberal education is an experience that is philosophical in the broadest sense. The particular subjects do not so much contain this quality as provide a possible means of approaching it. The liberal arts, then, include those subjects that can most readily be taught so as to produce an understanding of the modes of thought, the grounds of knowledge, and their interrelations, established and to be discovered.[13]

The fact is that corporation heads increasingly are recruiting employees on the basis of their potential for intellectual growth, their communication skills and their problem-solving ability, rather than on the basis of technical training for specific jobs. In our fast-changing world in which technical expertise is soon outdated, business executives are even beginning to recognize that liberal education is the best preparation for even a satisfactory *first* job. Stanley Marcus, the Harvard-educated president of Neiman-Marcus of Dallas, has taken advertising space to proclaim that "a liberal arts education is the best qualification for future Neiman-Marcus executives."[14] Under these circumstances, the Carnegie Commission's recommendation to relegate working class and black students to vocational training programs at community colleges and to deny them the authentic liberal arts education demanded by business leaders is, what Frank Riessman, editor of *Social Policy*, terms, "duping the poor." According to Riessman:

An attempt is being made to dupe the Blacks and to persuade them that higher education is really a lot of abstract baloney that at best provides false credentials for the professionals (the assumption being that there is no significant, advance professional knowledge)...There is a real danger, however, that poor people may be persuaded that they are getting a union card via relevant, work-oriented courses and that they don't need any of that highfalutin' college stuff. That would be a terrible pity, and a gross deception.[15]

In reality, the hoax of vocational training is even more tragic than simply duping the poor. For the latest research indicates that vocational education not only denies the poor access to liberal arts education, but that the basic assumption of vocational training—to provide students with marketable skills —is a fraud.

A major study completed by the National Institute of Education in 1980 on 1300 vocational students enrolled in public community colleges in Boston, Chicago, Miami, and San Francisco over a 28 month period, found that vocational education does not provide equal opportunity in the labor market for economically disadvantaged students. In many cases, the *vocational training makes no difference in the kind of jobs students secure.* Specifically, few students who completed the upper level programs included in the study—accounting, computer programming, and training as electronics technicians—obtained employment as a result of their vocational education. In fact, most *dropouts from the programs acquired the same kind of jobs as those who graduated from the vocational programs—but in neither case were the jobs in fields in which the students had received training.* According to the study's director, Wellford W. Wolms, "We found no evidence that vocational education plays an important role in equalizing students' opportunity in the labor market."[16]

PUBLIC EDUCATION IN MISSISSIPPI:
A PERPETUATION OF THE CLOSED SOCIETY

As stated in the introductory chapter, this book tests from the vantage point of higher education the endurance of Mississippi's "closed society." The unmistakable conclusion that emerges from this work is that racism persists and freedom of expression and inquiry is still repressed today in Mississippi higher education.

While racism and an absence of academic freedom have always characterized Mississippi's colleges (and many others), these policies are only indicators of the more basic problem in the state's (and nation's) public educational system. Universally, there is a crucial relationship between economic systems and popular education: in short, the status of the people's education is an excellent measure of the effectiveness of the governing class in exploiting its position. With characteristic trenchancy V.O. Key observed in his classic study *Southern Politics:*

> As sensitive an index as any of the efficacy of financial oligarchy—in the American milieu, at least—is the status of the education of the people. Universal education—with its promise of individual betterment—is the open sesame of American utopianism. And universal education, with its impact on the tax structure, unvariably comes into conflict with the oligarchical elements in American society for fiscal if not ideological reasons.[17]

The educational history of Mississippi and the U.S. offers a striking example of a governing class which has denied education to the people in order to keep them from perceiving their deplorable position. Indeed, America's faith in public education as an instrument of social progress has never manifested itself in Mississippi. Half of Mississippi's population—the Blacks—traditionally have been virtually excluded from reaping the benefits of a public education. The state's politicians have considered education of blacks a genuine threat, believing that, if educated, blacks would become dissatisfied. The tenor of black education in Mississippi was set by neo-Populist governor and senator James K. Vardaman who, in 1903, said: "When I speak of educating the people, I mean the white people...Why squander money on [Negro] education when the only effect is to spoil a good field hand and make an insolent cook?"[18] Mississippi generally has spent five times as much per pupil to educate whites as it has for blacks.[19] Similarly, the average salary per white teacher has exceeded that of black teachers by nearly 300 percent.[20]

Equally revealing is the fact that Mississippi's political leaders likewise have kept the state's white population highly uneducated. Mississippi has no public kindergarten.[21] It is the only state which does not now have a compulsory school attendance law.[22] Teacher salaries in Mississippi have always been the lowest of any state in the nation.[23] Not surprisingly, these policies have resulted in start-ingly low achievement by Mississippi students. For example, the results of a national testing, administered to over sixty-five thou-sand Mississippi fifth and eighth graders in the spring of 1971, showed an achievement level of only one-half of the national norm.[24]

But the real problem with Mississippi's white schools has been what can only be described as "thought control" aimed at perpe-tuating white racism. The governing class traditionally has used the race issue to divert the discontents of poor whites, thereby killing off or minimizing pressures for improved governmental services. Mississippi's leaders, working through the youth activi-ties division of the White Citizens' Council, have attempted, with considerable success, to indoctrinate the state's public schools with racist propaganda. In the late 1950s and early 60s the council conducted a white supremacy campaign in Mississippi's high schools, with speeches and books that depicted blacks as lazy, thieving, and cowardly. With the full cooperation of school superin-tendents, the council's representatives spoke to students in nearly every high school in the state, acquainting them with "the neces-sity of keeping our white race white" and pointing out "what has happened to nations that have experienced racial amalgamation."[25] Many Mississippi schools actually used the council's pamphlets to teach race relations. The following was used in the third and fourth grades:

> God wanted the white people to live alone. And he wanted colored people to live alone. The white man built America for you. White men built the United States so they could make their rules. George Washington was a brave and hon-est white man. It is not easy to build a new country. The white men cut away big forests. The white man has always been kind to the negro. We must keep things as God made them. We do not believe that God wants us to live together. Negro people like to live by themselves. They like to go to negro doctors. They like to go to negro schools. Negroes use their own bathrooms. They do not use the white people's bathrooms. The negro has his own part of town to live in. This is called our Southern Way of Life. Do you know that some people want the negroes to live with the white people? These people want us to be unhappy. They say we must go to schools together. God has made us different. And God knows best. They want to make our country weak. Did you know

that our country will grow weak if we mix the races? It will. White men worked hard to build our country. We want to keep it strong and free.[26]

Thought control still flourishes in Mississippi's high schools today in only a slightly more subtle form than in the 1950s. Since 1974, the only state history textbook offered to ninth grade Mississippi public school students has been *Your Mississippi.* a blatantly racist version of the state's history. Among its many revisions of history, *Your Mississippi* denies the existence of black revolts against slavery. "The Civil War was a perfect time for slaves to revolt," the book states, "Yet they never did. In many cases, the slaves actually kept the plantations going while the masters were fighting."

The book also distorts black gains made during Reconstruction and treats the virulently racist post-Reconstruction period as a positive development. "Both city and county governments were thought to be corrupt [during Reconstruction]," the book laments. "Most of the city and county offices were held by Blacks. Finally, in 1875, the old hatred began to fade. Mississippi was back under the control of the native whites." The book also describes the Ku Klux Klan as a secret "social and fraternal club" that required its initiates to "ride across the countryside in bed-sheet and hood to serenade his best girl. This frightened the Blacks." Thoughout the book the term "Mississippian" is used only in reference to whites.[27]

Mississippians are little different, basically, from other Americans except that a heavy toll has been exacted from them by such a system of thought control. Yet, tragically, the rest of the nation appears to be moving down the same educational path which Mississippi has already traveled. Specifically, Mississippi's closed society ordeal directly relates to the current controversy concerning the principal purpose of U.S. higher education. For is not the trend toward vocationalization and class stratification in our universities now producing a *similar closed society for America?*

The essential element of the Mississippi closed society is racism, which as Gunner Myrdal aptly pointed out is a "white problem." Perhaps the most obvious methods available at the college level in attempting to diminish racism are: an appropriately structured liberal arts curriculum, and the mixing of persons from different races on the same campus. Unfortunately, the vocationalization and stratification of U.S. colleges, so strongly encouraged by the Carnegie Commission on Higher Education, undermine both of these strategies.

The vocationalization of the college curriculum means that most white students are taught primarily technical skills. As such, these students are not exposed to the liberal arts and humanities courses which might help them develop tolerance toward persons of different racial and cultural heritages. Certainly few white college students learn much of the black experience in the U.S. As Clyde Z. Nunn observes:

> The 1970s have seen a resurgence of the shortsighted and narrow view of schools as preeminently places to train for occupational roles. Learning to be an accountant will be of little social value if the person is unprepared to live in a pluralistic world that will increasingly demand comingling of people.[28]

Thus, it is doubtful that graduates from our vocationally oriented colleges will be able to free their minds from prejudice.

What of the white students enrolled at *elite* universities? Admittedly, these students may receive a well-rounded liberal arts education which has as its goal enlightment of the mind. However, the class and race stratification in higher education means that there are very few blacks or other minority students at the elite universities for white students to mingle with. This is no accident, for the Carnegie Commission explicitly recommended the fragmenting of culture of the college community:

> We recognize that some of these options reduce the chances of a common culture among college graduates within which people communicate, but this has been happening anyway, and we believe the gains will outweigh the losses.[29]

Indeed, the Carnegie Commission's recommendations have largely succeeded in keeping black and working class students at the commmunity college level or in external degree programs, so that they do not appear on elite campuses, or enroll in such numbers, as to have no significant social impact on the elite college community.

Chapter Thirteen

THE PURGING OF DISSIDENT PROFESSORS AT U.S. UNIVERSITIES

As long as speech is ineffective, it's free—but not when it begins to threaten the rulers of the empire.

—H. Bruce Franklin
Stanford University, 1971

The foregoing case study of the University of Southern Mississippi has painted the picture of a university in which racism is rampant and academic oppression is the fate of professors who criticize the status quo. In this chapter, it will be demonstrated that *all* universities, even the most elite institutions, function, in one way or another, like USM. For colleges do not operate in isolation from general societal forces. As such, the pro-capitalist, racist, and sexist ideology which permeates society is recreated in microcosm in the university setting. Thus, the same authoritarian social relations which exist in society are mirrored in academia.

Academic freedom basically means the right of a scholar to the free search for truth and its free exposition. The maintenance of academic freedom is indispensable if universities are to contribute to the life of society, because if professors lose their jobs for what they write and say, they will not be able to effectively question and challenge accepted doctrines. In our highly technological and pluralistic society, universities have become a principal means of acquiring new knowledge and new techniques for social and scientific progress. "Without freedom to explore, to criticize existing intitutions, to exchange ideas, and to advocate solutions to human problems, faculty members and students cannot perform their work, cannot maintain their self-respect. Society suffers correspondingly."[1]

Many recent Supreme Court decisions contain sweeping language suggesting that teachers have broad constitutional rights of free speech in their classroom work. The court observed, for example in 1967, that academic freedom is "a special concern of the First Amendment, which does not tolerate laws that cast a pall of orthodoxy over the classroom."[2] In another decision, the court declared that college teachers have a First Amendment right to resist legislative scrutiny of their classroom conduct. The opinion in *Sweezy v. New Hampshire* broadly proclaimed that:

> To impose any strait jacket upon the intellectual leaders of our colleges and universities would imperil the future of our Nation. No field of education is so thoroughly comprehended by man that new discoveries cannot yet be made. Particularly is that true in the social sciences, where few, if any, principles are accepted as absolutes. Scholarship cannot flourish in an atmosphere of suspicion and distrust. Teachers and students must always remain free to inquire, to study and to evaluate...[3]

Despite the Supreme Court's eloquent rhetoric in support of academic freedom, *academic oppression* has always been the fate of one group of professors, *those who criticize the status quo*. Black, Feminist, and Marxist professors have experienced severe recrimination simply because they have tended to oppose some of the rules established by those running the universities. In the minds of those in power, challenging authority apparently is synonymous with challenging the capitalist "social" system.

THE ROLE OF THE UNIVERSITY IN CAPITALIST UNITED STATES

The primary reason why academic freedom is denied to critics of the status quo is that the capitalist establishment controls higher education in the U.S. by its domination of the board of trustees in which the ultimate governance of universities is vested. The business elite presence on boards of trustees is overwhelming according to Rodney Hartnett's 1968 national survey of more than 5000 college trustees. In general, trustees are male, white (fewer than 2 percent in the sample were black), Protestant, well-educated, financially well-off, and Republican—two thirds identified their own political and social views as close to those of Richard Nixon. The dominant occupation of trustees is corporate management. Significantly, the Hartnett study found that a majority of trustees claimed to be involved in *all important policy making areas* of the university, including decisions on faculty appointments, changes in the undergraduate program, and instructional methods. Roughly two-thirds of the trustees maintained that they and/or the college administration, as opposed to the faculty, should have the *only* say on faculty tenure decisions.

For our purposes, the most revealing finding of Hartnett's extensive study of college boards is that decisions of the trustees generally are based upon a business philosophy which places little value upon the norm of academic freedom. Specifically, Hartnett found that more than half of the trustees agree that "it is reasonable" to require faculty members to sign a loyalty oath, and two-fifths feel that the administration should "control the contents" of the student newspaper. Moreover, over two-thirds of the educational elite favor a screening process for all campus speakers, and nearly half feel that students already punished by local authorities for involvement in matters of civil disobedience off the campus should be further disciplined by the college. Given the conservative attitudes and social class backgrounds of trustees, it is hardly surprising that academic freedom for professors who are critical of the status quo is a rare phenomenon indeed.[4]

In the last few decades, trustees have increasingly imposed their reactionary vews on the academic decision making process. Since 1945, the pressure for firing controversial faculty members has usually come from the college administration and quite frequently from the boards of trustees, rather than from the local community, state legislature, or faculty. Typically, the cause for dismissal has been the ideological views of faculty members, rather than incompetence in carrying out their academic responsibilities. Referring to faculty firings in the years 1967 to 1970, Lionel S. Lewis and Michael N. Ryan concluded'

> Since nearly all cases saw the trustees and the administration on one side of the dispute, and the faculty on the other, it

would appear that administrators and trustees are in league to maintain the status quo. This is a marked departure from the expectation that one of the primary functions of the administration is to protect the academic freedom of faculty from the uncultivated laity.[5]

Recent actions of the board of regents of the University of California's multi-campus, billion-dollar educational enterprise well illustrate who controls U.S. universities and on what criteria "academic" decisions are made, In the fall of 1968, over the opposition of the academic senate, the regents of the University of California voted to withhold regular college credits for a series of speeches by Eldridge Cleaver at the Berkeley campus. In June 1970, these same regents voted to remove professor Angela Davis from the faculty of UCLA, contrary to the recommendation of her department and the decision of the chancellor of UCLA.

It is instructive to examine the composition of the University of California's board of regents. Four of the twenty-four regents are elected state officials—the governor, lieutenant governor, state assembly speaker, and superintendent of education. The other twenty appointed regents, serving sixteen-year terms, sit on a total of sixty corporate boards. According to David N. Smith, these corporations include some of the largest firms in California, such as Western Bank Corporation, United California Bank, AT&T, Pacific Telephone and Telegraph, Western Airlines, Southern California Edison, Pacific Mutual Life Insurance, Northern Pacific Railway, Lockheed Aircraft, and the Los Angeles Rams and the California Angels.[6]

Of course, the trustees of the most prestigious *private* universities hold directorships in the nation's very largest corporations and banks. For example, trustees for the country's top three private universities—Harvard, Yale and the University of Chicago—hold positions such as: Chair of the Board of Chase Manhattan Bank, Chair of the Board of IBM, Chair of the Board of Atlantic Richfield Co., Chair of the Board of Cowles Publication (largest U.S. newspaper chain), Director of Republic Steel Corp. and of Inland Steel Corp., publisher of the *Washington Post* and *Newsweek,* Governor of the New York Stock Exchange, etc.[7]

Despite the illusion of faculty participation in the academic decision making process, university trustees, acting through a new managerial class of well-paid and well-coopted administrative bureaucrats on campus, rule academia in 1980 as arbitrarily as ever. In this era of rising educational costs and declining student enrollments, budgetary stringency has become the paramount concern of the university administration. Faculty tenure, the cornerstone of academic process, is rapidly being eliminated. Academic freedom itself has given way to a sort of cost-accounting in which professors at many universities must turn in periodic work sheet forms, indicating that they have performed all "required duties" each day. This business philosophy of university trustees and administrators is well expressed by Professor Reed Whittemore in an article appropriately entitled, "Faculty Survival: Coping with Managers." Whittemore claims that those who control academia

> want the university to be like a community college except in that it has big-time athletics. They want it to provide remedial-writing classes, and training in the trades. They want it to be a clean, well-lighted place for getting on with the business of America. In serving these purposes, they can be as tolerant of the spirit of free inquiry, of speculative research, and of projects devoted to other than pragmatic, positivist values as the southern fundamentalists were during the great Darwin crisis. And naturally the managers' job at a university, especially a state university, is to act as a buffer between such intolerance and the faculty itself. Usually the managers accomplish that by not letting the faculty surface.[8]

Perhaps the most ominous development in university governance in recent years is that the U.S. government is openly siding with university trustees and admininstrators in their oppression of the faculty. Most noteworthy in this regard is the retreat by the Burger Supreme Court from the court's traditional defense of academic freedom to its new posture of buttressing the reactionary philosophy of university trustees. With its decision in the Yeshiva University case of February 1980 (*National Labor Relations Board v. Yeshiva University)*, the Supreme Court dealt a devastating setback to the faculty union movement in higher education.

The high court ruled that Yeshiva University did not have to engage in collective bargaining with faculty members because professors are not rank-and-file workers but "managerial employees," and thus are excluded from coverage under the National Labor Relations Act. Ironically, the court outlawed unionization at Yeshiva by arguing that faculty members already possess the very power they were seeking: managerial authority. Incredulously, the court claimed that faculty members are managerial because "their authority in academic matters is absolute"; indeed, the court concluded that faculty "substantially and pervasively operate the enterprise."[9] Plainly, the Supreme Court has now cast its lot on the side of university trustees as defender of the capitalist establishment.

In order to understand why challenges to authority are not tolerated in U.S. universities, one must examine the function the university performs in a capitalist society. Professor Sam Bowles has persuasively demonstrated that schools have evolved in the United States to meet two vital needs of capitalist employers: to train a disciplined and skilled labor force, and to provide a mechanism for social control in the interest of political stability.[10] In short, by transmitting to students those traditional values which enhance the power of the dominant class in society, professors contribute, to a significant degree, in reproducing the class structure from one generation to the next. When professors begin to actively subvert these functions, they must be purged; how could it be otherwise when these persons are employed by a capitalist society?[11]

While certain faculty members, particularly blacks and feminists, periodically challenge specific policies of university administrators, the political ideology of one group of professors— Marxists and radicals—is perceived by university administrators as posing a threat to their very existence. For this reason, university administrators, as the ultimate apologists and defenders of capitalism, have systematically punished and purged Marxist and radical professors.

Quite clearly, the greatest of all dangers to the capitalist system is that a sizeable number of people should endorse socialism and the elimination of privilege and inequality. In its various disciplines the university acts to legitimize capitalism, not by incessantly extolling the virtues of the capitalist status quo, but by subtly channeling criticisms of capitalism into acceptable alternatives and by rejecting the extreme socialist alternative to them. As Ralph Miliband astutely observes:

> Provided the economic base of the social order is not called into question, criticism of it, however sharp, can be very useful to it, since it makes for vigorous but safe controversy and debate, and for the advancement of "solutions" to "problems" which obscure and deflect attention from the greatest

of all "problems," namely that here is a social order governed by the search for private profit.[12]

One important reason why nothing more than mild criticism of capitalism is tolerated in academia is that most well-intentioned academicians sincerely believe that the free enterprise system is an essential part of the creed of freedom itself, and that therefore socialism is antithetical to a "free society." As reported in a 1978 survey conducted by Everett C. Ladd, Jr. and Seymour Martin Lipset, college teachers overwhelmingly support capitalism as a system; the radical left among professors has remained fairly constant during the last decade, at only 2 to 3 percent.[13]

The deep faith in U.S. capitalism of many teachers as socialized members of a capitalist society ensures that the campus curriculum remains within acceptable limits. Similarly, the prevailing consensus of opinion at most universities produces an atmosphere of hostility towards political unorthodoxy, such as radicalism. Thus, in an address delivered in 1961 to the Alumni Association of Harvard and entitled "The Age of the Scholar," Dr. Nathan M. Pusey, then president of Harvard, defended his economics faculty and other Harvard professors in the following terms:

> Can anyone seriously charge that these men and others in their department are subverting the American way of life?...[The Harvard faculty] is almost completely directed toward making the private enterprise system continue to work effectively and beneficially in a very difficult world.[14]

THE PURGING OF DISSIDENT PROFESSORS, 1970-1980

Before describing the conditions surrounding the firing of dissident faculty in the 1970s, it is helpful to place this period in historical perspective. Lionel S. Lewis and Michael N. Ryan have analyzed all contested dismissals reported in the *American Association of University Professors Bulletin* from 1916 to 1970, a total of 217 cases. They found that the reasons for faculty dismissals from institutions of higher learning since World War II have been drastically different from the factors which previously were pivotal. Specifically, in the period from 1916 to 1945, the most common causes for faculty firings were problems of interpersonal relations, incompetence in carrying out academic responsibilities, and administrative necessity, i.e., insufficient budgets. However, since 1945, the *ideological* position of the complainant has been most crucial as the ground for dismissal.

During the McCarthy years of the 1950s, countless faculty members were victims of the pervasive paranoia generated by the Cold War. A systematic attempt at that time to rid American universities of suspected subversives through loyalty oaths, disclaimer affidavits, certificates of allegiance, and pledges of patriotism resulted in wholesale faculty firings.[15] Dismissals based on ideological conflicts continued unabated throughout the 1960s. During the early 1960s, most disputes centered around the issues of racial integration, opposition to nuclear war, and liberal attitudes toward sex, while in the second half of the decade, general opposition to the Vietnam War became a salient issue.[16]

Of particular interest is the fact that a significantly larger number of faculty dismissals occurred during the last period studied, from 1967-1970, than in all other periods. While the average number of contested dismissals between 1916 to 1967 was 4.0 per year, with virtually no variation from period to period, the number of cases per year for the 1967-1970 period rose sharply to 8.5. Writing in 1971, Lewis and Ryan concluded: "It would appear that the security of academics was greater during the right wing vigilanteeism of the 1950s than today."[17]

What has been the status of academic freedom for Marxist and radical professors in the 1970s? While no systematic updating of the Lewis and Ryan study has been undertaken, a perusal of issues of the *AAUP Bulletin* and *The Chronicle of Higher Education* suggests that academic oppression continued unabated in the 1970s, at least at the level of the 1967-1970 period. It is impossible to detail here all the significant cases of academic oppression in the 1970s, though such a compilation certainly would include: the unconstitutional dismissal of Morris Starsky from Arizona State in 1972 (with help from the FBI's COINTELPRO program); denial of tenure to Harry Edwards in 1977 by the University of California at Berkeley (also with FBI prodding); and the continued blacklisting of Staughton Lynd from academia, a decade and a half after he was denied tenure from Yale

In order to understand what it is like for Marxist scholars in academia today, we will describe in some detail the cases of perhaps the four most prominent victims of academic oppression in the 1970s: Angela Davis, H. Bruce Franklin, Grant Cooper, and Bertell Ollman. The first three professors were fired outright because of their political beliefs; the fourth was denied an appointment for the same reason. The American Association of University Professors censored the offending universities in the Davis and Ollman cases. The courts reinstated Davis and Cooper in their jobs and even ordered that the offending universities award Cooper five years back pay. However, the most revealing pattern in these cases is that in all four incidents, the firing decision (non-appointment decision in the Ollman affair) was made not by the faculty or administration of the respective universities by rather explicitly by the board of trustees, the stalwart defender of capitalism. The unmistakable conclusion is that, as Professor Eugene Genovese stated in 1978, "There is growing evidence of what we used to call McCarthyism."[18]

ANGELA DAVIS, UCLA (1970)

In June 1970, Angela Davis was denied reappointment for a second year as acting assistant professor of philosophy at UCLA by action of the Board of Regents of the University of California. Actually, the 1970 action of the regents represented the second time in less than a year that it had fired Professor Davis. In July 1969, following newspaper reports identifying her as a member of the "Che Lumumba Club," Davis admitted membership in the Communist Party. The board of regents responded by firing Davis, basing their dismissal on resolutions which it had adopted in the 1940s and 1950s, affirming the university's dedication to "search for truth in its full exposition," its commitment to the freedom of the human mind, and its responsibility to protect the university from those who seek to destroy that freedom. The resolutions— asserting that freedom was "menaced in a world-wide basis" by the Communist Party, which sought control of thought and expression, and that therefore membership in the party was incompatible with teaching and the search for truth—directed the university administration to terminate any person found to be a member of the party.[19]

In a series of meetings in October 1969, the UCLA faculty protested the regents' firing of Professor Davis and unsuccessfully attempted to persuade them to reverse the dismissal. Members of the UCLA faculty then initiated a lawsuit challenging the constitutionality of the regents' regulations forbidding employment of Communists. The trial court held that the regents' resolutions violated the First and Fourteenth Amendments to the Federal Constitution, as well as provisions of the California constitution, "because they automatically excluded from employment by the University...solely by virtue of such membership, any person who is a member of the Communist Party." Accordingly, the court declared illegal any expenditure of funds to implement any of the regents' anti-Communist resolutions.[20] Thus, under court order UCLA was forced to reinstate Davis as a professor and restore academic credit for her courses.

Determined to get rid of a professed Communist faculty member, the regents insisted on maintaining a direct surveillance over Angela Davis's status at UCLA. Immediately following her reinstatment, several regents raised questions about three public speeches Davis gave in October 1969—two at campuses of the University of California and one off campus—as grounds for dismissal. Pursuant to a request of the regents, the UCLA chancellor appointed a confidential ad hoc committee to investigate Davis's conduct both in and outside the classroom. In May 1970, much to the regent's chagrin, the ad hoc committee followed the decision of the philosophy department by recommending the reappointment of Angela Davis for the 1970-71 academic year; the UCLA chancellor reported to the regents that he intended to reappoint Davis. The regents responded by relieving the chancellor of further authority over the Davis appointment, and, for a second time, voted to fire her. While the immediate basis for the regents' decision was the content of Davis's public utterances, obviously this reason was a mere pretext for the board to achieve the original objective of enforcing its rule.

In 1972, the American Association of University Professors placed UCLA on its list of censured administrations, and, in an unprecedented action, it directed censure specifically against the board of regents of the University of California. (Censure is the AAUP's method of informing the academic community that conditions seriously violating academic freedom have not been corrected at an institution.) The final conclusion of the investigation committee merits quotation in full:

> The features of the extracurricular speeches to which the Regents took exception, and which appear to be a main basis for their decision, are features which in most instances were not shown to be violations of AAUP standards of academic

responsibility; and in any case the Regents failed to show that they demonstrated, in light of the whole record, unfitness for a position on the faculty of the University. Consequently, the unfavorable decision of the Regents in reliance on these features of the speeches must be judged to be a violation of Miss Davis's academic freedom.[21]

BRUCE FRANKLIN, STANFORD UNIVERSITY (1972); UNIVERSITY OF COLORADO (1974)

In January 1972, Stanford University fired H. Bruce Franklin from his job as associate professor of English, making him the first *tenured* faculty member to be fired from a major university since the 1950s, and the first tenured professor from Stanford ever. After having his teaching application rejected at scores of colleges during the next two years, Franklin was offered a position for 1975 by the English department at the University of Colorado at Boulder. Before the air cleared, Franklin had added another first to his record: the first initial appointment ever rejected by the Board of Regents of the University of Colorado. Franklin's case clearly was a *cause celebre*.

Franklin possesses most impressive academic credentials. He is author of 11 books, 100 articles; a recognized expert on Herman Melville; teacher of the first scholarly course in science fiction, and uniformly laudatory student evaluation of his teaching performance. However, he has been an avowed, outspoken Maoist since 1966. For five years, Franklin's radical activities at Stanford consisted only of occasional speeches. Although he did discuss Marx in the classroom, none of his colleagues ever found fault with either his teaching or his scholarship. Then came the fateful events of 1971.

The Stanford administration fired Franklin for participating in two anti-Vietnam War activities in early 1971. Specifically, Franklin was charged with leading the clapping and chanting from the audience which disrupted a scheduled speech of Henry Cabot Lodge at Stanford on January 11, and with advocating an allegedly illegal action, a demonstration at the school's Computer Center which resulted in students occupying the facility for a few hours—but causing no damage—and leaving upon order of the police. (A research organization was conducting a project at the Computer Center which was known to involve plans for carrying out an amphibious invasion, possibly of North Vietnam.) The very day following the demonstration at the Computer Center, Stanford President Richard Lyman fired Professor Franklin, suspending him immediately without pay, and barring him from the campus except for the hours between one and five during which time he was permitted to gather evidence to use at a future hearing regarding his conduct.

Stanford spent $180,000 and thousands of precious hours in seeking justification for its firing of Franklin, the cost of six weeks of hearings on the Franklin affair before the Stanford Faculty Advisory Board. In its report, issued on 5 January 1972, the seven-person board unanimously acquitted Franklin of the charge of preventing Lodge from speaking, but unanimously agreed that he was guilty of helping to incite students to occupy the Computer Center. The report dwelled on the "high likelihood of future transgressions" on Franklin's part and concluded, "We are highly dubious whether *rehabilitation* is a useful concept in this case." [Emphasis in the original.] On January 20, President Lyman hailed the trustees' ratification of the faculty advisory board's decision to fire Franklin as a "landmark." In his statement, the president depicted Franklin's presence on campus as endangering the very existence of Stanford, arguing that to permit the free expression of ideas like Franklin's will "bring to a halt the functioning of one of the greatest strongholds of free expression in the world today—the American university."[22] Of course, the president made no comment about the real cause of the campus disorder: Stanford's close and continuing involvement with the U.S. Defense Department, which then was relentlessly and viciously bombing the people of Indochina.

The stakes involved in the Franklin case were underscored by the behind the scenes role played by the FBI. Under the amended Freedom of Information Act, the ACLU in 1975 obtained part of Franklin's FBI file—enough to indicate that he had been the subject of harassment and massive surveillance in a campaign to "neutralize" him. The FBI had attempted to discredit Franklin through false rumors, bogus letters, unfavorable newspaper articles written by a cooperative reporter, and anonymous contacts with trustees, alumni and parents of Stanford University students.

When Professor Franklin was fired from Stanford in January 1972, he had reason to expect a bright future in his profession.

Given his distinguished record as a scholar of American literature, it seemed likely that many universities would be anxious to hire him. However, every teaching application Franklin submitted was quickly rejected. Finally, in December 1973, Franklin wrote the Department of English at the University of Colorado to apply for one of six positions being advertised. Following a public lecture Franklin delivered at the University of Colorado at the invitation of the school's English department, the department voted twenty-six to five to recommend him for a three-year contract as associate professor. Franklin's appointment was endorsed by the dean of arts and sciences, the provost, the chancellor, the president, the student government, many students and faculty members of the university and both the state's major daily newspapers.

Despite this overwhelming support, the University of Colorado Board of Regents on 25 April 1974, rejected Franklin's appointment by a vote of 8-1, with the only woman on the board voting in favor of Franklin. The vote against Franklin was based on an "anonymous" packet of information, including an edited version of the already edited Stanford rationale for the firing, and at least one article critical of Franklin supplied to the Colorado regents by the FBI. During the roll call, several regents explained why they were voting against the appointment. One said that Franklin's behavior at Stanford led him to believe that it is sometimes necessary to *protect freedom of speech by denying it.* Another regent denied that Franklin's appointment was rejected for reasons of behavior and admitted that the issue was, and always had been Franklin's political beliefs, which this regent found repugnant."[23]

Perhaps, Franklin, himself, summarized the Colorado misadventure best. At one point in the regents' deliberations, Franklin spent an hour with the chair of the board of regents, a banker from Greeley, Colorado, at the latter's place of work. According to Franklin, "I walked into the First National Bank of Greeley to see a bank president and convince him to hire a Marxist. What kind of a chance do *you* think I had?"[24]

GRANT COOPER, UNIVERSITY OF ARKANSAS AT LITTLE ROCK (1974)

Grant Cooper is the son of a prominent physician who was

president of the Little Rock school board during the integration crisis of 1957, when Arkansas Governor Orval Faubus called out the National Guard to prevent the integration of Central High School. His father, Dr. W.G. Cooper, Jr., is not only on the University of Arkansas at Little Rock (UALR) Board of Visitors; the family has donated more than $250,000 to the university over the years. Despite his family ties, Grant Cooper was fired from his position as assistant professor of history at UALR in 1974 because of his political beliefs. Apparently anti-Communism is stronger than blood.

Grant Cooper was a member of the Maoist-oriented Progressive Labor Party. His troubles began in September 1973, when a campus newspaper at UALR reported that Cooper, whose beliefs were well-known on campus, was being told by the school's administration to keep them to himself. The *Arkansas Gazette,* the state's Pulitzer Prize winning liberal daily, put the story on the front page. The reaction to the making public of Cooper's radical beliefs was immediate and thunderous. The John Birch Society, the Veterans of Foreign Wars, various American Legion and church groups, and twenty-three state legislators united to file suit in Chancery Court to have Cooper's salary cut off. While denying that they were threatening the university, the legislators spoke of calling the state legislature into special session to close UALR if Cooper were not fired.

The UALR faculty and student body staunchly defended Cooper. The university chapter of the American Association of University Professors passed a virtually unanimous resolution of support for Cooper. A student referendum favoring Cooper's retention was approved overwhelmingly. However, the political pressure upon the university mounted steadily. The Arkansas legislature passed a "non-binding" resolution for the immediate removal of Cooper by a seventy-eight to three vote; the three negative votes were cast by the three black members of the House. Governor Dale Bumpers sent his "wholehearted" support to the movement to fire Cooper. The governor also praised the UALR administration's handling of the case, and said that neither the AAUP nor anyone else should have cause for complaint. Cooper was not removed immediately, but was "non-reappointed effective of May 1975," allegedly for reasons having to do only with his poor performance as a teacher.

Cooper's troubles were not over. On 20 February 1974, he went on trial in Little Rock, charged with what can best be termed "thoughtcrime." He was tried for allegedly violating six Arkansas criminal statutes which make it a felony to belong to, or even to teach about, any group calling for the "violent overthrow of the U.S. Government or the State of Arkansas," or any group defined as subversive by the state legislature. At the trial Cooper freely discussed his belief in the ultimate inevitability of revolution. The court found Cooper guilty and ordered UALR to cut off his pay effective April 1974, even though the university had renewed his contract for another year.[25]

In July 1979, a full five years later, a federal district court ordered the *reinstatement* of Cooper at UALR on the grounds that Cooper's acknowledgement of his political beliefs was protected by the First Amendments to the federal Constitution. The court also awarded Cooper back pay equal to the difference between what he had earned as a public school teacher and what he would have earned as an assistant professor at UALR.[26]

BERTELL OLLMAN, UNIVERSITY OF MARYLAND (1978)

The most celebrated and perhaps most foreboding "academic freedom" case U.S. higher education witnessed during the 1970s was ignited by the decision of the President of the University of Maryland in July 1978, to reject Marxist Professor Bertell Ollman's appointment to head the university's government and politics department. Liberal and progressive commentators almost universally viewed the Ollman incident as the tip of an ominous return to the McCarthyite repression of the 1950s in academia.

Ollman is a renowned Marxist scholar who, since 1967, has taught political science at New York Unversity. He received his D. Phil. degreee from Oxford University and has held fellowships at the University of Chicago and Columbia University. His book, *Alienation: Marx's Conception of Man in Capitalist Society,* is used at more than 100 universities in the United States and abroad. In addition to his work as a Marxist scholar, Ollman is the recent inventor and marketer of a board game, "Class Struggle," which has enjoyed significant popularity.

In February 1978, the University of Maryland's 12 member Search Committee, after considering more than 100 scholars, nominated Ollman to head the university's government and politics department with the rank of full professor. Ollman came strongly recommended both by his peers—Zbigniew Brzezinski had recommended Ollman, his former colleague at Columbia University's Russian Research Center for the position at Maryland—as well as his colleagues at NYU, who had indicated that he was a most undogmatic Marxist. On March 15 after having obtained approval of the chancellor, the University of Maryland provost offered the position to Ollman, subject to the approval of the president and the board of regents. Within a week, Ollman accepted the offer.

On 18 April 1978, the Maryland campus newspaper ran the headline, "Marxist Eyed for Top Post." The very next day, on April 19, three members of the board of regents of Maryland condemned the Ollman nomination because of the professor's political beliefs. The secretary of the board said. "He'll [Ollman] never get on there. We've [the regent's] got the final say. I'm not for it. I don't think a Marxist should be at a state institution in a position of that caliber. We have too many of those kind of people from New York down here now." In a similar vein, the vice chair of the board was quoted as saying, "I would be very unhappy with that kind of appointment because of Ollman's Marxist beliefs." The next day, on April 20, in a statement widely reported in the press, Acting Governor (and gubernatorial candidate) Blair Lee, expressed serious concern over Professor Ollman's Marxism, declaring: "We are dealing with a state-supported university and there is, I think, a question of whether it's wise to make such an appointment...It may kick up quite a backlash of sorts among citizens, legislators..."[27]

The backlash, indeed, was immediate. The chair of the committee in the Maryland State Senate which handles the university's budget stated, "They might have gone a little far this time." Threats of budget cuts circulated throughout the legislature. Almost overnight, the Ollman issue became a national *cause celebre.* At its national convention, the American Legion protested the Ollman designation and several syndicated columnists resorted to redbaiting, most notably Evans and Novak, who made public "this unspoken concern within the academic community: The avowed desire of many political activists to use higher education for indoctrination."[28]

On 20 July 1978, John Toll, the newly installed president of the University of Maryland announced to the board of regents that he was taking the all but unprecedented action of rejecting the chancellor's recommendation of Ollman. The president claimed that his decision was based on academic, not political grounds, but declined to explain his position, other than to say that he had concluded after consulting certain unspecified "expert opinions" that Ollman was not "the best qualified person we can reasonably hope to get."

Reaction to Ollman's rejection was overwhelming. The Search Committee chair called President Toll's decision, "shameful, self-serving, inadequate as an explanation." The *New York Times* editorialized that "the spread of divergent ideas can never hurt as much as their suppression."[29] In June 1979, the American Association of University Professors formally voted to censure the University of Maryland, concluding that the refusal to approve the appointment of Ollman, apparently on the basis of his political ideology, was a blatant violation of academic freedom. In its formal report, the AAUP stated:

> The willingness of several of the Regents to intervene in the decision purely on the basis of Professor Ollman's Marxist views surely threatened academic freedom, and the additional view that the President ought to discuss the matter with them *in the event that he was disposed to approve* certainly placed the President under pressure not to approve the appointment, whatever his view of the merits.[30]

The broader meaning of the Ollman affair for academic freedom is well expressed by Marxist Professor Eugene D. Genovese, president of the Organization of American Historians:

> There is no question in my mind that there is a great deal of political discrimination again and it's getting nastier and nastier...The real question is that if this kind of attack can be made on Ollman and in this public way, it feeds the climate of repression...But he's really fighting a battle that is very important in terms of rolling back a McCarthyite offensive that in a much more subtle form is taking place today-...There are substantial forces in the country that are pushing for a top to bottom return to those methods.[31]

Chapter Fourteen

INSTITUTIONALIZED RACISM AND SEXISM IN ACADEMIA

Higher education performs a critically important function for American capitalism: the dividing and ranking of students for later entry into a highly hierarchic job market. In short, higher education has a virtual monopoly on entrance to middle and upper-level positions in the class structure. The education system, and American universities in particular, have served the capitalists' interests by perpetuating inequalities generated elsewhere in the capitalist system. The effectiveness of the educational system in social class tracking is most impressive. On balance, the available data suggest that the number of years of schooling attained by a child depends upon the social class standing of their father at least as much as it did fifty years ago.[1] Equally important, the acceptance by most Americans of the myth of equality of opportunity through education has legitimized the role of the university in reproducing the existing social division of labor.

In the preceeding chapter, we argued that the upper class in the U.S. controls the main decision making bodies in higher education, the boards of trustees of colleges and universities. Through these bodies, the upper class has established "rules of the game" which appear egalitarian in their ostensible intent, but which have the practical effect of maintaining the unequal class system. The most prominent of these principles is that so-called

144

excellence in schooling should be rewarded, a rule which is operationalized through the use of "objective" tests of academic performance to determine access to universities. As Samuel Bowles states,

> given the capacity of the upper class to define excellence in terms of which upper-class children tend to excel (e.g., scholastic achievement), adherence to this principle yields inegalitarian outcomes (e.g., unequal access to higher education) while maintaining the appearance of fair treatment.[2]

The use of entrance qualifications for the purpose of social class tracking is most evident in higher education's lowest rung—the community college. The community college utilizes the principle of excellence by enabling private universities and major state colleges to deny access to those citizens who do not meet their qualifications. Thus, while private universities are predominantly attended by middle and upper class youth, community colleges are attended mainly by working class and poor youth, who are highly disproportionately black and Hispanic. Moreover, social class tracking continues even *within* the community college. Terminal vocational training programs, in contrast to curricula preparing students for transfer to four-year colleges, are filled by those from low income backgrounds. In the end, community college students are placed in occupations very similar to those of their parents.[3]

In short, U.S. universities operate in a manner which might be called "institutionalized classism." The genius of the university system is that, like the capitalist economic system of which it is a part, it buttresses the belief that equality of opportunity actually exists in the U.S. and that each person, as the architect of their own destiny, must blame themselves, rather than "the system" for their failures. The latent ideology of the university system, reinforced by the community college movement, is that "everyone should have an opportunity to attain elite status, but that once they had a chance to prove themselves, an unequal distribution of rewards is acceptable."[4]

Needless to say, the group which is victimized most severely by the social class tracking of American higher education are blacks. Relatively few blacks are admitted to prestigious white universities and far fewer are awarded diplomas. Not surprisingly, in 1976, 69 percent of all bachelor's degrees received by blacks were granted by predominantly black colleges.[5] Channeling of black students into black colleges, to community colleges and to vocational programs within community colleges is capitalism's response to the demands of blacks for access to positions of power in the American stratification system.

What is particularly onerous about the current racism in academia is that intellectuals are doing the capitalists' bidding by providing the scholarly underpinnings for the new racism. Since the early 1970s, an articulate and powerful segment of the academic world has condemned even the federal government's modest commitment to "affirmative action." Intellectuals have attacked the program as systematically and vigorously as if it were a diabolical plot, an "egalitarian juggernaut," in the words of Professor Sidney Hook, that according to sociologist Nathan Glazer threatens to "undermine the very foundation of our society."[6]

The immediate cause for professors' opposition to affirmative action apparently is its perceived threat to their status in academia. While professors do not generally receive financial remuneration commensurate to their long years of study in graduate school, they receive the status benefits that accrue to members of the "intellectual elite." The status privileges enjoyed by the white male power elite in academia is a "perk" which it is determined to defend. In the words of Lilli S. Hornig, speaking in 1972 at a conference of Women in Higher Education sponsored by the New York State Education Department:

> Affirmative Action...presupposes that everyone truly desires a world of equal opportunity for men and women of all races and creeds. Unfortunately this assumption is not yet justified; the reason why Affirmative Action programs are so bitterly criticized is precisely that when equal opportunity is granted to all, those who have heretofore been privileged will have to give up some of what they regard as their natural prerogatives.[7]

Finally, intellectuals have a special reason to oppose the demands of minorities, and blacks in particular, to have access to positions of influence in academia. Many intellectuals hold a Social Darwinist world view in which the "white culture" which they labored so diligently in graduate school to master is perceived as "superior" to any other. According to Joel Dreyfuss:

> The neo-conservatives line up against minority and Third World demands because they have a vision of the West as a

fortress against (non-white) barbarism. They believe Western civilization to be man's greatest achievement and that
the forces of dissidence, here and abroad, want to loot the
treasure house. This philosophy also reserves all wisdom
and rationality to the elite (i.e., themselves).[8]

MINORITY ENROLLMENT IN AMERICAN UNIVERSITIES
IN THE ERA OF AFFIRMATIVE ACTION

Just how close has this nation come to equalizing educational
opportunities in college for all Americans? The most useful definition of this concept appears in a report from the Institute for the
Study of Educational Policy at Howard University:

> Three distinct but related concepts are used to measure
> [equal educational opportunity]: These are access—the op-
> portunity to enroll in college; distribution—the type of insti-
> tution attended and the field of study; and persistence—the
> opportunity to remain in college and complete training in a
> timely fashion.[9]

"Access—the opportunity to enroll in college..." In the egalitarian mood of the 1960s and early 1970s, the federal government
passed a series of legislative acts and executive orders which
acknowledged and attempted to remediate long-standing patterns
of discrimination against minorities. As applied to higher education, these measures were generically known as "affirmative
action" programs. The most obvious yardstick for measuring the
impact of affirmative action programs would be comparative statistics charting the relative status of minorities. It is to this analysis that we now turn our attention.

The number of blacks attending colleges in the country more
than doubled in just seven years—from 522,000 students in 1970—
to 1.1 million in 1977.[10] Similarly, the number of minority students
enrolled in law and medical schools increased dramatically—
almost 300 percent —from 1968 to 1978. In 1978, blacks constituted
10.8 percent of the nation's total college enrollment, a share that
nearly equals the proportion of blacks in the total population—
roughly 12 percent.

In reality, these statistical increases in minority enrollment
provide little cause for celebration. For one thing, these figures
must be interpreted in the context of the starting points on which

they are based. For example, it was not until 1969 that blacks represented even 3 percent of total medical school enrollments; and in the years preceding, 80-90 percent of black medical students were enrolled in only two black institutions—Meharry Medical College in Nashville and Howard University—leaving the number of blacks in predominantly white medical schools at *less than one per institution*. Similarly, in 1969, in the entire country there were only forty-four Chicano first-year medical students (out of a total first-year enrollment of 10,422), only ten mainland Puerto Ricans, only seven Native Americans.[11]

A second difficulty with the general undergraduate statistics is that they fail to acknowledge that though the total black population is represented almost proportionately by the percentage of black students, the under twenty-five black population is not. In 1978, 25.7 percent of white youth eighteen to twenty-four were enrolled in college, compared with only 20.1 percent for blacks.[12]

"Distribution—the type of institution attended..." A serious shortcoming of the data on overall enrollment gains of minority students is that they cannot be viewed in isolation from the quality of the types of colleges enrolled in. Specifically, the overall statistics mask the grossly uneven distribution of minority enrollments between four-year universities and underfunded two-year junior and community colleges. While minority enrollment at the undergraduate level has increased steadily since 1969, it has actually declined, sometimes drastically, at the most prestigious universities. For example, the black undergraduate enrollment at the University of California at Berkeley dropped by half in just five years from over 1400 in 1972 to 733 by February of 1977. The projected black undergraduate enrollment at Berkeley in the 1978-79 academic year was 300—approximately the same as it was in 1963.[13]

Indeed, much of the gains in minority college enrollment is accounted for by increases in enrollment in two-year institutions. In 1976, community and junior college enrolled 36 percent of the nation's black full-time college students, 45 percent of the Hispanic students, 32 percent of the Asians, and 47 percent of the Native Americans. By contrast, only 26 percent of white fulltime students were enrolled in community and junior colleges. Needless to say, the quality of education received by minority students in these institutions is lower than that of their white counterparts studying at four-year colleges. According to Michael Olivas, senior research fellow for the Study of Educational Policy. "Two-year students are less likely to take baccalaureate degrees than are four-year enrollees, are less likely to have campus residential subsidies, and are less likely to be exposed to higher-quality faculty."[14]

"Distribution, the field of study..." Black students today are still greatly underrepresented in the college enrollment in many significant fields as the following enrollment statistics demonstrate: agriculture and natural resources (2.1 percent); architecture and environmental design (4.5 percent); biological sciences (6.6 percent); and physical sciences (4.3 percent). Blacks represent 4 percent of the enrollment in dentistry, 5.9 percent in medicine, and 4.5 percent in law.

Not only are blacks significantly underrepresented in disciplines which offer rich job opportunities, but black degree holders are concentrated in the traditional fields of education, where employment prospects in the 1980s are quite bleak. Specifically, while only one in every five white bachelor degree holders in recent years has been in education, one in every three black bachelor degree recipients has majored in education. At the master's and doctoral degree levels the racial imbalance is even greater; indeed, three of every four advanced degrees awarded to blacks has been in education. According to Temple University Vice President Bernard C. Watson, "What clearly emerges is a picture of black Americans entering higher education in increasing numbers but continuing to enroll in traditional fields, many of which offer poor prospects for employment and career advancement over the next several decades."[15]

Most critical of all in evaluating the progress of minority enrollment in higher education is the unmistakable fact that the progress that was made between 1965 and 1975 has already begun to erode in the last five years. For example, in each of the years since 1974, the percentage of first-year medical school enrollments for minority groups (other than Asian-American and Cuban-American) has steadily declined. Specifically, black students accounted for only 6.1 percent of medical school enrollment in 1979, compared to 7.5 percent in 1974; the current figure represents a regression to the 1970 level.[16] Similarly, total minority law school enrollment has declined in the years since 1976, when such students represented 8.1 percent of the enrollment. Minority enrollment at the University of Pennsylvania Law School, for instance, fell from a high of 47 first-year minority students in 1976 to only 28 in 1978. The situation in most other professional and graduate schools is comparable, if not worse. For example, minority-group enrollment in graduate programs at Stanford University dropped from a 1973-74 peak of 533 to 388 in 1978-79.[17] Most lamentable of all is that these declining enrollment figures reflect the status of minorities in graduate school *before the Bakke decision,* which portends even more serious numerical setbacks in minority enrollments in graduate and professional schools. For the academic year 1980-81, there were *no* blacks among the 100 students in the entering class at the University of California at Davis Medical School, the defendant in the *Bakke* case.

THE EXPERIENCE OF BLACK STUDENTS AT WHITE COLLEGES

"Persistence—the opportunity to remain in college and complete training in a timely fashion..." Obviously, the end product of college enrollment is college graduation. Yet, the evidence strongly suggests that colleges today provide limited access but not degrees to thousands of black Americans.

While affirmative action programs have produced a drastic increase in the number of black students enrolled in traditionally white colleges, the number of blacks who *graduate* from these institutions has risen very little. In 1979, over one million black students attended predominantly white colleges and universities, about four times the number attending traditionally black universities.[18] Yet, even though only a fifth of today's black students are in black institutions, those schools granted *half the college degrees* blacks received in spring 1979. More important, perhaps, is that that half the graduates of black colleges went on to get a second degree within five years of completion of their undergraduate education,[19] a statistic which strongly suggests that it is the *white college rather than the black student which is at fault.* At any rate, the attrition rate of black students at white colleges is staggeringly high—approaching four times the rate at black colleges. Clearly, white colleges are often little more than "revolving doors" for black students, who enter in September and are dismissed the following May.

The reasons for the enormous attrition rate of black students at white colleges are complex, but one point is indisputable: racism is at the core of the problem. For one thing, very few strong role models in the form of either administrators or teachers are provided by white colleges to black students. Data as recent as 1977 show that 79 percent of the key administrative positions in U.S. colleges are held by white men; white women hold 14 percent; minority men 5 percent; and minority women, 2 percent.[20] In 1978, less than 3 percent of U.S. college faculties were black—and disproportionately untenured.[21] The statistics for the University of California at Berkeley and Harvard University, widely regarded as the nation's leading academic institutions, glaringly reveal the status of black faculty members in academia. In 1974, of 1408 faculty members, at Berkeley, only 13 were black and only 22 of over 4800 ladder-rank faculty members—less than half of one percent—were black![22] In 1979, Harvard had only 5 black tenured professors out of a tenured faculty of 352.[23]

One of the basic causes of the extremely high black student attrition rate is the almost complete lack of any real commitment in academia to the education of blacks. The tragic fact is that black youth still receive a grossly inferior education in the nation's elementary and secondary public schools, twenty-five years after the Supreme Court's *Brown* decision. What is needed are programs of systematic educational remediation and concentrated enrichment, designed to raise the academic level of black students. Yet, such programs are virtually nonexistent in white colleges. For example, an extensive three-year (1976-79) federally financed study of the nation's nursing schools found that black student retention is high only where college faculty members are directly involved in such activities as special tutoring and counseling sessions with black students. Not surprisingly, however, the study also found that virtually the only faculty members in non-black colleges who were involved in such retention programs for black students were black teachers.[24] Indeed, as Elias Blake, president of Atlanta's Clark College says, the typical attitude of the faculty at white institutions is, "Send us qualified students; then we'll educate them."[25]

Richard Roderiquez, himself a doctoral product of the affirmative action program, describes the tragedy of the lack of a staff of trained tutors and professors committed to implementing affirmative action:

> These students, it's true, were usually offered tutoring programs by academic officials, but such programs were often not well staffed and they couldn't correct many years of

inferior schooling with a crowded hour or two of instruction each week. Not surprisingly, among those students with very poor academic backgrounds there were few who completed their courses of study. Many dropped out, some suffering mental breakdowns, all blaming themselves for their failure. Though little has been said about such students, their shabby mistreatment by schools that used them as statistical evidence of social reform is the saddest chapter in the whole story of affirmative action.[26]

Perhaps the underlying reason why relatively few black students receive diplomas from predominantly white colleges is the atmosphere of racism that permeates the white campus. While outright racial clashes are rare at most colleges, black students frequently must contend with a steady undercurrent of petty insults. A series of race-related incidents at Dartmouth College in early 1979 is typical of the racism prevailing in academia today. On February 23, a campus maintenance worker defiled a mock graveyard that a black student organization had set up as a monument to black victims of apartheid in South Africa. Two days later, much to the dismay of Native American students, three white students dressed in feathers and loincloths skated onto the ice during a hockey game, while the band played and thousands of spectators cheered them on.[27]

Black students at historically white universities in the South generally are totally isolated from the mainstream of campus life. Blacks comprise only a minute fraction of the student body at these colleges. For example, at the University of Texas at Austin, the largest university in the South, in 1979 blacks constituted only 2.4 percent of the 42,000 student enrollment.[28] Of the 21,000 students at Texas A&M in 1979, only 66 were black and 50 of them were athletes.[29] Not surprisingly, blacks still room together, dine together, and together endure virtual exclusion from white fraternities, sororities, and other campus activities. Particularly insulting to black students are the huge Confederate flags which are flown in front of fraternity houses at a number of southern universities. One black student at a predominantly white southern university put it this way:

> It seems as if we are an unwanted intrusion on this campus. Although there are 23,000 students here, only 300 are black. There are just three black professors...And while black athletes play key roles on the football, basketball, and track

teams, the university does little to insure the academic success of those black students who happen to be nonathletes.[30]

Racism is just as rampant at northern universities. Take "enlightened" Harvard University, for example. The sign in front of the Afro-American studies building at Harvard was stolen so many times during the 1978-79 academic school year that it finally had to be moved indoors. The same year, a Harvard instructor repeatedly returned papers to the wrong one of the two black women undergraduates in his government class.[31] One black student who transferred to Tuskegee Institute after two years of straight A's at Harvard, explained, "Although the instruction at Harvard was good, I found the atmosphere to be culturally alien and sterile.[32] Another black student who left Harvard to pursue a less "prestigious" degree at Howard University confessed, "I just couldn't continue to face the hostility I perceived."[33] As Harvard's black dean of students grimly reported in 1979: "You can say that a code of conduct exists between white and black that says, 'We're going to co-exist and call it integration.' "[34]

A significant manifestation of racism in academia which directly affects black students is the ongoing dismantling of black studies programs in those white universities that established them in the late sixties and early seventies. While in 1971 there were over 500 black studies programs in colleges across the United States, in 1980 there were less than 200. The irony is that even at their zenith, these programs were never intended to be anything other than what Professor C. Eric Lincoln calls "educational placebos." The black studies programs were backed by administrations initially only for "political" reasons—specifically, to avoid confrontations with militant black students following the assassination of Dr. Martin Luther King. From their inception, these programs have had an "adjunctive" aura which stigmatized the students and professors associated with them, since universities seldom made a serious effort to fund, staff, or regulate them in a way that would lend them institutional prestige.[35] For example, the black studies program at the University of Michigan has, in nine years, had eight changes in directorships.[36]

Now that the confrontations of the sixties are all but forgotten, many universities "have adopted a strategy to permit their black studies programs to languish and deteriorate until they appear to be dying of natural causes."[37] The basic ploy is for universities to discourage students from enrolling in existing black studies programs. Eugene Matthews, a black student in Harvard's class of 1980 reports, "I was told not to take many black studies courses because law schools don't look favorably on them."[38]

The negative propaganda is proving very effective. Black and white enrollment in undergraduate course offerings at the University of Michigan's black studies programs has dropped from approximately 150-175 to 50 and below. At Harvard in 1979, there were only ten Afro-American studies majors. Universities now are phasing out their black studies programs, arguing that there is too little interest in the programs to justify them in terms of dollar costs per student when compared with other disciplines, especially in a declining economy. The black studies scenario has now played itself out: what began as an attempt on the part of white universities to co-opt black students has regressed to an exercise in hypocrisy and bad faith.

The nature of racism and discrimination against black students in academia today is extremely well expressed by Professor Barry Phillips of the University of Massachusetts in Boston:

> In the final analysis the threat to full minority acceptance in the universities of this country comes from persistent racism and from aggravation of that racism by those whose interest it serves...Members of the academic community who a decade ago actively resisted minority efforts to enter our universities actively resist them now: fraternity walls drip with racist spray-paint, faculty and administrative offices drip with 'I knew they couldn't hack it' pieties. The passive non-resister has turned resister, resentful of the minority students' failure to shuffle in gratitude for toleration of their claims on an education, rebuffed in the attempt to impose all the white man's cultural ways, or perhaps simply frustrated in the effort to eliminate the effects of twelve years of abysmal schooling and three centuries of racial oppression in two semesters of Freshman Comp. And for at least some of the supporters of increased minority enrollments, the stacks of government pamphlets and university press-releases have provided a pillar for complacent collapse.[39]

INSTITUTIONALIZED SEXISM IN
AMERICAN UNIVERSITIES

While there is some evidence that university administrators and faculty are beginning to internalize the social unacceptability of racism, institutionalized sexism flourishes, as ever, in academia. Indeed, it remains an unpleasant fact that "the basically decent, liberally-educated people who administer universities and colleges in the United States have, on a widespread and systematic basis, practiced discrimination against women in hiring, promoting, and to a lesser extent in setting salaries."[40] The continuing sexism in academia is well-captured by the sentiment expressed in former Harvard University President Nathan Pusey's cryptic comment, "We shall be left with the blind, the lame, and the women."[41]

The actual evidence of discrimination against women in U.S. universities is well documented, In 1979-80, women accounted for only 25.9 percent of the nation's fulltime faculty in higher education. Nationally, women are relegated to the lower academic ranks of the lower-prestige institutions. Numerically, women faculty constitute 26 percent of two-year college faculties and 23 percent of four-year college faculties, but only 15 percent of university faculty ranks. In addition, women are heavily concentrated in the lower faculty ranks. The data on fulltime instructional faculty on 9-month contracts for 1980 show that while women comprised 51.8 percent of all instructor positions and 33.9 percent of assistant professorships, they made up only 19.4 percent of associate professorships, and a mere 9.8 percent of full professorships. (Women on 12-month contracts constituted an even lower 18.0 percent of associate professorships and 7.6 percent of full professorships.)[42]

Quite revealing is the fact that the elite institutions show the greatest discrepancies between women and men with respect to overall total numbers and rank distribution. For example, in 1974-75, the number of women faculty members in the ranks of associate and full professors at Princeton, Yale, Harvard, Columbia combined was a mere 55 out of 1429, or 2.7 percent.[43]

Not surprisingly, income disparities between women and men faculty members are very substantial. In fact, for 1979-80, average salaries for white men exceeded those for women *at every academic rank* for both 9- and 12-month contracts. For men on 9-month contracts, the average salary was $21,941 compared to $17,922 for women. For 12-month contracts, the difference was even greater—$27,039 for men and $19,816 for women—a gap of 36.5 percent.[44]

Finally, women are poorly represented in policy making positions in universities. A 1970 survey of 450 colleges and universities found that there were on the average only 2.6 women department heads per institution. No institution with over 10,000 students had a woman president; 21 percent of all colleges lacked any woman trustees, and another 25 percent had only one. The proportion of administrative posts held by women also was quite small, except in women's colleges.[45] Nor has the status of women in university administration improved in the past decade. Data as recent as 1977 show that white women hold 14 percent and minority women hold 2 percent of the key administrative positions in U.S. colleges.[46]

Of course, these figures give only *prima facie* evidence of discrimination against women faculty. Conceivably, the low status of women in academia could be explained by their own inadequacy rather than by discrimination. However, the qualitative data confirm that women professors are at least as competent as are male faculty. Studies have indicated that women doctoral recipients have somewhat greater academic ability than their male counterparts.[47] Women's durability on academic jobs is slightly greater than men's. Studies attempting to measure teaching effectiveness tend to show no difference between female and male teachers.[48] Most significantly, despite the almost universally accepted belief that women do not produce, the facts are that women with Ph.Ds publish as much as male Ph.Ds.[49] It may well be that women professors are *superior* in academic competence to men when one takes into account the discrimination against women in academia.

These data plainly indicate that the panoply of laws and executive orders known as affirmative action has not redressed the effects of sexism in academia. Indeed, the government's record in affirmative action cases is quite dismal. All regional offices of the Equal Employment Opportunity Commission have up to ten-year backlogs of complaints awaiting investigation and cases awaiting litigation. Similarly, the Office of Civil Rights within H.E.W. has been slow to move on complaints against academic institutions. The results of a few sex discrimination cases which have been brought to trial also have been disappointing. In fact, the original intent of Title VII of the Civil Rights Act of 1964 has been undermined by judicial decisions which now require that plaintiffs demonstrate not only discrimination but also the university's *intent* to discriminate—a far more difficult issue.[50]

Given the costs—in terms of time, money, emotional strain and jeopardy to career—of bringing anti-discrimination suits against a particular institution, many women faculty have been understandably reluctant to take legal action. Emily Abel, a California historian, and Gloria De Sole, an affirmative action officer at SUNY/Albany, after gathering extensive accounts of women professors who brought legal action against their universities, conclude:

> Most of them have horror stories to tell: retalitory letters describing them as troublemakers addressed to department chairs at other institutions where they have applied for jobs; ostracism and intimidation at institutions where they have been denied promotion and subsequently brought suit; feelings of loneliness and isolation.[51]

Affirmative action cases have been unsuccessful, in part, because the major culprit in institutionalized academic sexism, the "Old Boy Network," is an elusive, hard to pin down, informal system. Through Old Boy Networks, department heads consult with their professional colleagues—usually exclusively men—in determining who to hire for faculty vacancies, on the grounds that candidates so selected will be "effective colleagues." Hiring through this process discriminates against women because the "old boys" usually do not take women graduate students or women professors seriously and therefore rarely recommend them to their professional acquaintances for positions. Ellen Cantarow's analysis of the Old Boy Network in English applies equally for all academic disciplines:

> It was an Old Boy at a nearby prestigious university who, at fall hiring some years ago, told a male friend of mine, "Save the chicks until last and hire them for Freshman Comp. They always need the jobs." It was the pen of some Old Boy that scratched, on a female job candidate's application to a California state college..."She's a medievalist. But do we need just another medievalist? Perhaps we should rule her out on the basis that she's six feet high, rawboned, and awkward."[52]

The central figure in the discrimination against women professors is the male department head who frequently holds subtle prejudices against professional women, although he usually is wholly insensitive to the fact that he is discriminatory toward women. One element in this pattern is the inability of male department heads to distinguish between women professors and their own homemaker wives, believing that female faculty are basically housewives rather than totally committed professionals. This state of mind causes male employers to actually presume that women professors are genuinely pleased to accept part time faculty positions at low salaries as "a nice way to spend their afternoons." Male department heads often use tortured rationalizations to refuse salary increases and promotions to competent women faculty. Professor Alice Rossi describes perhaps the most common of these peevish sexist gripes: "Since most academic women, if married, have husbands in academic or professional fields with more than adequate incomes of their own, department chairmen are sometimes motivated not by a woman's performance on the job, but personal resentment of the higher style of life a joint household of career people can enjoy."[53]

The discrimination directed against women faculty is but a continuation of the institutionalized sexism which is endemic to all levels of American education. From elementary school through graduate school, women experience an educational process which rewards female passivity, instills in girls and boys stereotypic sex roles, and above all, *does not take the female mind seriously.* Curriculum content consistently excludes or deprecates the female experience, often expresses hostility to women, condones physical violence against women, and teaches women that the "real" goal in life is to seek male approval, ultimately in marriage. And, of course, this indoctrination is all expressed in blatantly sexist language and grammar.[54]

Attitudes toward women are particularly discriminatory within graduate departments, the highest rung in the educational ladder. Male professors tend to have totally different expectations about the performance of women and men graduate students. This sexism is well illustrated by the following series of quotations from male professors at various graduate schools in the United States:

"Any girl who gets this far has got to be a kook."

"I know you're competent and your thesis advisor knows you're competent. The question in our minds is are you *really serious* about what you're doing?"

"Have you ever thought of Journalism (to a student planning to get a Ph.D. in political science)? I know a lot of women journalists who do very well."

The admissions committee didn't do their job. There is not one goodlooking girl in the entering class."

You have no business looking for work with a child that age."

"I'm sorry you lost your fellowship. You're getting married, aren't you?"

We expect women who come here to be competent, good students; but we don't expect them to be brilliant or original."

You're so cute. I can't see you as professor anything."[55]

Success in almost all professions requires the learning of crucial trade secrets which usually is provided to the neophyte by a sponsor or protege. Unfortunately, male graduate school professors habitually refuse to serve as sponsors to women graduate students. Unlike their male peers, women graduate students generally are afforded very limited opportunities for interaction with colleagues, are not promoted or mentioned by eminent (male) sponsors, are not producers of joint authorship with well-known (male) professors, and are not sponsored for jobs.[56]

Not only are women graduate students denied the positive self-image which develops from the acceptance and recognition of their professors, but they face the particularly degrading prospect of sexual overtures from their male professors. These seductive gestures may produce humiliation and even intellectual self-doubt in women graduate students. "Even if turned aside, such gestures constitute mental rape, destructive to a woman's ego. They are acts of domination as despicable as the molestation of the daughter by the father."[57]

THE CONTENT OF LIBERAL ARTS EDUCATION: A REFLECTION OF WHITE CULTURE

The content of education offered in the U.S. even at the most elite liberal arts colleges such as Harvard, Yale, and Berkeley, is racist, sexist, nationalist, and pro-capitalist in orientation. These biases prevail because they are consistent with the overriding integrative function of schooling in the United States: "perpetuating the social, political, and economic conditions for the transformation of the fruits of labor into capitalist profits."[58] This section will demonstrate that the textbooks used in the country's elite colleges reflect the sexist, racist, and exploitative values of white culture. These ideologies dominate the curriculum because the white male establishment which determines the developmental path of U.S. educational systems is resolved in perpetuating the stable functioning of the society in which it enjoys a privileged status.

We begin our analysis by surveying the depiction of women and blacks in general history textbooks. Unlike their treatment of white men, historians inevitably assume that women and blacks possess an innate "nature." For example, historian Page Smith, in his book *Daughters of the Promised Land* declares that "Anyone who writes about women has to confront, sooner or later, the question of the nature of women"; he goes on to conclude that "A woman 'is'; a man is always in the process of becoming."[59]

As Professor Ruth Rosen cogently points out:

> The assumption that women, or any other social group, have an "identifiable nature" is a crude form of pseudo-biological determinism. Such assumptions are always at the root of racist and sexist thought.[60]

Of course, the "nature" of women invariably is presented in stereotypical terms such as: docile, passive, coy, fragile, inane, deceitful, childlike, and capricious. In a similar vein, until recently, historical analysis had concluded that black slaves were the happy, mindless servants of their beneficient masters. White male historians have unquestioningly accepted these stereotypical characterizations women and blacks as eternally true, biologically determined facts, rather than as the socially conditioned responses of an underprivileged and oppressed social group or the end result of their own racist and sexist attitudes.

Professor Ruth Rosen's excellent survey of women in historical writing shows that only a select few women are included in "mainstream" texts;[61] when women do appear in history texts, they are generally dismissed with the easy familiarity of a superior or discussed in terms of their appearance rather than their achievements Rosen cites the two historical gems as evidence of the misrepresentation of women by white male historians: women are not as sexually motivated as men because they do not respond to traditionalist (sexist) pornography; women rarely make great chefs because, according to historian Page Smith, "A woman's cooking is personal. She cooks for those she loves and wishes to nuture; thus her cooking is sacramental."[62]

As further evidence of the biases and lack of sympathy toward women in historical textbooks, Professor Rosen offers the following preface to *Everyone Was Brave: The Rise and Fall of Feminism in America* written by historian William O'Neill:

> This book, then, is first of all an inquiry into the failure of feminism...To begin with, I have avoided the question of whether or not women ought to have full parity with men. Such a state of affairs obtains nowhere in the modern world and so, since we cannot know what genuine equality would mean in practice, its desirability cannot fairly be assessed.[63]

As Rosen suggests, if the word "black" were substituted for "women," and "white" for "men" so that we were dealing with racism rather than sexism, "I begin to wonder whether this would be considered serious history or simply racist propaganda."[64] Indeed, a case can be made that the mocking condescension in scholarly writings is at least as great toward women as it is toward blacks.

Not only does the content of the education presented in elite liberal colleges validate white men even as it invalidates women, but the information itself is conveyed in sexist language and grammar. Perhaps the most subtle way in which the language used in virtually all college textbooks represents women as a derivative, or a subset of men, is the linguistic convention known as "generic Man" (or what linguist Wendy Martyna has called "He-Man" grammar). By this language convention, the same word "man" that is used to refer to "male human beings" also is used in the same generic sense to refer to "all human beings." The same generic principle that makes "Man" both male and sex indefinite is supposed to apply as well to pronouns. Thus, in standard college textbooks, the third person singular pronoun "he" is both masculine and sex-indefinite.[65] But, if this is really true, as Mary Ritchie Key points out, then the following statement should sound perfectly natural:

> No person may require another person to perform, participate in, or undergo an abortion against *his* will.[66]

The reason why sexist language persists is clear. Language is a powerful influencer of the perceptions and interactions of individuals in society. By talking about matters in certain ways, people develop the habit of thinking substantively in terms of these same concepts. Above all, language, then, is used by the dominant white male elite in higher education to *reinforce the status quo,* thereby facilitating the perpetuation of sexist attitudes and practices while inhibiting social change.[67] Specifically, men use sexist language and content to depict women as mentally incompetent and dangerously erratic to justify male domination of the institutions— educational and otherwise—in society.[68]

Undoubtedly, the white male leaders of the United States are hopeful that women, too, will see themselves as the language sees them: as sex objects, as trivial, and ambivalent about their status as complete human beings. According to Adrienne Rich:

> Sexist grammar burns into the brains of little girls and young women a message that the male is the norm, the standard, the central figure beside which we are the deviants, the marginal, the dependent variables.[69]

In addition to sexism, college textbooks exhibit a decided bias in favor of white Anglo-Saxon culture and a corresponding deprication of the culture of virtually all non-Western peoples. While the atrocities committed by Americans against Native Americans and black slaves are sometimes alluded to in college U.S. history textbooks, the prevailing white supremacist bent is revealed by what is *ommitted* from historical writings. For example, it is rarely noted that Native Americans and blacks have not been the only non-white groups in this country to suffer because of their skin pigmentation. As Manuel Mendoza and Vince Napoli remind us:

> Japanese-Americans were herded into concentration camps during World War II, but not German-Americans. The United States dropped an atom bomb on Japan, but not on Germany. The Louisiana territory was purchased from the French, and the Russians were paid for Alaska; but we took California, Arizona, New Mexico, and Texas from the dark-skinned Mexicans.[70]

Every effort is made by the educational establishment to minimize the exposure of white students to the reality of the black experience in the U.S. in an attempt to preserve the continuity of the dominant Anglo-Saxon culture. This precautionary strategy of suppressing knowledge about the black heritage is openly being practiced in 1980 at elite Harvard University. In April 1980, during his first week as chair of the Afro-American Studies Department at Harvard, Professor Nathan Huggins told students majoring in the department:

> Afro-American studies is not a valid academic discipline nor field of scholarly study. The department will not be dedicated to studying Afro-American Studies from a Black perspective, nor will there be any emphasis on the study of contemporary Africa as it pertains to the Afro-American experience in the new world.[71]

Besides sexism and racism, college textbooks at the prestigious liberal arts colleges reflect a staunchly nationalist and procapitalist bias in which the business system and the military establishment are subject to virtually no critical analysis. Textbooks in history and political science invariably incorporate the "consensus" school, which is strongly nationalist, emphasizes the national consensus and national integration, and downplays any divisions in society, especially those based on class. Little or nothing is mentioned of popular insurgency in U.S. history, radical trade unionism, slave revolts, or other elements of militant working class traditions of the country's historically oppressed. The pervasive influence of the "consensus" school in social science textbooks is well demonstrated by a selection from a recently published textbook designed for use in college courses in U.S. government. Thus, Grant McConnell writes:

> American politics has been largely free of class divisions and American political thought has had little to offer on this subject. This lack is the consequence, as Louis Hartz has said (echoing Tocquesville) of the fact that Americans were "born equal" without having had to become so. There has been a profound consensus on the large issues that in other countries have been subject to the overriding fact of class conflict.[72]

The camouflaging of genuine diversity and conflict in the U.S. is an ongoing process which requires the constant rewriting of history, not very different from the system depicted in Orwell's *1984*. John McDermott prophetically suggested in 1969 that the history of popular resistance struggles of the 1960s in the U.S. would be conveniently rewritten. According to McDermott:

> It has often crossed my mind that when liberal historians two decades hence write the chronicle of the Southern freedom movement of the early 1960s or of the anti-Vietnamese War movement of today, they will find imaginative and persuasive reasons to show that the first was really part of the New Frontier and the second of the Great Society. It was thus that their predecessors have managed to reduce the richness and variety of popular revolt in the 1930s to the bureaucratic dimensions of a Washington-based "New Deal."[73]

The overriding theory in sociology for the past two decades is the so-called "structural-functional" school of thought, which argues that the existing social structures in a society have evolved to their present institutional arrangement, because they are the most functional to serve the needs of that society. Accordingly, the sociologist tacitly accepts the structure of American society, which includes an unmodified system of private property and its attendant social relations, as well as the existence of a gigantic military establishment. Thus, sociologists conduct their research and report their findings with a decidedly conservative bias, confining their inquiries to the nature and operations of society's institutions, but not daring to examine critically the existence of the basic institutions and processes of society themselves.

Consider sociology writings regarding remedies for poverty. Willard Waller, in an influential paper which helped to establish the model for the "scientific" approach to social problems, wrote:

> A simpleton would suggest that the remedy for poverty in the midst of plenty is to redistribute income. We reject this solution at once because it would interfere with the institution of private property, would destroy the incentive for thrift and hard work and disjoint the entire economic system.[74]

The overwhelming bias not to disturb the routine functioning of society-as-it-is means that in nearly every recent textbook on social problems, the sociologist treats symptoms rather than solutions: "criminals, not the law; mental illness, not the quality of life; the culture of the poor, not the predations of the rich; and so on."[75] This kind of analysis comes very close to suggesting that whatever is, is right.

CONCLUSION

Oppression, racism, and sexism in academia do not operate in isolation from one another; instead, they reinforce each other in serving the interests of the capitalist system. The primary functions of the university under capitalism are to transmit to students the traditional values which maintain the power of the dominant class, and to track students in a manner which perpetuates the inequalities generated elsewhere in .he capitalist system. Because they pose a threat to the capitalist system, Marxist and radical professors who actively subvert these functions must be purged from academia, thus creating the strange paradox of academic oppression.

Racism has historically been an essential stabilizing force for capitalism. By focusing the resentment of lower income whites toward blacks and away from capitalism, racism has reduced the ability of these groups to forge a united political movement which might threaten the capitalist system.[76] One is struck by the fact that the *myth of "excellence" or so-called mertiocracy in academia has served as a functional equivalent to such racism,* by deterring potential political dissent. The myth of educational excellence and the accompanying myth of existence of equality of opportunity in academia forcefully legitimize the stratification system. Indeed, the myth of excellence is a manifestation of the "blaming the victim" syndrome, which functions to minimize the formation of political opposition to the capitalist system by blacks and poor whites. For "as long as one adheres to the 'reward excellence' principle, the responsibility for unequal schooling appears to lie outside the upper class, often in some fault of the poor—such as their class culture, which is viewed as lying beyond the reach of political action or criticism."[77]

Sexism in academia is especially pernicious because the principle of rewarding excellence cannot conceivably be used to rationalize discrimination against women students and professors, whose academic records are at least equal to men's. "The real issue continues to be ingrained institutional and social prejudice that renders most white males incapable either of recognizing or appreciating the merit that serious women scholars have always possessed."[78]

The evidence has demonstrated that academic oppression, racism and sexism have pervaded academia throughout the 1970s.

Marxist and radical, and recently-hired women and black professors can expect to be the most vulnerable to the layoffs planned by
many universities in the current era of economic retrenchment. In
the late 1970s, black studies and women studies programs were cut
to the bone at many universities. There is already mounting evidence of cutbacks in minority recruitment, scholarship aid and
academic support services in the post-Bakke period. In short, there
is every reason to expect that oppression, racism, and sexism in
academia will continue unabated in the 1980s.

Chapter Fifteen

THE CONDITION OF BLACKS IN THE STATE OF MISSISSIPPI

The history of the United States records a continuous clash between the ideal of equality and the tyranny of racism. Equality as a goal to aspire to was embodied in the first paragraph of the Declaration of Independence in 1776. While white racism in the U.S. is also as old as the beginning of the Republic—the Constitution explicitly states that a black is equal to three-fifths of a white— it is only in relatively recent times that it has been perceived as a social problem. Gunnar Myrdal's book, *An American Dilemma* (1944), began with these lines: "There is a 'Negro Problem' in the United States, and most Americans are aware of it...Americans have to react to it, politically as citizens and...privately as neighbors." Myrdal forced the American conscience to confront the fact that the so-called "Negro problem" was really white racism which therefore is a "white problem." "America," he wrote, "is continuously struggling for its soul."[1]

In this chapter, we will analyze the condition of blacks in 1980 in the state of Mississippi, while the next chapter compares these findings to the status of blacks in the nation as a whole. Resistance to the Civil Rights Movement was fiercest in Mississippi, a state notorious in the fifties and sixties for the Ku Klux Klan, lynchings, shotguns in the night, police dogs and fire hoses. Our investigation will demonstrate that while race relations in the twenty-five years since the Supreme Court's historic desegregation decision of 1954 have appeared to improve considerably, in reality they have changed to a "respectable racism." But, then, as the state with the largest black population, the burden of the "American Dilemma" has always rested most heavily on Mississippians.

Because of the Supreme Court's highly questionable distinction between de jure segregation and de facto segregation, the North was not forced to confront the agony of desegregating its schools until the 1970s. As the next chapter will detail, the advances in racial equality in Mississippi, however modest, have clearly *not* been exceeded by the rest of the country. Indeed, the judgment of Samuel DuBois Cook, President of Dillard University, that "racism has exerted tyranny over the mind of the white South on every level and in all aspects of public and institutional life,"[2] applies today in equal measure throughout the entire nation.

The concept of equality contains five separate ideas that generally are used in varying combinations by democratic theorists— political equality, equality before the law, equality of opportunity, economic equality, and social equality.[3] In assessing the status of blacks in Mississippi and the nation in 1980, we will consider the degree to which each of these types of inequalities have been achieved. It should be noted that in practice these different types of equalities tend to form a continuum, with the first one, political equality, being the easiest to achieve, while social equality is the most difficult to reach.

POLITICAL EQUALITY

Political equality includes two separate points, equality at the ballot box and equality in the ability to be elected to public office. The Civil Rights Movement of the 1950s was based on the premise that the right to vote for blacks, i.e., political equality, was crucial to the achievement of full equality. Dr. Martin Luther King, Jr. eloquently expressed linkage on 17 May 1957, the third anniversary of the Supreme Court's *Brown v. Board of Education* decision:

> Give us the ballot, and we will no longer have to worry the federal government about our basic rights. Give us the ballot, and we will no longer plead to the federal government for passage of an anti-lynching law. We will, by the power of our vote write the law on the statute books of the South, and bring an end to the dastardly acts of the hooded perpetrators of violence. Give us the ballot.[4]

The right to vote was effectively denied to blacks in Mississippi until 1965 when Congress passed the Voting Rights Act. As a consequence of this law, the proportion of the state's black population which registered to vote increased dramatically from a mere 5.2 percent in 1960 to 71.0 percent in 1970.[5] Nevertheless, extralegal obstacles to full black political participation still exist in Mississippi. As late as 1974, the U.S. Civil Rights Commission reported: "Acts of violence against blacks involved in the political process still occur often enough in Mississippi that the atmosphere of intimidation and fear has not cleared."[6] In balance, the legal right of Mississippi blacks to register and vote largely has been improved.

The record for black Mississippians in the other essential aspect of political equality, the ability to be elected to public office, also shows some changes. In 1965, Mississippi had fewer than fifteen local black officials, most from all-black towns. However, by 1978, Mississippi had 303 black elected officials—15.2 percent of whom were women—the second largest number of any state in the country. Nevertheless, all but four of these black elected officials held only municipal school board, or in a few cases, county offices, rather than federal, statewide, or regional offices. The four black officials at the statewide level held seats in the 122-member state House of Representatives; none of the 52 state Senators in 1978 were black.[7]

Before 1979, the vastly increased black voter registration in Mississippi had not resulted in the election of black state legislators because the state legislature had juggled the election system to minimize the impact of the black vote. Specifically, the maintenance of multi-member, county-at-large legislative districts diluted the state's black vote. In June 1975, the U.S. Supreme Court invalidated Mississippi's apportionment plan, marking the fourth consecutive time the state's lawmakers had designated an unconstitutional seating plan.[8]

Finally, in 1979, Mississippi's legislative districts were apportioned by a federal court ordered plan following the conclusion of a fifteen-year-old reapportionment suit. In the November 1979 elections, seventeen blacks won seats in the state House of Representatives while two blacks were elected to the state Senate, becoming the second and third black senators in Mississippi since Reconstruction. With these victories, total black elected officials in Mississippi neared the 350 mark, more than any other state in the nation. Despite such substantial recent gains, the number of black elected officials in Mississippi today is hardly proportionate to the black population: only 7 percent of the state's elected officials are black and only 12 percent of the legislative representatives are black, while the state's black population is 37 percent.[9]

Even at the county level, blacks are prevented from winning elections because of gerrymandering—drawing election district lines with the intent to minimize black voting strength. The 1970 census reported that there were twenty-five black-majority counties in Mississippi; however, because of outrageous gerrymandering, none of these are controlled by black officials. In Holly Springs, Mississippi, for example, although the city and surrounding county are 60 percent black, the mayor is white, the police chief is white, four of the county's five supervisors are white, four of the city's five alderman are white and only three blacks are on a police force of fifteen. In nearby Lexington, Mississippi, in order to maintain their political superiority, whites diluted black voter strength in 1969 by *un*incorporating certain areas of the city—heavily black populated areas—that could have increased black voter strength by as much as 50 percent.[10]

The maps of Mississippi's county districts display an Alice-in-Wonderland appearance. One of the typically bizarre examples of "creative" gerrymandering is County District Number One in Pearl River County. The district has a long—twenty-seven-mile-long leg, one mile wide running down into the city of Picayune where most of the county's black population lives.[11] Until black Mississippians are able to thwart these extra-legal political stratagems devised by the white power structure, they will remain unable to translate their voting numbers into a proportionate number of black officeholders and therefore will not achieve political equality.

EQUALITY BEFORE THE LAW

Equality before the law means that all persons will be treated in the same manner by the legal system, regardless of race, wealth, or the type of crime involved. As a stronghold of diehard segregation, Mississippi in the 1960s was notorious for its unequal treatment before the law for dissenters from the official orthodoxy, whether black or white. In the early sixties, freedom riders were regularly arrested upon their arrival in the state and tossed in jail.

On 12 June 1963, Medgar Evers, field secretary of the state NAACP was fatally shot down at the front door of his home. The white man charged with Evers's murder was not convicted, despite the presence of his *fingerprints on the murder weapon.* In the summer of 1964, three civil rights workers, Andrew Goodman, James Chaney, and Michael Schwerner were brutally murdered in Nebosha County with the full complicity of local law enforcement officers. And in May 1970, two black students at Jackson State University were killed by Mississippi law officers in a confrontation on campus.

What progress has been made in the past decade toward achieving equality before the law for blacks in Mississippi? The 1970s have witnessed fewer outright killings by Mississippi law enforcement officers. Gone is the legacy of the days when the candidate for governor who could "yell 'Nigger' the loudest" would be elected. The massive black voter registration of the 1960s has resulted in state-wide candidates now courting the black vote covertly, but usually with only symbolic gestures. For example, in June 1973, Mississippi Governor William Waller, in an act unparalleled in Mississippi politics, declared a statewide observance of ceremonies marking the tenth anniversary of the assassination of Medgar Evers.[12] However, as we enter the 1980s, there still are far too many examples of blatant violations of blacks' constitutional rights to be sanguine about the Mississippi criminal justice system. Consider the following cases:

On the night after Thanksgiving in 1978, nightriders fired shots with a high-powered rifle into three Jackson, Mississippi houses of worship—one Jewish synagogue and two black churches, one Baptist and one Islamic. News of the nightrider attacks was suppressed by orders of the Jackson police chief.[13]

In January 1979, in Holly Springs, Mississippi, a black prisoner was found dead in his cell, hanging by a rope from the ceiling with his hands and feet tied. The Marshall County Coroner ruled the death a suicide. Following a massive protest movement by the area's blacks, the Marshall County Board of Supervisors held a special hearing in February 1978 in which witnesses detailed beatings in county jails. One woman stated that the jailor allowed a man to enter her cell and rape her.[14]

In May 1978 the home of Henry Boyd, Jr., a paralegal with the North Mississippi Legal Services, a federally funded organization, was firebombed and his back and front porch lights were shot out.[15]

In response to these acts of violence, officials of the United

League of North Mississippi, a civil rights organization founded in 1966, wrote the area's U.S. attorney, complaining about his poor track record in prosecuting civil rights violations: "There is an air of hopelessness on the part of many black citizens in north Mississippi concerning the attitude or seeming attitude toward the vindication of their constitutional rights as black American citizens."[16]

In January 1978 a federal judge awarded a man serving time in the federal penitentiary in Atlanta $2500 in his lawsuit against two captains of the Tupelo, Mississippi police department for beating confessions out of him. Following the federal court's decision, complaints of police brutality about these same two policemen began reaching Tupelo's board of aldermen. (Prisoners in the past had frequently charged at trials and in complaints to the FBI that the pair's success came from beating confessions out of suspects.) Despite the overwhelming evidence against the policemen, on 24 February 1978, the seven-member Tupelo board of aldermen voted six to one not to fire the officers. The sole dissenting vote was cast by the only black alderman.[17]

The rise of black protest against police brutality in Tupelo has been met by the militant resistance of the Ku Klux Klan. The Klan has precipitated a continuous series of incidents in Tupelo since the spring of 1978, which appear to have the support of the local policemen. For example, the Klan rally held on 6 May 1978, at a city-owned recreation center in Tupelo, was attended by "ninety-nine percent of the city's cops, the chief of police and the mayor." The mayor reportedly received a standing ovation for his speech before the Klan.[18]

In some of these confrontations the Tupelo police overtly aided the Klan. At a Klan rally on the courthouse steps on 10 June 1978, a white lay minister exclaimed to Klan Imperial Wizard Bill Wilkinson, "You symbolize hatred, You call yourself a Christian!" Wilkinson directed some Klansmen to take care of the minister. Robed Klansmen broke from their close-knit ranks and dragged the man to the ground; the minister offered no resistance. Tupelo police stepped in, saying, "Let us have him," and began striking and gagging the minister, then slammed him to the ground, handcuffed him, and hauled him to a van. He was charged with inciting a riot.[19]

Individual blacks who measure their daily lives against earlier times acknowledge a vast increase in their civil rights. Reuben V. Anderson, who in 1978 was elected judge of the County Court of Hinds County, thus becoming the first black county judge in Mississippi history, reminisces, "When I was growing up in high school, I was afraid to even walk at night other than in black neighborhoods. The parks that you see around Jackson, I never walked in them at all while I was a child."[20] In a similar vein, Clare Collins Harvey, a funeral homeowner in Jackson, Mississippi, observes, "Just being able to breathe free air and not being called 'gal,' or 'nigger' are very important changes. Equality isn't here fully, but the fear at least is gone."[21]

Obviously, contrasted to the crude indignities of the past, blacks have made significant progress toward being accorded equal legal treatment in Mississippi. However, the fact remains that of the 154 prisoners executed in Mississippi between 1930 and 1974, 124 (or 80 percent) have been black, including all 21 persons executed for the crime of rape.[22] As the many examples of legal atrocities perpetuated against blacks catalogued above indicate, overcoming the legacy of the past will not be an easy task. Genuine equality before the law is not yet a reality in 1980 for black Mississippians.

EQUALITY OF OPPORTUNITY

Equality of opportunity means that no *artificial* barrier will keep any person from achieving what one's ability and hard work can gain for them. According to this concept, a person ought to be able to move up or down within the class and social system depending solely upon one's ability and application of that ability. In applying this standard to Mississippi, the fundamental issue to be examined is: Has racial discrimination served as an artificial barrier against blacks preventing their achieving social mobility commensurate with their ability?

The United States has always considered public education to be the primary means of achieving its commitment to equal opportunity. This critical function of education in American life was forcefully articulated in the *Brown v. Board of Education* decision:

> Today education is perhaps the most important function of state and local governments... It is the very foundation of good citizenship. Today, it is a principal instrument in awakening the child to cultural values, in preparing him to adjust normally to his environment. In these days, it is doubtful that any child may reasonably be expected to suc-

ceed in life if he is denied the opportunity of an education. Such an opportunity, where the state has undertaken to provide it, is a right which must be made available to all on equal terms.[23]

In 1979, on the twenty-fifth anniversary of the *Brown* case, Kenneth Clark, the social psychologist whose work influenced the decision, reiterated the burden placed on public education: "History demonstrates that the American public school system has been the chief instrument for making the American Dream of upward social, economic and political mobility a reality..."[24]

What has the *Brown* decision meant for blacks in Mississippi? For the first decade following the case, Mississippi officials simply refused to desegregate the state's school system at all. Despite the court order that desegregation proceed "with all deliberate speed," it was not until the federal government enforced Title IV of the 1964 Civil Rights Act terminating federal funds to recalcitrant school districts that the very first school in Mississippi desegregated. But once the flood gates were opened, desegregation proceeded at a fairly rapid pace. The fact of the matter is that in 1979, the U.S. Civil Rights Commission reported that the Southeast region of the country had by far the highest proportion of desegregated schools, and Mississippi, by virtue of its heavy black population, had one of the least segregated public school systems in the nation.

However, the tragic fact is that desegregation of the Mississippi public school system, far from providing the conduit to the American Dream of equality of opportunity, has not necessarily improved the quality of education for the state's black population. On first glimpse, this conclusion appears to be incorrect. After all, Mississippi can now no longer spend five times as much per pupil to educate whites than blacks or even pay white teachers three times the amount given to black teachers, as it did before the *Brown* decision. Two factors converge to produce this disheartening conclusion: the inequitable system of financing the Mississippi education system, and the absence of black role models for black students.

Mississippi spends less per pupil on its public school system than any other state in the nation. Worse, yet, is the fact that because the school system is largely locally financed, the quality of a child's education depends primarily on the wealth of the local community. Many blacks in Mississippi live in school districts that simply cannot raise enough money to properly support their schools. Ironically, underfunding of black schools, a central issue in the 1954 *Brown* desegregation suit is still a serious detriment to quality education for blacks in Mississippi.

The picture becomes even more complicated when one examines what has commonly happened to tax rates and assessment practices in many Mississippi school districts since the advent of desegregation Particularly in rural areas where the black population is especially large, whites have dropped out of the public schools to attend private segregation academies, leaving blacks with the public school system or what remains of it. Based upon her exhaustive study of school finance in the South, Linda Williams explains the usual pattern:

> Tax rates and school spending levels in many communities were either cut or allowed to stagnate, so that white parents would have money left over from taxes to send their children to private segregated academies. Many a school system which previously operated on a blatantly 'separate and unequal' basis, with poorly funded black public schools and richer white ones, now shifted its strategy of discrimination, and began operating a system of poorly funded, nominally desegregated (mostly black) public schools, while in fact indirectly supporting a parasitic chain of academies.[25]

Williams cites the school district of Anguilla in the predominantly black Delta area to illustrate the pattern of school finance in Mississippi. Prior to desegregation in 1968, the Anguilla district had a white enrollment of 24.7 percent; the tax rate was 25 mills. By 1975, the white enrollment had dropped dramatically to 2.3 percent and the tax rate had fallen correspondingly to only 14 mills. And, while property wealth in the state increased by 63 percent in the period, in Anguilla it rose by only 24 percent, giving rise to suspicions that, in addition to the substantial cut in the rate, property assessments were deliberately being kept low. The result was that local school revenue per pupil increased by only $26, compared to the state average of $85 per pupil. Clearly, the inequitable system of financing public education in Mississippi makes a mockery of the intent of the *Brown* decision: to assure equal expenditures for educational purposes for all pupils, regardless of race.[26]

While almost all white children have withdrawn from the public schools in the Anguilla school district, there are actually some Mississippi towns in which *no* whites attend public schools.

For instance, the public school system in the predominantly black town of Lexington, Mississippi, is 100 percent black. At the Lexington attendance center, there are 595 students and 27 teachers, all of whom are black. After the federal courts mandated school desegregation, whites pulled their children out of the public schools and opened up the private Center Holmes Academy in 1970, which is 100 percent white. The pullout has had devastating effects upon the all-black Lexington public schools. Underfunding has resulted in poor facilities, virtually no educational materials for students and extreme overcrowding. Although class size is supposed to be limited by law to twenty-eight students, most classes contain well over forty students.[27] Ironically, Lexington today is the recreation of the very same totally segregated school system which was outlawed in the *Brown* decision.

The public school systems in many of Mississippi's middle-sized towns (which contain only modest black populations) are both adequately financed and well integrated. The problem in these schools, however, is the paucity of role models. i.e., blacks in positions of authority, for black students. Take Tupelo, Mississippi for example, a town which is approximately 18 percent black:

> Of twenty-two first grade teachers in the school system, one is black.
>
> Of roughly 100 teachers in the high school, nine are black.
>
> Of fifteen janitors for the schools, fifteen are black.
>
> Of about fifty employees in the food services, forty-nine—the exception being the manager—are black.[28]

Tupelo High School illustrates well the plight of black students in so-called "integrated" schools. The student body at Tupelo High is 18 percent black; however, although there are 13 black women teachers, there are no black males teaching academic courses full-time, no black counselors, and no black head coaches in the major sports. Under the circumstances, it is not surprising that the academic achievement level of black students is far below that of whites. Indeed, various studies show that black children in the pre-1954 dual school system in the South had far more motivation to achieve than they are receiving under the integrated system today, primarily because role models for black youth have largely disappeared.[29] CBS News Correspondent Ed Bradley concluded his 1979 analysis of Tupelo High School with this observation:

> For black students at Tupelo High, integration has been a tradeoff: a loss of black role models and control in return for much improved educational facilities. But the education here seems geared to middle-class students, white and black. So, although the Tupelo administration and faculty are first-rate, it is still likely that if a student is both black and poor, it would be difficult to break the cycle that entraps him. Those black students who are well-motivated and probably middle-class benefit most from integration.[30]

In summary, public education has not been an effective mechanism of mobility for blacks in Mississippi because the educational system has been totally undermined by overall underfunding, an inequitable system of financing, and the displacement of black teachers. In the predominantly black rural areas of the state, schools are largely resegregated, while in the more racially balanced towns, black role models for black youth have been dismissed. In short, the promise of the *Brown* decision—that equality of opportunity could be achieved through public education—has not occurred in Mississippi because the state has never committed itself either to desegregation or to providing a system of quality public education. Thus, while some poor white children have been denied an opportunity to improve their "life chances," Mississippi's black students, at the bottom of the socioeconomic ladder to begin with, are those most victimized by the lack of justice in Mississippi's school system.

ECONOMIC EQUALITY

The fourth aspect of egalitarianism is economic equality. Strictly speaking, economic equality means that every individual within a society should have the same income. However, because only a tiny proportion of Americans favor complete leveling of income, the more common definition of economic equality is that every individual within a society must be guaranteed some level of economic *security*. In other words, a minimum standard of living for all should be established. As will be seen, extreme levels of poverty often effectively bar individuals from achieving equality of opportunity, legal equality, and even political equality.

The rationale behind the Civil Rights Movement of the 1950s and the 1960s was the belief that many of the economic problems that blacks face as a race could be solved through voting and the acquisition of political power, either by electing black officials or by playing brokerage politics with white officials. In short, the hope was that political equality would translate to economic security. But have the few gains in black political representation resulted in long-range economic public policy payoffs for the state's black population? It is to this question that we now turn our attention.

The bottom line is that there is a low correlation, if any, between the rise of black elected officials in Mississippi in the past fifteen years and improvement in the socioeconomic conditions of the majority of black people. The fact is that Mississippi is the poorest state in the U.S. for whites as well as blacks. But, the average family income for blacks in the last twenty-five years has remained only slightly above half that of white family income. In 1979, the unemployment rate was *four times higher* for blacks than for whites. One-third of the black population of Mississippi now depends on food stamps.

Despite such extreme poverty, the state government has made no attempt whatsoever to provide even a semblance of economic security for the poor, most of whom are black. Indeed, Mississippi consistently captures fiftieth place in state surveys of social programs and spending: it is the state with the lowest per capita spending for schools, unemployment compensation or aid to families with dependent children.[31] Despite its failure to provide social services and economic relief to poor blacks, Mississippi burdens the poor with extraordinarily heavy taxes. Although it is the poorest state in the nation, Mississippi depends heaviest on the sales tax, a regressive tax which disproportionately hurts poor people. Specifically, Mississippi received 45 percent of its general revenue funds for the 1979 state budget from its 5 percent state sales tax, a proportion which is more than twice the national average.[32] At the same time, many communities continue to reduce the millage rates on their property taxes, the tax used to finance the public school system.

The reality of life for Mississippi's blacks is far from the picture offered in investment brochures promoting the "New South." Simply put, the widely heralded industrial development in Mississippi has mainly bypassed the rural areas where most of the state's black population lives. Typically, rural Mississippi blacks work as sharecroppers on cotton farms and live in shacks with a single wood-burning stove, often lacking toilet facilities. According to a report on health care in the South prepared in 1974 by the Southern Regional Council, nearly half the homes in Tallachatchie County, Mississippi (which is 60 percent black) have no indoor plumbing. The infant mortality rate among blacks in the county is 41 per 1000 births compared to only 9.7 for whites. For a population of 20,000 people there were eight doctors, none black. Slightly more than 60 percent of all the people were living below the federal poverty level. As Steven Suitts, executive director of the Southern Regional Council explains: "It all relates back to the tradition of white folks using black folks as cheap labor."[33]

A vicious poverty and politics cycle prevails in many rural Mississippi counties. In these areas, blacks live in such extreme poverty that they effectively are prevented from participating actively in the electoral process. Black sharecroppers are intimidated by the handful of white families who control the county's entire economy from exercising their potential political power. William McGee of the Mississippi Action for Community Education, a former sharecropper, observed in 1978:

> People on the plantation still wait for the bossman to tell them how to vote...It's hard to talk about civil rights or upgrading their lives in church because the landowner owns the church building too and they're afraid he'll tear it down. If they get in trouble with the man, they won't have a place to meet.[34]

Not surprisingly, in many Mississippi counties where black sharecropping predominates, black majorities have been unable to elect any black officials at the county level. The hope of the Civil Rights Movement—to translate political clout into economic rewards—has a hollow ring in rural black Mississippi.

Perhaps the bleakest result of extreme poverty among Mississippi blacks is the rapid disappearance of the state's black farmer and landowner. Mississippi had more black-owned farms than any other state. However, the latest figures (in 1974) show that blacks own only about 5 percent of the state's farmland; they had lost 39.6 percent of their land holdings between 1969 and 1974. Since 1969, blacks have been losing land in Mississippi at a rate of almost 2000 acres a week; at the present rate of land loss there will be no black farmers left in the state by 1990.[35]

Blacks are being forced off their lands through several "legal" devices, principally the following: (1) tax sales—the taking of tax delinquent property by the state and auctioning it off to the highest bidder; (2) estate sales—the taking of land by the state when an heir is unable to raise sufficient cash to buy out the share of other heirs who want to sell farm land; and (3) mortgage foreclosure—the loss of mortgaged property due to delinquent debt.[36] Clearly, the underlying reason for the rapid decline in black landowning is the dire poverty of the black farmer. Indeed, life for the black Mississippi farmer who is not forced off the land is hardly comfortable. In 1975, the median income for Mississippi black farmers was only 43 percent of median income for white farmers—$4857 compared to $11,237.[37]

The economic conditions of blacks living in towns and cities in Mississippi closely parallel that of their rural counterparts. In Holly Springs, for example, the average black person in 1979 earned less than $3000 a year, had a tenth grade education and worked either in a factory or as a hired hand on a white-owned farm.[38] Twenty years ago, black families in Lexington, Mississippi, earned one-fourth as much as whites; today they earn one-third as much. Thirty-nine percent of Lexington's housing is substandard, most of it black-occupied. The much vaunted "black middle class" has totally bypassed Mississippi. In 1979, less than 1 percent of black families in the state earned $25,000 or more a year![39]

SOCIAL EQUALITY

In a narrow sense, social equality means that no public or private association may erect artificial barriers to activity within the association. Examples of this type of equality would be the lack of artificial barriers to use a public park or to membership in a country club. While social equality is a fairly intangible concept, it essentially means that people of different races, backgrounds, cultures, positions and incomes can interact socially and be equally accepted.[40]

Title II of the Civil Rights Act of 1964 forbids discrimination on the basis of race in places of public accommodation, such as lodging establishments, restaurants, motion picture theaters and other places of entertainment. Today, blacks generally have access to the public facilities of their choice throughout the state of Mississippi, except in relatively isolated cases.

However, racial discrimination in the use of *private* facilities is rampant in Mississippi in 1980, even in such vital areas as health care. Today, as a decade ago, most black Mississippians seek medical care from white physicians and not uncommonly must endure separate waiting rooms for black and white patients. For example, separate racial waiting rooms were maintained by the five white physicians in Lexington, Mississippi, in April 1979; one doctor still had "Colored" and "White" signs on his doors. Ed Bradley of CBS News reported the situation this way:

> For the black patients, a crowded, windowless, dark shabby waiting room; no lamps, tables, magazines; just the absolute minimum. The white patients enjoy a sunny airy waiting room with decent furniture and plenty of reading material.[41]

Because the physicians accept federal Medicaid funds, they are in violation of Title VI of the 1964 Civil Rights Act.

At the Holmes County Hospital in rural Mississippi, only three of the hospital's thirty nurses are black. Black and white employees eat in separate areas. No orderlies are allowed in the rooms of female patients unless accompanied by a nurse; all the orderlies are black.[42] At Madison General Hospital, a public hospital near Jackson, Mississippi, hospital physicians routinely refuse to touch black patients and make diagnoses after giving visual examinations.[43]

Whites who attempt to assist blacks in Mississippi still suffer serious recrimination. The Franciscan Sisters, a group of nuns who came to Lexington, Mississippi in 1973 from Wisconsin, have been severely abused for aiding blacks. "I can't walk down the street without whites calling me dirty names," says Debbie Sass, a 22-year old white woman working with the nuns. "When I came here I had no idea things like this were still going on." Since the Sisters have been working in Lexington, they have been evicted from three white-owned houses, their house has been egged by white youths, nails have been put daily under the tires of their car and they have been the constant target of verbal abuse. Sister Beverly Weidner observes:

> The whites like to tell us we're being used by the blacks and that we just don't understand. They tell us that blacks "know their place" and we should know ours. Many whites view blacks as they do a dog. It's okay for blacks to work for

you, or to maybe talk together—if blacks understand their place—but you *don't* invite your dog to dinner.[44]

Blacks and whites in Mississippi live in virtual physical isolation from each other, except for occasional contact at the workplace. Most towns and cities in the state have extremely high rates of residential segregation, with the black community literally confined to the "other side of the tracks." Despite school integration, spectators at high school football and basketball games sit apart in the stadium and field house bleachers. And, still, the taboo against interracial dating is as absolute as ever. Joe Washington, Jr., in 1979 was seventeenth in his class, a star basketball player and president of the student body at Tupelo High School. But even for successful black students, social equality is at best a distant hope. When asked if he ever went out with white women, Washington replied: "No, no. That's not allowed in Tupelo...That's the biggest sin, you know, probably in Tupelo." When pressed as to what would happen if he dated a white, Washington stated:

> Well, first of all, probably I'd—I'd hit rock bottom to tell you the truth...If that would happen with a white girl, you'd get looked at, first of all. Then it'd get spreaded around and it'd get talked about. Then it'd get back to the businessmen, and probably hard for you to get a job.[45]

Professor Ivory Phillips' 1979 case study of Rosedale, Mississippi, a predominantly black town in northwest Mississippi, offers a sober perspective to the much lauded racial progress in the state. Phillips observes:

> As one visits Rosedale today there is virtually no evidence of segregation in places. There are still, however, all-White private academies for elementary and high school children. Church services are still segregated. And, there still exists the all-White private Walter Sillers Memorial Park and the all-White V.F.W. The private vestiges of segregation seem to suggest that people are still segregationists at heart. They are only integrated out of fear or respect for the law.[46]

Perhaps, the state of race relations in Mississippi is expressed best by Irwin Walker, the first black to attend the University of Mississippi without a court order and presently director of the Urban League in Jackson, Mississippi. According to Walker, "their basic attitudes may not have changed, but there's no longer the type of overt racism that used to be rampant in the South."[47]

THE CONDITION OF BLACK WOMEN IN MISSISSIPPI

The greatest discrimination in Mississippi falls on the race and sex group that comprises almost one in four of the state's rural population: black women. Perhaps the most graphic way to describe the plight of black women in Mississippi is to analyze in depth the strike since February 1979 of 208 employees—almost all black women—of the Sanderson Farms chicken processing plant in Laurel, a town of 25,000 in the pine belt of southeastern Mississippi. As Susan Holleran of the National Organization of Women states: "In one place this strike embodies almost all the issues central to people who care about human dignity and basic rights—sexual harassment, discrimination against women and minorites, health and safety violations, inadequate pensions, union busting, intimidation by the Ku Klux Klan and other forces."[48]

"Sexual harrassment..." Workers at the Sanderson plant were routinely subjected to sexual advances from male supervisors. According to worker Gloria Jordan, "Some of the foremen would come up to you and rub you and hug you and everything. It happened to me a lot."[49] Workers who refused their foremen's sexual advances often were assigned to jobs which they were physically unsuited to perform, such as on the hanging dock. Several employees were terminated for resisting such overtures or for slapping their foremen in an attempt to protect themselves. Moreover, workers were allowed to use the lavoratory during non-break times *only three times a week,* and then had to explain to a foreman why they wanted to use the facility. Joanna Yates, a worker at Sanderson for five years, suffered a miscarriage in her fourth month of pregnancy because her foreman refused to permit her to use the bathroom.

"Discrimination against women and minorities..." Ellen Chinn recalls the advertisement that led her to her first job six years ago, "Want a better job? Come down to Sanderson Farms." Despite the barbaric working conditions in the plant, Sanderson Farms was one of the few places a black woman with limited formal education or job training could get hired in Laurel, Mississippi. Pay levels at Sanderson before the strike were at tne poverty level, barely above

the federal minimum wage. The starting salary was $2.95 an hour with some workers earning only $3.20 after twelve years. Of course black women were consigned to the lowest paying, dirtiest jobs.

"Health and safety violations..." Working conditions at the Sanderson plant resemble a page from a Dickens' novel. The work itself is extremely dirty and demeaning. Workers must first unload the 100,000 birds—workers do not call them chickens—from huge trucks which arrive at the plant periodically through the day. The birds are hung by their feet and then are transported through the plant in a mass production operation. The birds are killed by having their throats cut; feathers, innards, and other edible parts are removed; and then the birds are cut and distributed.

Employees who unload the chickens often must work covered with feathers, the ones who cut the chickens, with gore. The plastic aprons workers use cannot be kept clean and gore from the chickens produces a painful rash on arms and necks. Workers are expected to cut up five chickens a minute, a dizzying pace, and are constantly being yelled at by the foreman demanding faster work. Knives provided workers generally are dull and rusty which means that workers often cut themselves as they attempt to keep up with the line; workers who cut themselves must stay on the line and continue working.[50] According to Linnie Myrick:

> It's the hardest work I've ever done. And I was raised on a farm. I was on the saw line, sawing chickens, and they expected five chickens per minute, which I felt was too many chickens. Everyday they were hollering at us to cut more chickens. I've seen people beg to go home after eight hours and they wouldn't let them.[51]

"Inadequate pensions..." Not only was there no meaningful pension or insurance plan for workers at Sanderson, but there was no vacation policy and no seniority system. Work hours were indefinite and irregular: employees rarely knew when they went to work in the morning how long they would have to stay at the plant. Because there frequently was not a full day's work, employees seldom earned more than $300 a month. On other days employees were forced to work overtime. Workers who refused to stay were charged with a whole day's absence; three days absence within two months meant automatic dismissal. As one worker put it, "They just didn't treat us like human beings. They treated us worse than they treated the chickens."[52]

"Union-busting..." The employees of Sanderson Farms first organized a union in 1972 as an affiliate of the International Chemical Workers. For years Sanderson refused to even consider workers' grievances regarding working conditions. Finally, after negotiations failed to produce a new contract, workers went out on strike on 27 February 1979. Sanderson's last offer was a 50-cent-an-hour increase over 3 years; 45 cents of which would have been mandated automatically by minimum wage increases.

The bitterly fought struggle at the Sanderson plant is a classic strike, recalling the tumultuous 1930s. Sadly, the strike also demonstrates the severe obstacles the nation's labor movement faces in attempting to organize black women in low-paying jobs, especially in the anti-union, right to work South where many U.S. businesses and factories are now locating. Specifically, Sanderson's refusal to negotiate with the union has hardly affected business; the plant now is operating at near-capacity, for with the poverty and lack of knowledge about unions in the rural South, Sanderson has had little trouble hiring new scab workers to replace the striking employees.

Along with traditional methods of racist division, Sanderson has added the new sophisticated tactic of fighting unions by employing a wealthy union-busting law firm in an attempt to convince workers that unions are detrimental to their interests. The company continues to manipulate the labor laws which are weighted in favor of management. For example, Sanderson merely ignored the 1980 complaint of the NLRB which had cited the plant for violation of health and safety and child-labor laws. In a 29 October 1979 hearing before the NLRB, the Laurel workers charged that Sanderson Farms management was refusing to bargain in good faith. After fifteen months of foot-dragging, which objectively aided the company, the NLRB ruled on 22 January 1981 that Sanderson Farms management was guilty of "surface bargaining," or failure to bargain in good faith. Accordingly, the NLRB ordered Sanderson to return to the bargaining table, to rehire some 150 striking workers and to replace the scabs who had been operating the facility at near-capacity levels.

The immediate optimism of the striking workers appears to be somewhat premature. Sanderson Farms vice president Odell Johnson told reporters in February 1981 that the company would not even consider bargaining with the workers until it had appealed the NLRB decision through the courts. Johnson stated: "We feel the

NLRB ruling is an unfair ruling. We never thought we were guilty of unfair labor practices and just because the NLRB says so doesn't mean we're going to change our minds."[53]

So, while Sanderson continues to employ strikebreakers and refuses to negotiate, counting on time to wear down the stikers, the union local fights for survival as striking workers attempt to manage on strike benefits of only $15 a week.

"Intimidation by the Ku Klux Klan and other forces..." The protracted history of virulent racism in Laurel, Mississippi where Sanderson Farms is located, seriously deters the efforts of plant workers to organize and secure economic justice. Traditionally, Laurel has been a stronghold of Ku Klux Klan racist terror. In the 1960s, Laurel Klansmen were among those who murdered three civil rights workers in Philadelphia, Mississippi. Thus, succeeding generations of blacks in Laurel have been subjected to Klan terror, while white workers have effectively been discouraged from joining blacks in organizing unions.

Today, the *plant superintendent* at Sanderson Farms is a man who was indicted—and released—in connection with the 1966 fire-bombing of black civil rights leader Vernon Dahmer, a murder plotted by the Ku Klux Klan.[54] Not surprisingly, the racist traditions of Laurel have persuaded most of the small number of white workers in the Sanderson plant not to join the strike. However, the company is not adverse to using intimidation to divide black and white workers, as worker Archie Purvis explains:

> The company does things to keep whites out of the union. Take our vice-president, she was white. She got injured on the job. She was a cutter, and it messed up one of her arms, due to cutting for long hours and improper materials. When she returned to work, they put her back on that same thing, knowing it was going to aggravate her injury. That was to make her quit, because she was one of our long-time members. And she couldn't stand it, and she left.[55]

Despite the severe frustrations and hardships of the workers, the Sanderson strike continues past the two year mark, with no immediate likelihood of a resumption in bargaining. In a sense, the strike points out how dramatically the mood of the nation has changed. Had the strike occurred just ten or fifteen years ago, undoubtedly thousands of civil rights workers would have journeyed to Laurel to assist the striking workers in their struggle against plantation-like conditions. Still, the two hundred black women carry on their lonely bitter strike. As Gloria Jordan puts it, "We did not have any dignity when we worked for Little Joe [Sanderson]. Now we are not making any wages, but I say we have our dignity."[56]

The condition of black women in Mississippi parallels black women's dual victimization in the U.S.'s racist, sexist society. Black women face severe discrimination in the labor market, which often results in their living in poverty. In 1976, 31.2 percent of all black women over age 16 were impoverished, compared to 19.6 percent of similar black men, 9.8 percent of white women and 6.2 percent of white men. It may well be that discrimination against black women in the workplace is even more sexual than racial. For example, in 1974, black women had slightly higher educational attainment and job prestige than black men; however, black women were earning only 62 percent as much as black men were earning in terms of annual pay and 71 percent as much as black men in hourly earnings.[57] The primary reason for the low wages of black women is segregation of jobs by sex and the consequent concentration of black women into a few low paying occupations. Indeed, in 1977, a full 37 percent of black women held jobs as service workers. Clearly, employment discrimination against black women means that they have fewer resources and more barriers to overcome than any of the other groups in society.

Chapter Sixteen

RACIAL EQUALITY IN THE NATION: "RESPECTABLE" RACISM

Except for rare instances of racist obstructionist tactics by voting registrars, the right of blacks to register to vote in the United States is absolute. Certainly, one of the most dramatic indications of black progress in the last decade has been the increase in the number of black elected officials around the country. However, blacks in the country as a whole have been much less successful than blacks in Mississippi in translating their voting strength into electing black public officials. Whereas 6.4 percent of Mississippi's elected officials in 1978 were black, only 0.9 of the 522,294 elected officials in the nation are black. Women comprise a mere 18.7 percent of all black elected officials. Since blacks constitute more than 12 percent of the national population, the current number of black officials cannot be considered equitable representation. Nationwide, for every 100,000 non-blacks, there are about 286 non-black elected officials; for every 100,000 blacks, there are only 20 black elected officials.[1]

Because of the concentration of blacks in U.S. cities, a sizeable number of black mayors (182 in 1980) have been elected. In some cities, black mayors are now serving their second terms (Thomas Bradley in Los Angeles, Coleman Young in Detroit, Maynard Jackson in Atlanta) and even their third terms (Kenneth Gibson in Newark, Richard Hatcher in Gary). However, the electoral process makes no lasting promises to blacks. In the November 1978 election, several prominent black officials were defeated, including Edward Brooke (for re-election as Senator) in Massachusetts; Mervyn Dymally (for re-election as Lieutenant Governor) and Yvonne Braithwaite Burke (for state Attorney General) in California. In the same election the number of black state legislators was reduced from 194 to 285.[2] Only seventeen members of the U.S. House of Representatives are black; with the defeat of Senator Brooke there are now no black U.S. senators. Perhaps, most discouraging is the rapid decline in the rate of growth in the number of black elected officials in the country. While the annual increase in the number of black elected officials averaged 19 percent between 1969-1976, the annual increases in 1977, 1978, and 1979 were only 8 percent, 4 percent, and 2 percent, respectively.[3]

Even after the passage of the 1965 Voting Rights Act, subtle barriers have perpetuated the historic pattern of racial discrimination against black voters by diluting black participation in the electoral process. The most effective of these barriers—the at-large voting district—still exists throughout the nation, particularly in the South. There can be no doubt that the at-large voting district discriminates against blacks: for this electoral system allows whites to outvote even very substantial, but less than majority, black populations for *every legislative seat* in both city and county elections.

Between 1973 and 1980, the nation's federal courts began to dismantle at-large electoral systems on the grounds that they discriminate against black voters. However, on 22 April 1980, in the *City of Mobile v. Bolden,* the U.S. Supreme Court dealt a chilling setback to black voting rights. In a major departure from previous decisions, the Court ruled that plaintiffs cannot merely demonstrate that a particular at-large electoral system has a discriminatory effect; from now on plaintiffs must prove that an at-large voting system was *explicitly adopted or maintained* for its adverse effect upon blacks. If such motivation cannot be proved, said the Court, then the system will be assumed to be constitutionally neutral.[4]

Clearly, the court's decision will substantially reduce the number of blacks elected to public office in the nation. Blacks who are a numerical minority in an electoral district are now confronted with the ominous prospect of being frozen into permanent minority status, never achieving meaningful political power. Justice Thurgood Marshall bitterly denounced the ruling, stating in his dissenting opinion, "In the absence of proof of intentional discrimination by the state, the right to vote provides the politically powerless with nothing more than the right to cast meaningless ballots."[5] The League of Women Voters, not known for hyperbole, declared:

> We are shocked and dismayed...the Supreme Court has retreated from its obligation to protect the constitutional rights of minorities...has hidden the real issue, the continuing denial of basic constitutional rights to the minority citizens of this country.[6]

Ira Glasser, director of the American Civil Liberties Union, explained the grim reality of the court's decision:

> For now the U.S. Supreme Court has set us back. The Court has taken away a very powerful weapon, and proved once again that the effort to wipe away the stain of slavery and centuries of racial discrimination, even in such a fundamental area as voting rights, is far from over, and will be longer and harder than anyone imagined.[7]

The U.S. Justice Department, responding to the *Bolden* decision, immediately withdrew many voting rights discrimination suits, including one against Hattiesburg, Mississippi.

EQUALITY BEFORE THE LAW

The lack of equality before the law for blacks in the United States is dramatically evidenced in the country's criminal justice system. The U.S. imprisons a greater proportion of its population than does any other Western capitalist nation except South Africa. Racism clearly is the compelling factor in explaining this high imprisonment rate. Federal statistics indicate that of the approximately 400,000 persons in prison in the U.S., more than 300,000 of them are black. In 1973, the median U.S. incarceration rate for whites was 43.5 per 100,000—a rate which is lower than in many European countries, such as Great Britain, Denmark, Sweden, France and Italy. On the other hand, the median incarceration rate for blacks in 1973 was 367.5 per 100,000, *8.4 times the rate for whites*.[8]

United Nations Ambassador Andrew Young correctly pointed out that there are thousands of political prisoners in U.S. jails, most of whom are black *and* poor. For even some middle-class blacks can use their economic resources to circumvent a jail term. As sociologist Robert Staples puts it, "This society punishes only the poor and powerless who commit a crime."[9] (Even lawyers have a motto: "innocent till proven broke.") But, in addition to race and income, the criminal justice system discriminates on the basis of the type of crime involved. It is estimated that by far the largest single element in the crime cost in this country, accounting for over one-third of the total expense, is white collar crime. Yet, in the state of New York, the harshest penalty that can be meted out to white collar criminals is three months in prison and a $500 find, a penalty which is rarely imposed.[10]

The Supreme Court's 1976 decision to uphold the legality of capital punishment portends ominous consequences for a criminal justice system already wrought with racism. Of the 3859 prisoners executed in the U.S. between 1930 and 1974, 53.5 percent were black. Thus, blacks, who constitute about one-tenth of the population, make up over half of those executed. As of November 1978, 43.3 percent of those on death rows across the U.S. are black.[11] Of course some blacks do not even get their day in court. A 1977 study of seven urban areas revealed that 79 percent of the victims shot by police were black.[12]

The racism as well as sexism which permeate the criminal justice system are glaringly evident in the sentencing patterns for the crime of rape. From their inception, rape laws have been established, not to protect women, but to protect women's property value for men. The underlying rationale of these laws is that the rape of a married women wrongs her husband, while the rape of an unmarried women reduces the monetary value of her father's property investment. By this callous system of economics, the punishment for the rapist also depends upon the value of the merchandise (women) which allegedly is irreparably damaged. Thus, rape is far more likely to be prosecuted if the female victim is middle or upper class and is attacked by a lower-class male. Rape is least prosecuted if the victim is a black female, for the rape of poor, black women is not considered an offense against (white) men of power and substance. According to this logic, the most heinous crime is the sexual assault of a white woman by a black male, who is seen as a vengeful castrator, deserving the most severe punishment.[13]

The empirical data on rape convictions graphically demonstrate the racism of the criminal justice system. Most individuals convicted of rape serve a sentence of no longer than four years, except when the victim is white and the offender is black. The death penalty for the crime of rape is almost exclusively reserved for blacks; of the 455 men executed for rape from 1930 to 1974, 405 (89 percent) were black.[14] However, black males are not uniformly punished: "Of the four categories of rapist and victim in a racial mix, blacks received the stiffest sentences for raping white women and the mildest sentences for raping black women."[15] Wolfgang and Riedel's definitive study discovered that blacks who raped whites received the death penalty in 36 percent of the cases, while blacks who raped blacks were given it in only 2 percent of the time.[16] In short, while the sentencing patterns of rape convictions discriminate heavily against black men, the criminal justice system offers nothing in the way of protection of the legal rights or even the basic human dignity of black women.

EQUALITY OF OPPORTUNITY

Quality of education has traditionally been the instrument for achieving equality of opportunity and upward mobility in the U.S. Herbert Hoover posed the issue well when he said: "We, through free and universal education, provide the training of the runners; we give them an equal start; we provide in government the umpire of fairness in the race."[17] Tragically, public schools have nevei given blacks in the U.S. "an equal start."

Segregated public schools, which relegate blacks to an inferior education, have never been dismantled by the U.S. Supreme Court. While the *Brown* decision of 1954 outlawed de jure racial discrimination (defined as purposeful or intentional segregation), de facto school segregation, reflecting racially segregated housing patterns, has never been held unconstitutional. In *Milliken v. Bradley* (1974), the landmark case involving metro or cross-district desegregation, the Supreme Court held that racial isolation in Detroit's inner-city schools was not significantly the result of official state action or collusion by the several school districts in the greater Detroit area and therefore, a multi-district desegregation plan could not be required.[18] The pernicious effect of de facto school segregation is dramatically attested to by the fact that, in 1979, Linda Brown

Smith, the plaintiff in the landmark *Brown v. Board of Education* decision, returned to court to request that her case be "reopened" because, after twenty-five years of de jure segregation, the schools of Topeka, Kansas remain segregated.[19]

Largely as a result of the court's ill-conceived distinction between de jure and de facto segregation, discredited dual public school systems still predominate, especially outside of the South. In 1979, the U.S. Civil Rights Commission reported that for the nation overall, a full 46 percent of black students attend segregated schools. The two sections of the country with the greatest amount of school segregation are the Northeast, where 65 percent of black students attend segregated schools, and the North Central region where the figure is 68 percent.[20] In fact, the percentage of black students attending segregated public schools in such northern urban centers as New York, Philadelphia, Cleveland, Detroit, and Chicago was *greater* in 1978 than it was in 1954.[21] Thus, the formal integration of public schools masks a deeper and more significant pattern of resegregation.

Rather than serving as instruments of upward mobility for blacks, public schools, especially those in Northern urban centers, have become the chief *obstacles* to equality of opportunity. As Kenneth Clark observes, "They are for the most part institutions breeding despair, frustration and sowing the seeds of self-destruction and social instability."[22] The plain fact is that many U.S. public schools are providing scandalously inferior education to blacks, thereby turning young blacks into a permanent, functionally illiterate underclass.

It is no coincidence that the decline of the quality of public schools in the U.S. corresponded with their changing composition to a majority non-white student body in most large cities. As public schools in cities like Los Angeles, Chicago, and Boston have been ordered to integrate, white parents have responded by transferring their children from public to private schools and therefore have been unwilling to financially support the public school systems. Across the country, school budgets thought to be too high are being rejected. In November 1976, for example, Detroit voters rejected for a second time in three months a proposed five-mill increase in property taxes to support the financially crippled public schools.

Acceleration of the movement to private schools has increased the political support for such private subsidy proposals as Senator Moynihan's tuition tax credit plan. A measure passed by the U.S.

House of Representatives on 1 June 1978 (H.R. 12050) granted tax credits for tuition paid to private elementary and secondary schools. Referring to this bill, Dr. Benjamin Mays, former president of Morehouse College and currently president of the Atlanta Board of Education, asserted:

> The passage of such legislation by the federal government puts money in the pockets of the rich and well-to-do to pay for their children to go to private schools and will leave schools to poor whites and poor blacks...I believe it will be the beginning of the destruction of public education in this country which is at the heart of a democracy like ours, in which the founding fathers were interested in providing at least a high school education for every American.[23]

Although the Moynihan plan was not enacted into law in 1978, twelve different tuition tax credit bills have been introduced in Congress in early 1981; the chances are excellent that one of these proposals will be adopted.

Besides the devastating effects of shrinking resources allocated to public school, blacks are victimized by several other forces in U.S. education. Black educators, from teachers to principals, are being displaced at an alarming rate. It is estimated that between 1968 and 1976, 233,322 black teachers nationwide were displaced by discriminatory hiring and dismissals.[24] In addition, we are witnessing a phenomenon which has come to be known as "the student pushout." A student who has been "pushed out" is one who had been expelled or suspended from school under questionable circumstances or who, because of intolerable hostility directed against him or her, finally quits school. The percentage of blacks suspended or expelled from schools in the U.S. in 1976 was approximately 50 percent higher than for whites.[25] The Regents of the State of New York have estimated that less than 50 percent of public school students in New York City graduate and that the rates are three times higher among non-whites than among whites.[26]

The newest expression of race discrimination in U.S. education is the movement growing steadily across the nation to test students' competency in basic skills as a minimum basis for awarding high school diplomas. While taken at face value, competency testing appears to be a means of improving educational achievement, its practical effect is to discriminate against black students who are failing the tests at far greater rates than whites. In the most recent tests (1978-79), the ratio of black-to-white failure was four-to-one in Florida and five-to-one in North Carolina and Virginia.[27] Obviously, these test scores reflect the grossly inferior education provided to black youngsters by teachers who "have and communicate such low academic expectations and standards to minority children that they establish a self-fulfilling prophesy."[28] Rather than attacking the source of the problem—poor teaching—competency tests "blame the victim" by making students, most of whom are black, pay for the failure of the entire educational system.

Competency testing is likely to have devastating consequences for black students. By denying a high school diploma to a sizeable number of black youngsters, job opportunities will be cut off and black unemployment, already alarmingly high, will increase significantly. Ironically, the high failure rate of blacks on the competency tests will adversely affect the educational opportunities for even black students who *pass* the exam, as it will reduce the black admission quotas in many state universities which are based on the black-white ratio of graduating high school seniors in the state.[29] Perhaps most damaging of all, competencty tests, by officially labeling large numbers of black students as incompetent, not ony causes irreparable psychological damage to stigmatized blacks, but also reinforces the pathology of white racism.

A major study released in mid-1979 by the Carnegie Council on Children forcefully debunks the long-held U.S. myth that our eduational system produces equality of opportunity. The report concluded that the socioeconomic and race and sex status of a person, rather than natural ability, early training, or educational attainment, determine one's chances for success. Mean family income was found to be highly correlated with how students perform on standardized tests. The study concluded that educational programs do not improve children's life chances; the actual determinants of a child's future are class, race, and sex.[30]

A good test of this stratification model of social mobility is to compare the employment situation of black youth with that of white youth with equal or lower educational attainment. The startling fact is that in 1976 even white youth who were *high school dropouts* had lower unemployment rates (22.2 percent) than black youth with college education (27.2 percent), or black graduates from high school (23.6 percent). Indeed, the difference in income between black and white *professionals* is greater than the difference in income between blacks and whites holding nonprofessional jobs.[31] Clearly, racially discriminatory hiring undercuts the American goal of equality of opportunity, even for blacks who overcome the racism that pervades the educational process itself.

ECONOMIC EQUALITY

During the civil rights movement of the 1950s, the vote was seen by black leaders, if not as a panacea, certainly as a means of improving the quality of life for the black masses. The bottom line today is that the enormous progress made in the political arena, as evidenced in the dramatic increase in the number of black elected officials around the country, has not been translated into economic advancement for most blacks. While in an absolute sense, blacks have improved their economic status in the fifteen years since the Voting Rights Act of 1965; when one compares their progress with whites, it is apparent that the racial gap in jobs and income has widened considerably.

"The Election: Jimmy's Debt to Blacks..." read the *Time* magazine headline following the 2 November 1976 presidential election. The article opened with a quote from John Lewis, executive director of the Voter Education Project: "I wish—lord, how I wish—Martin [Luther King] were alive today. He would be very, very happy. Through it all, the lunch-counter sit-ins, the bus strike, the marches and everything, the bottom line was voting."[32] The black vote had an unprecedented impact on the 1976 presidential election. Approximately 90 percent of all black votes cast went to Jimmy Carter. The estimated number of black votes for Carter, 5.2 million, was more than three times his popular vote margin of 1.7 million. Black votes for Carter were responsible for his margin of victory in thirteen states, which accounted for 216 of the 297 electoral votes Carter received—almost four times his narrow 56 electoral vote victory margin.[33]

What did blacks receive from the Carter Administration in return for their decisive contribution to his election victory? The major black expectation from a Carter Administration was meaningful jobs, However, the only tangible employment legislation in Carter's term in office was the Humphrey-Hawkins full employment and Balance Growth Bill which was signed into law in

October 1978. In its final, badly watered down form, this legislation was basically a statement of policy goals, with no new commitment of funds to create jobs.[34] Beyond slightly more enlightened policies toward Africa, two major high-level appointments to Patricia Harris and Andrew Young (who subsequently was forced to resign), and a few patronage jobs, blacks received nothing from the Carter Administration. Indeed, the Carter "black agenda" consisted primarily of cuts in social services.

The significant economic gains achieved by blacks in the 1960s were reversed in the 1970s. In 1970, the median income of black families in the nation was 61.3 percent of white family income. However, this figure fell to 58.5 percent in 1974, and plummeted to 57.1 percent in 1978—a figure first reached in 1945. Another indication of the erosion of past gains is that the proportion of black families whose total income was above the government's "higher budget level" ($24,000), dropped from 12 percent in 1972 to only 9 percent in 1976. Such data do much to dispel the widespread impression that the black upper class has expanded in recent years.

The deteriorating economic condition of blacks is further evidenced by the fact that blacks in 1979 constituted over 30 percent of all persons living below the government definition of poverty. Indeed, 28 percent of black families live in poverty, compared to only 7 percent of the nation's white families. A whopping 42 percent of all black children in the U.S. live in poverty. The erosion of past economic gains is further demonstrated by current unemployment data. At the peak of the 1975 recession, the black unemployment rate was 1.7 times the white rate; by the first half of 1978, the black jobless rate was a record 2.3 times higher than the white rate.[35] In 1979, black unemployment had reached its highest level in history, 23.1 percent, according to the National Urban League's total unemployment index which includes the discouraged unemployed who have stopped their job seeking.[36] As Professor Herbert Hill, for many years national director of the NAACP, observes, "It is evident that a permanent black underclass has developed, that virtually an entire second generation of ghetto youth will never enter into the labor force."[37]

The so-called "tax revolt" of the white middle class culminating in the approval of Proposition 13 by two-thirds of California voters in June 1978 and by the wholesale defeat of candidates perceived as "soft" on tax cuts in the 1978 and 1980 national elections, portends a continued erosion of the economic position of blacks. An overriding belief of many persons who voted for passage of Proposition 13 to slash property taxes by 56 percent was that their taxes had been used to support "unnecessary" social programs that primarily benefited racial minorities. Suggestive of the long-range effects of the California vote was a Gallup Poll asking the state's voters which services they felt could most usefully be curtailed. The largest number, 69 percent, cited welfare payments to the poor, while 21 percent named mass transit—a service indispensable to blacks and Chicanos.[38] Parren Mitchell, leader of the Congressional Black Caucus, predicted that "every single human-resources program is going to be in danger. Medicare and Medicaid, welfare, the job programs."[39] Columnist Joseph Kraft of the *Washington Post* ominously wrote, "the immediate victims of this populist hedonism, unfortunately, are the poor minorities."[40]

SOCIAL EQUALITY

Perhaps the most accurate quantitative measure of the amount of social equality in a society is the degree to which people of different races are willing to live physically proximate to each other. Accordingly, our operational definition of social equality will be the level of residential integration that exists in the nation.

The National Advisory Commission on Civil Disorders (the Kerner Commission) reported in 1968 in stark and clear language that "our Nation is moving toward two societies, one black, one white—separate and unequal."[41] In the decade since the Kerner Commission's report, institutionalized racism has continued to prevent blacks from free access to housing in most U.S. communities. The latest (1977) analysis of black segregation in the country found that residential segregation levels in cities in the U.S. remained virtually unchanged between 1960 and 1970, declining overall by less than 1 percent. In fact, over half of the metropolitan areas in the country experienced net *increases* in residential segregation during this period, with decreases occurring only in the West. Segregation levels increased noticeably between 1960 and 1970 in cities with the largest proportion of blacks such as Newark, Washington D.C., Atlanta, Philadelphia, Detroit, and Cleveland. Using 1970 census data, we find that 75.1 percent of all black households would have to move in order to achieve racial integration in the nation's cities.[42]

Blacks have traditionally been excluded from living in suburban United States, where much of the most desirable housing stock is located. In 1977, the central cities of the United States were 22.8 percent black, while only 5.6 percent of the suburban population of the country was black.[43] As the National Commission on Urban Problems reported in 1968: "The suburbs, however, contain nearly half the *white* metropolitan poor—a figure which suggests that the suburbs discriminate more on the basis of race than on the basis of economic status."[44] Most blacks who do live in the suburbs are as segregated residentially as are their central city counterparts. So-called "snob zoning"—e.g., requiring single detached housing, large lots, expensive building code requirements—is the mechanism used to keep the bulk of blacks out of the suburbs.[45] In short, whites in the U.S. appear staunchly determined to maintain spatial as well as social distance in relation to blacks.

CONCLUSION: "RESPECTABLE" RACISM

Racism and inequality for blacks is a U.S. tradition which appears to be intransigent. Our analysis has demonstrated that blacks have made little progress toward achieving equality with whites in the past decade except in the area of electoral politics, and even there the ability of blacks to influence the national political process remains rather feeble. Perhaps the most revealing finding of our study is the fact that the level of inequality for blacks appears to be fairly uniform throughout the nation. Indeed, we have found a striking similarity between the condition of blacks in 1980 in the state of Mississippi, the most die-hard segregationist state, and in the nation as a whole in all five types of equalities examined.

Specifically, while the number of black elected officials in both Mississippi and the nation has increased dramatically since the Voting Rights Act of 1965, the white majority has refused to permit blacks to operationalize black power, to translate political clout into improved economic conditions. Professor Mack H. Jones of Atlanta University properly cautions that in assessing black political power one must distinguish "between having power and being associated with those who have it, between participating in the decisional process and actually influencing the outcome of that process, and between the symbolic trappings of political power and political power itself."[46]

In terms of equality before the law, there has been a considerable decline in recent years in incidents of violence against blacks committed by law enforcement officers or with their tacit approval. However, violence of this type has not disappeared in either Mississippi or in northern cities. To cite one notorious case in point, in August 1978, when the leader of MOVE, a black religious sect in Philadelphia surrendered to police, walking out of his headquarters with his hands over his head, he was kicked and beaten severely by four policemen, as one high-ranking officer looked on. Neither the Philadelphia Chief of Police nor Mayor Frank Rizzo took any action to reprimand or prosecute the policemen.[47]

Several developments in 1980 testify to the continuing inequality of treatment accorded blacks by the U.S. legal system. The unsolved waves of murders of blacks in cities such as Atlanta, the acquittal of whites in deaths of blacks in Greensboro, N.C. and Miami, among other places, and the unsolved assault which nearly claimed the life of Urban League president Vernon Jordan are examples of such ominous and foreboding events. In its January 1981 report to the White House and Congress, the U.S. Commission on Civil Rights noted with alarm, "widespread acts of animosity, such as cross burnings and vandalism of churches and synagogues, and a rising number of civil disorders triggered by violent treatment of minorities by law enforcement officials." Now that Strom Thurmond and not Edward Kennedy, as head of the Senate's Judiciary Committee, will be conducting hearings on President Reagan's judicial nominees to the federal bench, genuine equality under the law for blacks appears to be an even more distant prospect.

As has been documented, quality public education as the conduit to upward mobility has never been provided to blacks in either Mississippi or in the nation for basically the same reasons. School integregation has generally meant that white parents have pulled their children out of public schools, leaving these schools largely resegregated and desperately underfunded. Blacks today are receiving a grossly inferior education, are being suspended and expelled from schools at alarming rates, have been denied black role models as teachers or principals, and finally, are having their high school diplomas withheld because of racist competency tests.

The economic position of blacks vis-a-vis whites today is roughly the same in Mississippi as it is in the nation at large. For the past two decades, the average family income for blacks in both

Mississippi and the nation has hovered at slightly above half that of white family income. During this same period, almost one-third of the black population of both the state and the nation have lived below the poverty level. In 1979, the unemployment rate for blacks was approximately three times the white rate in the country, compared to four times the white rate in Mississippi. Finally, the achievement of genuine social equality for blacks in Mississippi and the nation, if measured in terms of white acceptance of blacks as their equals, is still a utopian dream.

One must sadly conclude that a substantial level of pure racism still festers in the U.S. A survey of racial attitudes in the nation conducted by Louis Harris in the Fall of 1978 reveals that 49 percent of whites believe that "blacks tend to have less ambition than whites," 36 percent hold that "blacks want to live off the handout," and one white in four believes that "blacks have less native intelligence than whites."[48] According to a recent poll conducted by Stanford University professor Seymour Martin Lipset, "most whites accept the reality of at least some racial discrimination, but see black problems as stemming essentially from the moral failings of individuals."[49] In short, the stereotype of the lazy and shiftless black persists in the white American mind.

An extensive national opinion survey administered in 1978 by the Gallup organization reveals additional gloomy news for the future progress of blacks. The survey found that white Americans rank "the problem of black Americans" as the very lowest—thirty-first—of an array of thirty-one domestic and international issues, below even such concerns as "communism in France and Italy," "mass transit," and "Communist China."[50] Whites seem to have taken the posture that blacks have made such substantial progress that their plight need no longer be a matter of major concern. In 1979, columnist Carl T. Rowan astutely observed, "Whites don't want to feel to blame for the still depressed level of life of black Americans so they are inclined to see big progress where almost none exists."[51]

By the late 1970s, white racism had evolved from its nastier blatant form. No longer fashionable in polite conversation to explicitly race-bait, racism today is more respectably expressed in the code words of "merit," "educational quotas," "reverse discrimination," and "tax revolt." Take the much proclaimed Proposition 13 movement, for example. While part of the impetus on the part of the white middle class to cut their property taxes was simply a reaction against inflation, it was quite clear that there was a racial difference in the perception of the issue. Over 90 percent of blacks voted against Proposition 13 while 75 percent of whites voted for it. Jimmy Breslin commented:

> The blacks are one of the reasons for the tax revolt, but almost nobody mentions them or the code word for them, welfare, because this could cause charges of racism to be aimed at the tax revolt and once again the poor would have ruined everybody's pleasure.[52]

What has occurred in the last decade is that the Civil Rights Movement has shifted from an effort by blacks to secure basic constitutional rights to an attempt by blacks to advance their economic standing in society. While whites grudgingly capitulated to black demands for political equality, they remain today determined as ever to resist any reduction in their standard of living. During the affluent decade of the 1960s, whites were willing to support some of the Great Society programs. However, once inflation began to burden middle class whites, they were left with only two viable options: to make blacks and the poor pay more taxes or to provide them with fewer services. Because openly placing higher taxes on blacks and the poor is not socially respectable, "Proposition 13 and its progeny offer a politically acceptable cover for penalization of the economically vulnerable."[53] The election of Ronald Reagan in 1980 was an overt expression of the narrow callousness of voters who favor reducing the level of public services that benefit blacks and the poor.

In short, racism in the early 1980s no longer takes the form of racial lynchings (although there has been widespread violence concerning busing and neighborhood integration) or exclusion from the voting booth, and the like. Today's racism is subtle and "respectable." Whites rationalize that black inequality is due to moral failings of blacks rather than to white racism. Joel Dreyfuss calls this the "New Racism":

> The New Racism is particularly dangerous because it attempts to deprive blacks of the validity of their grievances...The new strategy is simple but admittedly brilliant: it denies the existence of racism and accepts no responsibility for inequality. The effect of such an attitude places black demands in the position of being outrageous.[54]

Basically, what we have observed is that racism has evolved through three stages in the last half-century: from individual racism to institutional racism,[55] and more recently, to respectable racism. Overt acts of violence against blacks by individual whites, such as the bombing of a black church, are comparatively rare today. Institutionalized racism, in the form of public policies and social arrangements which perpetuate the lack of proper food, shelter and medical facilities for blacks, continues unabated. Institutionalized racism serves the psychic needs of whites for it places no clear responsiblity on any individual for the condition of blacks; "a consequence of this is to absolve everybody of the responsibility for 'objectively' racist outcomes such as segregation in residence and education."[56] Today's respectable racism, by denying the existence of racial discrimination and by propagating the myth of enormous black progress, provides the ultimate absolution of the white community's responsiblity for the condition of blacks in the U.S. Regardless of the form white racism has taken, it remains "an American Dilemma." As Myrdal articulated two generations ago, the so-called "Negro problem" is a "white problem" a deeply-rooted sickness which only whites themselves can cure.

CHAPTER ONE

1. This historic clash of educational ideals is thoroughly described in Laurence R. Veysey, *The Emergence of the American University* (Chicago: University of Chicago Press, 1965).

2. Carnegie Commission on Higher Education, *The Open-Door Colleges* (New York: McGraw-Hill Book Co., 1970), p. 16.

3. *Ibid.,* p. 1.

4. Samuel Bowles and Herbert Gintis, *Schooling in Capitalist America: Educational Reform and Contradictions of Economic Life* (New York: Basic Books, 1976), p. 212.

5. Jackson *Clarion-Ledger,* 16 May 1972, p. 6.

6. James W. Silver, *Mississippi: The Closed Society* (New York: Harcourt, Brace and World, 1963), p. 6.

7. For an excellent analysis of the Southern identity, see C. Van Woodward, *The Burden of Southern History* (Baton Rouge: Louisiana State University Press, 1960), pp. 3-25.

8. Peter Schrag, "A Hesitant New South: Fragile Promise on the Last Frontier," *Saturday Review* 105 (12 February 1972): 52.

9. Marshall Frady, "Discovering One Another in a Georgia Town," *Life* (12 February 1971): 46D.

10. Timothy McNulty, "Old Problems Persist in the 'New South'," *Chicago Tribune,* 17 June 1978, p. 9.

11. Janice Castro, "In Mississipipi: The KKK Suits Up," *Time* III (26 June 1978): 7.

12. Samuel DuBois Cook, "Democracy and Tyranny in America: The Radical Paradox of the Bicentennial and Blacks in the American Political System," *Journal of Politics* 38 (August 1976): 290.

13. Lerone Bennett, Jr., "Old Illusions and New Souths," *Ebony* 26 (August 1971), 37.

14. Manning Marable, "The Post-Movement Reaction," *Southern Exposure* 7 (Spring 1979): 60.

15. Manning Marable, "Tuskegee and the Politics of Illusion in the New South," *The Black Scholar* 8 (May 1977): 16.

16. Julian Bond, "Better Voters, Better Politicians," *Southern Exposure* 7 (Spring 1979):69.

17. B. Drummond Ayres, Jr., "South's 'Seg' Schools Are Now Part of the System," *New York Times,* 17 June 1976, sec. 4, p. 1.

18. The leading early study of political intolerance was: Samuel A. Stouffer, *Communism, Conformity, and Civil Liberties* (Garden City, N.Y.: Doubleday & Co., 1955). The results of a 1973 replication of the

Stouffer study were published in: Clyde Z. Nunn, Harry J. Crockett, Jr. and J. Allen Williams, Jr., *Tolerance For Nonconformity* (San Francisco: Jossey-Bass, 1978).

19. Bernard Murchland, "The Eclipse of the Liberal Arts," *Change* 8 (November 1976): 22.

20. Henry Steele Commager, "Our Schools Have Kept Us Free," *Life* 29 (16 October 1950): 46.

CHAPTER TWO

1. Powell, "Academic Martial Law at Southern: McCain Zips Dissenting Lips," 4: *Student Printz,* 8 May 1969, p.1.

2. *Student Printz,* 11 September 1969, p. 1.

3. William D. McCain, "Our American Heritage," paper read before the meeting of the All American Forum III, Hattiesburg, Mississippi, 17 July 1972.

4. William D. McCain, "Reminiscences of the United States Archivist in Italy, 1944-45—Director William D. McCain on Military Leave from Mississippi Department of Archives and History," *Journal of Mississippi History,* 34 (February 1972): 8-9, 18, 18-19, 27-28.

5. *Student Printz,* 25 April 1972, p. 3. Is it any surprise that in 1967, at General McCain's initiative, USM became the first university in the nation to open its doors to the U.S. Army Reserves for summer encampment? The university annually receives some $300,000 in direct monies from the presence of the Reservists. *Student Printz,* 7 July 1971, p. 1.

6. Gilbert T. Saetre, *The Pride 1920-1970* (Hattiesburg: University of Southern Mississippi Press, 1969), p. 74.

7. Lew Powell, "Academic Arrogance at Southern," *Mississippi Freelance,* I (June 1969): 4.

8. William D. McCain, "The Administration of David Holmes, Governor of the Mississippi Territory, 1809-1817," *Journal of Mississippi History* 24 (November 1967): 328.

9. "The American Historical Association and the AAUP: A Joint Inquiry into an Issue of Attribution," *AAUP Bulletin,* 57 (Winter 1971): 528-32.

10. Mrs. Racine had no legal grounds for charges of plagiarism because her thesis was not copyrighted.

11. "The American Historical Association and the AAUP: A Joint Inquiry into an Issue of Attribution," 529.

12. New Orleans *Time-Picayune,* 13 February 1972, p. 1.

13. *WE,* II (15 September 1970), 3.

14. Hattiesburg *American,* 13 December 1971, p. 17.

15. William D. McCain, History is Being Made in Mississippi Now," *The Citizen* 7 (November 1962): 6-8.

16. Jackson *Clarion-Ledger,* 8 February 1964, pp. 1, 8.

17. *Student Printz,* 31 January 1967, p. 1.

18. Hattiesburg *American,* 24 May 1955, p. 1.

19. William D. McCain, "Our Heritage," paper read before meeting of the All American Forum III, Hattiesburg, Mississippi, 17 July 1972.

20. Personal observation.

21. *Student Printz,* 20 April 1967, p. 3.

22. *Student Printz,* 4 February 1971, p. 1.

23. *Student Printz,* 11 February 1971, p. 1.

24. William D. McCain, Report before meeting of the Student Senate of the University of Southern Mississippi, Hattiesburg, Mississippi, 13 March 1972.

CHAPTER THREE

1. James W. Silver, "Mississippi: The Closed Society," *Journal of Southern History* 30 (February 1964): 5.

2. James Meredith, *Three Years in Mississippi* (Bloomington: University of Indiana Press, 1966), p. 79.

3. The following account relies heavily upon Ronald A. Hollander, "One Mississippi Negro Who Didn't Go To College," *The Reporter* 17 (8 November 1962): 30-34.

4. Kennard didn't believe in a forced, violent integration of schools; he even offered to take night courses at MSC. He eloquently explained his position in a letter to the Hattiesburg *American:* This had led me to request that I be permitted to enroll at Mississippi Southern College, without a court order to do so. I, too, am a solid believer in the ability of the individual states to control their own affairs. I believe that if this state should lead out with only the smallest amount of integration it would never worry about Federal intervention...The thought of presenting this request before a Federal court for which that would bring about, makes my heart heavy." Hattiesburg *American,* 26 January 1960, p. 10.

5. Hollander, "One Mississippi Negro Who Didn't Go to College," 32.

6. *New York Times,* 16 September 1959, p. 33.

7. Hattiesburg *American,* 29 September 1959, p. 1.

8. Hollander, *op. cit.*

9. With characteristic trenchancy James Meredith observed: "Mississippi society is very legalistic, and no injustice is committed against a Negro without some semblance of an excuse (the excuse can be real or imaginary). Where there is no excuse Mississippi creates one, as in the Mississippi Southern-Clyde Kennard case." Meredith, *Three Years in Mississippi,* p. 84.

10. Comedian Dick Gregory sent private investigators to Hattiesburg to seek out the truth in the Kennard case. After discovering that Kennard was innocent, Gregory offered to bring Roberts, the youth who committed the actual theft, to Chicago and locate a job for him if he would testify in Kennard's behalf. Roberts refused, fearing retaliation against his family in Mississippi. Tom Dent, "Portrait of Three Heroes," *Freedomways* 5 (Spring 1965): 257.

11. Silver, *Mississippi: The Closed Society,* p. 94.

12. *Southern School News,* 7 (June 1961), 4.

13. James Silver points out that of all the hypocrisies indulged in by those who perpetuate the closed society, some of the most insidious appeared at the expense of the gentle Kennard in the Mississippi newspapers. The Jackson *Clarion-Ledger* on 28 January 1963, reported: "Gov. Ross Barnett hastened admission of a negro convict suffering cancer, into University Hospital here the other day. At the time, he reported he didn't know the man was in serious condition. That is true. Now, the case of Clyde Kennard, the negro who once tried to enter Mississippi Southern University, we understand that the man has not been neglected. Hugh Boren (assistant to Governor Barnett) tells us that Supt. C.E. Breazeale and doctors at Parchman have been fully aware of and have been closely watching the Kennard case. Apparently, outsiders were more worried about Kennard than the authorities who actually knew the man's illness and were attending to it as appeared necessary. Boren says that the negro is not nearly so bad off, prison doctors think, as new stories have pictured." Silver *Mississippi: The Closed Society,* 95.

14. Bradford Daniel and John Howard Griffin, "Why They Can't Wait: An Interview with a White Negro." *The Progressive* 28 (July 1964): 18-19.

CHAPTER FOUR

1. *Southern School News* 7 (June 1961), 4.

2. Hollander, "One Mississippi Negro Who Didn't Go to College," 32.

3. John B. Hudson, "The Spoils System Enters College: Governor Bilbo and Higher Education in Mississippi," *New Republic,* 64 (17 September 1930): 123.

4. Clarence Cason, "The Mississippi Imbroglio," *Virginia Quarterly Review* 7 (April 1931): 238. The day before Governor Bilbo delivered he announcement to the press he called Hugh Critz, the director of public relations for Mississippi Power and Light, into his office. "Mr. Critz," the Governor is reported to have asked him, "if you were elected president of Mississippi Agricultural and Mechanical College, would you have any objections to the removal of faculty members and employees who have made themselves obnoxious to me?" Critz answered in the negative, and the next day was appointed president of the college. Critz knew the college well; in fact he struggled five long years there to receive his only degree—a B.S. Hudson, "The Spoils System Enters College: Governor Bilbo and Higher Education in Mississippi," 123.

5. Aubrey Keith Lucas, "The Mississippi Legislature and Mississippi Higher Public Education: 1890-1960," (unpublished Ph.D. dissertation, Dept. of Education, Florida State Univeristy, 1966), p. 92.

6. Allen Cabanies, *The University of Mississippi: Its First Hundred Years* (Hattiesburg: University and College Press of Mississippi, 1971), p. 145.

7. *Ibid.,* p. 146.

8. *Ibid.,* p. 145.

9. Hudson, "The Spoils System Enters College: Governor Bilbo and Higher Education in Mississippi," 124.

10. *Ibid.*

11. Cabaniss, *The University of Mississippi: Its First One Hundred Years,* p. 146.

12. Hudson, *op. cit.,* 124. When consideration was being given to replacing the head of the Ole Miss Department of Greek, Governor Bilbo said to his cohorts, "Is there any one in my gang who can teach Greek?" There was a silence. The department remained intact. An individualistic professor of chemistry, recognized as brilliant, said that Bilbo wished to fire him, but when asked why he remained, Dr. Fogelsong replied, "Hell, they couldn't spell my name." A. Winfall Green,

The Man Bilbo (Baton Rouge: Louisiana State University Press, 1963), p. 75.

13. Cabaniss, *The University of Mississippi: Its First One-Hundred Years,* p. 147.

14. W.F. Minor, "Hope Held for College Board," New Orleans *Times-Picayune,* 16 April 1972, sec. 2, p. 2.

15. *Southern School News,* 10 (September 1963), 14.

16. W.F. Minor, "Hope Held for College Board," New Orleans *Times-Picayune,* 16 April 1972, sec. 2; p. 2.

17. *Southern School News,* 10 (January 1964), 11.

18. *New York Times,* 15 June 1958, p. 68.

19. *New York Times,* 6 June 1958, p. 25.

20. *New York Times,* 7 June 1958, p. 10. The NAACP noted pointedly that, "No question was raised as to Professor King's mentality when he advocated segregation and attacked this association and the Supreme Court of the United States in a series of newspaper articles in Mississippi which was syndicated to many southern daily papers." *New York Times,* 7 June 1958, p. 10.

21. King's wife filed a petition for a writ of habeas corpus. The petition charged that the state had violated Mississippi law by holding King's lunacy hearing in Jackson, instead of Oxford where he was arrested, or in Gulfport, where he lived. Mississippi law required that lunacy hearings be conducted in the country of residence or where the person involved was taken into custody. *New York Times,* 6 June 1958, p. 68. Governor Coleman reassured all civil libertarians by saying, "All his legal rights will be fully preserved." *New York Times,* 6 June 1958, p. 25.

22. Russell Barrett, *Integration at Ole Miss* (Chicago: Quadrangle Books, 1965), p. 33.

23. New Orleans *Times-Picayune,* 31 August 1958, p. 10.

24. Walter Lord, *The Past That Would Not Die* (New York: Harper Row, 1965), p. 76.

25. For a complete account of Reverend King's "assaults upon windmills," see Jack Anderson, "The Checkered Career of Clennon King," New Orleans *Times-Picayune,* 15 September 1977, p. 15.

26. "Academic Freedom in Mississippi," *AAUP Bulletin* 51 (Autumn, 1965), 347; Silver, *Mississippi: The Closed Society,* p. 319.

27. *Ibid.*

28. *Ibid.,* p. 62.

29. W.F. Minor, "Last Mixing Fight May Be Costliest," New Orleans *Times-Picayune,* 18 November 1973, sec. 2, p. 2.

30. New Orleans *Times-Picayune,* 22 June 1974, p. 1.

31. W.F. Minor, "Last Mixing Fight May Be Costliest," p. 2.

32. Ken Vinson, "Trustees of the Closed Society," *Ave Maria* (1June 1968): 21.

33. For details of Vinson's case, see "The University of Mississippi," *AAUP Bulletin* 56 (Spring 1970), 79.

34. Ken Vinson, ::Mississippi's Master Racist," *Change* (September-October 1970): 23.

35. Hattiesburg *American,* 23 February 1955, p. 1.

36. The administrative assistant most actively concerned in the screening was a former member of the FBI who worked closely with Mississippi Senator Eastland's Internal Security Committee and who appeared to have no particular academic qualifications himself except that he had been in charge of FBI training. "Academic Freedom in Mississippi," 348.

37. Barrett, *Integration at Ole Miss,* p. 32.

38. Silver, *Mississippi: The Closed Society,* p. 109; "Academic Freedom in Mississippi," 348.

39. Vinson, "Mississippi's Master Racist," 23.

40. *Ibid.*

41. Vinson, "Trustees of the Closed Society," 22.

42. Tom Ethridge, "Mississippi's Notebook," Jackson *Clarion-Ledger,* 2 December 1966, p. 8.

43. "The University of Mississippi," 82.

44. Vinson, "Trustees of the Closed Society," 22.

45. John H. Carter, "A Boll Weevil Six Feet Long," *Library Journal* 94 (15 October 1969)' 3616.

46. *Ibid.,* 3618.

47. *Ibid.,* 3616. See also "The University of Mississippi," 82; and Curtis Wilkie, "Mississippi Muzzle," *Nation* 208 (3 February 1969): 132.

48. John N. Carter, "The Return of the Boll Weevil," *Library Journal* 95 (15 May 1970): 1817.

49. Newspaper columnist Willson F. Minor, who has covered Mississippi politics for over a quarter of century, states "Roberts has been in the forefront of each stance which has put the institutions in academic hot water. He has also been the architect of board policies which have put the board very deeply into the purely administrative functions of the colleges." W.F. Minor, "Hope Held for College Board," New Orleans *Times-Picayune,* 16 April 1972, sec. 2, p. 2.

50. The "M.M." actually stands for Malcolm Mette.

51. Vinson, "Mississippi's Master Racist," 24.

52. By the scant margin of 6-5, the Board of Trustees voted that it was powerless to withhold Meredith's diploma. The majority sentiment was that denying Meredith's diploma would result in automatic

discreditation of all Missisipppi colleges and that it would be declared illegal by the courts. *Southern School News* X (September 1963), 14.

53. Vinson, "Mississippi's Master Racist," 23.

54. Testimonial banquet for M.M. Roberts given by William D. McCain, Hattiesburg, Mississippi, 19 April 1972.

55. Vinson, "Trustees of the Closed Society," 22.
check one 55 and 56.

56. "Mississippi Muzzle," pp. 132-33.

57. Carter, "A Boll Weevil Six Feet Long," 3616.

58. Letter from M.M. Roberts, President, Board of Trustees of State Insitutions of Higher Learning, State of Mississippi, Hattiesburg, Mississippi, 10 March 1970. The letter is reprinted in Ed Williams, "M.M. Raps MSU's 'City Slickers, Foreign Ideologies,' " *Mississippi Freelance* I (March 1970), 1.

59. See *New York Times,* 19 April 1970, p. 84; *Newsweek,* 75 (30 March 1970): 83.

60. *Student Printz,* 11 December 1969, pp. 1, 4.

61. *Student Printz,* 21 April 1970, pp. 1, 2.

62. The entire resolution is reprinted in *Playboy,* 17 (April 1970): 57-58.

63. *Student Printz,* 11 December 1973, p. 2.

64. New Orleans *States-Item,* 23 August 1974, p. 12.

65. Hattiesburg *American,* 8 September 1978.

66. Hattiesburg *American,* 1 September 1978.

67. Hattiesburg *American,* 8 September 1978.

68. Hattiesburg *American,* 23 October 1978.

69. Hattiesburg *American,* 15 November 1978.

CHAPTER FIVE

1. William D. McCain, Report before the meeting of the Student Senate of the University of Southern Mississippi, Hattiesburg, Mississippi, 13 March 1972.

2. Hattiesburg *American,* 10 November, 1972, p. 27.

3. In June 1973 workmen installed "lifts" under the seats in the balcony in an attempt to remedy the problem.

4. *Student Printz,* 29 September 1970, p. 2.

5. *Student Printz,* 12 November 1970, p. 4.

6. *Student Printz,* 5 December 1972, p. 1.

7. *Student Printz,* 29 April 1971, p. 20.

8. The tone of Cox' book is indicated by its very last paragraph: "There is no doubt as to the nation's ability to repatriate the Negro. Repatriation is possible! It is necessary! If we do not repatriate the Negro, our race will become negroid and our culture will decay. If we do repatriate the Negro, our civilization is to increase, and our future belongs to God." Earnest Sevier Cox, *White America* (Los Angeles: Noontide Press, 1966), p. 194. The editor's introduction in the recently published paperback edition of *White America* states: "Copies of all editions are extremely hard to come by and expensive when found. Until publication of this NOONTIDE PRESS Classics Series the book was readily available only from University Microfilms, of Ann Arbor, Michigan, for $15 per copy." It should have added, "or at the USM library."

9. *USM Faculty Handbook* (1971), 57.

10. Author's observation, 19 September 1972.

11. Interview with Ed Fleming.

12. The USM catalogue explicitly states that "members of the faculty of USM above the rank of instructor cannot become candidates for a doctoral degree at this institution." *USM Bulletin Graduate Program* (1972), 23. In 1971-72 this dean was a doctoral candidate at USM while he served as dean. Of course, at Southern a dean is not necessarily above an instructor.

13. Interview with George Ethridge, USM student, Winter, 1972.

14. *Perspective USM* 31 (29 March 1971), 5.

15. Christopher Jencks and David Riesman, *The Academic Revolution* (Garden City, N.Y.: Doubleday, 1969), p. 61.

16. William D. McCain, Report at the Freshman Orientation Program of the University of Southern Mississippi, Hattiesburg, Mississippi, 6 September 1971.

17. Jackson *Daily News,* 10 March 1972, p. 7.

18. Jackson *Daily News,* 27 May 1972, p. 4.

19. W.F. Minor, " 'Degree Factory' Duplication Is Hit," New Orleans *Times-Picayune,* 21 April 1974, sec. 2, p. 2.

20. Interview with Mary Louise Norwood, a USM student, Summer 1972.

21. Claude E. Fike. Report before the meeting of the College of Liberal Arts Faculty of the University of Southern Mississippi, Hattiesburg, Mississippi, 9 May 1972, p. 8.

22. The dean of the university said: "We paid a lot of attention to *The Keyhole.* I really felt that it was an honest expression of the students and it was information that was gathered under, I thought, very controlled kind of circumstances where we could trust it. You have no idea how much help *The Keyhole* gave to people." Interview

with Charles W. Moorman, dean of the university, University of Southern Mississippi.

23. *Student Printz,* 14 March 1972, p. 1.

24. Interview with editor of *The Keyhole,* 11 April 1972.

25. *Student Printz,* 31 October 1972, p. 5.

26. *Student Printz,* 19 October 1972, p. 2.

27. *Student Printz,* 4 February 1971, p. 1.

28. *Student Printz,* 2 February 1971, p. 2.

29. *Student Printz,* 25 March 1971, p. 1.

30. According to the road manager to the Allman Brothers Band: "Some of the Band members were arrested for alleged possession of narcotics in Grove Hill, Alabama just prior to their scheduled appearance at the University of Southern Mississippi. There were no convictions of any kind for violations of the Alabama State drug laws." Letter from William H. Perkins, road manager of the Allman Brothers Band, 8 January 1973.

31. *Student Printz,* 3 May 1973, p. 1.

CHAPTER SIX

1. This number includes both undergraduate and graduate majors. William Hatcher, "Reflections on the Self-Study Report of the Department of Political Science," (February 1973), 2.

2. G., "A Look at Congressional-Executive Relations in Foreign Policy Making with Emphasis on the 'Cuban Missile-Crisis' of 1962: The President as the Leader" (Hattiesburg, Mississippi: Winter Quarter 1971), pp. 1, 4, 14, 17.

3. G. once told me that he almost gave me "$100 bill toilet paper" as a Christmas present, but that he was afraid I might not understand. The point, as G. explained it, was that "Some people burn their paper money with cigars, but I could use mine to..." Instead, G. gave me figurines of all the U.S. presidents, mounted in a cardboard box.

4. Letter from William Hatcher to all USM department chairmen, 25 June 1971.

5. Orley B. Caudhill, "The Americans, the World and the Future," *The Southern Quarterly* 9 (October 1970): 12. 19. 23; (January 1971), 168-70.

6. Letter from William Hatcher to M.M. Roberts, 4 February 1971.

7. Two pages of the Poltical Science Department's Self-Study Report of 1973 were devoted to the cooling problems of the classrooms. To quote a short excerpt: "The mechanism regulating the temperature gets out of order several times a year, and then the temperature is definitely either too hot or too cold. If a teacher tries to get relief by opening windows, that upsets the ventilation of other rooms, and the situation is worse. Although the Building and Grounds people are accommodating, it usually takes several days and sometimes more than one adjustment to get the temperature right." "Self-Study of the Department of Political Science" (31 January 1973), 17.

8. Interview with Jerry E. Falls, 1971.

9. Bill A. was the department's very first graduate student to reach the Ph.D qualifying examinations. K. naturally enjoyed the honor of being Bill's major professor. Apparently, K.'s verbal blast at Doumas reflected K.'s firm belief that Doumas was out to sabotage Bill's candidacy.

10. *US,* No. 8, p. 4.

11. *US,* No. 4, p. 1; No. 6, p. 2; No. 8, p. 1. Copies of *US* can be obtained by writing to Hugo Johnson in Meridian, Mississippi, or to the Southcentral Regional Office of the Anti-Defamation League of New Orleans, Louisiana.

12. "A Guide to Graduate Study in Political Science 1972," (Washington: American Political Science Association, 1972), 3-14.

13. Letter from William Hatcher to Aubrey K. Lucas, dean of the graduate school at the University of Southern Mississippi, 8 August 1971.

14. Interview with Q., Fall 1970.

15. Interview with Kenn Kerr, Winter 1971.

16. Harold P., "The Minor Parties of the United States," (Hattiesburg, Mississippi: Fall Quarter 1970), pp. 8, 13.

17. Letter from William Hatcher to Linda F. Keith, 12 January 1973.

CHAPTER SEVEN

1. Sidney Hook, *Academic Freedom and Academic Anarchy* (New York: Cowles Book Co., 1969), p. 34.

2. *Student Printz,* 9 September 1971, p. 8.

3. *Student Printz,* 6 February 1973, p. 1.

4. *Student Printz,* 23 January 1969, p. 1.

5. Charles Moorman, *Sapientia Ex Fondo Hibernico,* The Dean's Annual Report to the Faculty of the Unversity of Southern Mississippi (Hattiesburg, The Faculty Meeting, 3 September 1971), p. 12-14.

6. Jackson *Clarion-Ledger,* 16 May 1972, p. 6.

7. *Student Printz,* 10 September 1970, p. 1.

8. *Perspective USM* 26 (7 September 1970), 8.

9. *Ibid.*

10. *Perspective USM* 27 (11 October 1971), 5.

11. *Perspective USM* 26 (7 September 1970), 8.

12. *USM Faculty Handbook* (1971), 35.

13. Letter from William Hatcher to the USM Bookstore, 27 May 1970.

14. Letter from Jesse Gore, Manager of the USM Bookstore, to Charles W. Moorman, Dean of the University, 28 May 1970.

15. Letter from Charles Moorman, Dean of the University, to William Hatcher, 1 June 1970. Chair Hatcher wrote to Claude E. Fike, Dean of the College of Liberal Arts, on 2 July 1971: "There is a new edition of...and we need very much to keep up to date—the edition currently being used does not contain the 1968 & 1970 election results. The new one does." The letter came back to Hatcher with the following note from Dean Moorman written on it: "On the new text for PS 101, give bookstire one year to get rid of *600* copies. Please tell the students who won in 1970." Letter from William Hatcher to Claude Fike, Dean of the College of Liberal Arts, 2 July 1971.

16. *Perspective USM* 27 (11 October 1971), 5.

17. Note from Charles W. Moorman, Dean of the University, to Claude E. Fike, Dean of the College of Liberal Arts, 12 October 1971.

18. Claude E. Fike, Report before the meeting of the College of Liberal Arts Faculty of the University of Southern Mississippi, Hattiesburg, Mississippi, 9 May 1972, pp. 6-7.

19. Hook, *Academic Freedom and Academic Anarchy,* p. 73.

20. Minutes of the meeting of the Curriculum Committee of the College of Liberal Arts, 1 September 1971.

21. Claude E. Fike, *op. cit.,* p. 8-9.

22. Memorandum from Claude E. Fike, Dean of the College of Liberal Arts, to the author, 9 February 1972.

23. Charles W. Moorman, *Sapientia Ex Fondo Hibernico,* The Deans's Annual Report to the Faculty of the University of Southern Mississippi (Hattiesburg: The Faculty Meeting, 3 September 1971), pp.7-8.

24. Interview with Cedric Evans, 9 September 1971.

25. *Student Printz,* 26 October 1972, p. 1.

26. *Student Printz,* 1 February 1973, p. 1.

27. *Student Printz,* 6 February 1973, p. 1.

28. Robert E. Kuttner, Paper read before the meeting of the 17th Annual Leadership Conference of the Citizen's Council of America, New Orleans, Louisiana, 2 September 1972.

CHAPTER EIGHT

1. Zbigniew K. Brzezinski, *The Permanent Purge, Politics in Soviet Totalitarianism* (Cambridge: Harvard University Press, 1956), p. 38.

2. Figures on faculty turnover were compiled from the respective bulletins of the University of Southern Mississippi.

3. While one can estimate the number of teachers fired at Southern, no statistic will reveal directly the number of professors who have internalized the policy of constraint for both on-campus and off-campus utterances and activities.

4. *Student Printz,* 20 April 1967, pp. 1, 3.

5. Jackson *Clarion-Ledger,* 8 February 1964, p. 8.

6. Powell, "Academic Martial Law at Southern: McCain Zips Dissenting Lips," 4.

7. *Ibid.,* p. 1. The inevitable suit was filed in April 1969 by the mother of a Columbus, Mississippi teenager. The Mississippi legislature on 14 April 1972 invalidated its 1926 law prohibiting the teaching of evolution.

8. Morgan notified the university on 1 July 1969 that he was resigning "primarily because of lack of the administration's cooperation in the conduct of his department." Hattiesburg *American,* 1 April 1969, p. 2.

9. *Shelton v. Tucker,* 364 U.S. 479 (1960).

10. *Mississippi State Conference of AAUP et al. v. Holmes Chairman of the Board et. al,* (N.D. Miss. 1966).

11. Interview with W.D. Norwood, Jr., 17 May 1972.

12. *Ibid.*

13. Wood received a letter, dated 18 July 1972, from the Director of Student Activities, confirming the fact that he would be serving as faculty advisor to the ACLU Chapter. Six weeks later Wood received a notice, dated 7 September 1972, announcing that his one-year contract for the 1972-73 academic year would not be renewed.

14. Interview with Fred Bergerson, 19 January 1971.

15. *Student Printz,* 19 May 1970, p. 2.

16. *University of Southern Mississippi Faculty Handbook* (1971), 13.

17. The resolution called for a "full scale investigation of the firings by an elected committee composed of full time faculty members." *Student Printz,* 29 September 1970, p. 3.

The USM AAUP Chapter has long been harassed by the administration. Some years ago, an associate professor at Southern who had become eligible for tenure found himself among those "being advanced tenure" on a list sent out by the President's office; but before any further action had been taken the President heard a rumor that the professor was being "investigated by the FBI" and removed his name from the list. An AAUP committee tracked down the rumor which proved to be without substantial foundation. At the time, the professor was president of the campus AAUP Chapter. "Academic Freedom in Mississippi," p. 350.

18. Charles W. Moorman, *Sapientia Ex Fondo Hibernico,* The Dean's Annual Report to the Faculty of the University of Southern Mississippi (Hattiesburg: The Faculty Meeting, 3 September 1971), p. 2.

19. Powell, "Academic Martial Law at Southern: McCain Zips Dissenting Lips," p. 4.

20. Lew Powell, "A Seg Theoretician Becomes an Activist and Seems to Like It," *Mississippi Freelance* I (March 1970): 3.

21. Prior to his departure to Chicago in August 1968 to serve as a delegate to the National Democratic Convention, Posey had been given a contract raising his salary to $1400—a figure in line with other members of his department; on his return, he found that his raise had been cut to $400. Although the ax formally was wielded by Dean Fike, it had the approval of General McCain—himself an unsuccessful candidate for a seat on the state's Regular (all-white) delegation. Posey issued the following statement: "With little prospect of advancement at this university, and the financial sacrifice entailed by staying under such circumstances, I was forced to resign." Powell, "Academic Martial Law at Southern: McCain Zips Dissenting Lips," 1.

22. Report of the Advisory Council Ethics Hearings, 14 July 1969, pp. 4-6.

23. *Ibid.* p. 7.

24. Interview with Charles W. Moorman, Dean of the University, 1971.

25. After being subjected to salary discrimination for five years, Scarborough said in 1974 that he knows "how it feels to be treated like a nigger." He added, "I don't blame blacks for their resentment and for wanting to do what they can to overcome discrimination." Interview with William Scarborough, Spring 1974.

26. Interview with Charles W. Moorman, Dean of the University, Fall, 1971.

27. Interview with X., Spring 1972.

28. The administration did offer I. a token $400 to teach one course for the Fall Quarter of 1972. I.'s regular teaching load was four courses per quarter, for which she received $3200 per quarter. Therefore, the administration effectively offered I. one-quarter of her normal work load at one-eighth pay. I. rejected the preposterous proposal. Interview with I., 13 July 1973.

29. A quixotic crusader for campus reform, Becky was somewhat of a institution at Southern. The fact that Becky seldom wore a bra was taken as *prima facie* evidence of her moral degeneracy. At a president's luncheon on 28 September 1971, the dean of the university explained that the new fountain under construction in front of the administration building was "for Becky in the nude."

30. Interview with Cedric Evans, Fall 1972.

31. *Student Printz*, 1 February 1973, p. 1.

32. Interviews with Cedric Evans and Sanford Wood, Spring 1973.

33. Interview with W.D. Norwood, Jr., 17 May 1972.

34. The Dean said: "A unique program of Creative Writing is taking shape in Dr. Norwood's fertile brain." Charles W. Moorman, *Quo Vadis, Becane?* The Dean's Annual Report to the Faculty of the University of Southern Mississippi (Hattiesburg: The Faculty Meeting, 16 December 1969), p. 15.

35. Apparently, the administration representative spying on the meeting missed Norwood's crucial remark to the group: "I cannot join a campus chapter of the Civil Liberties Union precisely because it is likely to be attacking the Administration, and I as chairman of the Department of English, am part of that Administration." Interview with W.D. Norwood, Jr., 17 May 1972.

36. *Ibid.*

37. William D. McCain, Report before the meeting of the Student Senate of the University of Southern Mississippi. Hattiesburg, Mississippi, 13 March 1972.

38. It happened that Z. got married to someone at Florida State the following summer and didn't assume her position at Southern after all. She later was fired from Florida State. It seems Z. was president of the AAUP chapter there.

39. Letter from Robert Cochran to Marice C. Brown, acting chair, department of English, 16 July 1971.

40. Letter from Robert Cochran to the author, 13 January 1977.

41. Norwood's predecessor as chairman of the English department had been dismissed from that post after serving only one year.

Since the other professor had formal tenure, Norwood had to be the one to be terminated.

42. Interview with W.D. Norwood, Jr., 17 May 1972.

CHAPTER NINE

1. Hollander, "One Mississippi Negro Who Didn't Go To College." 33.

2. Interview with J.C. Gardner, 17 July 1972.

3. Interview with Willie C., 15 February 1973.

4. Silver, *Mississippi: The Closed Society,* p. 152.

5. New Orleans *States-Item,* 25 August 1973, p. 1-12; New Orleans *Times-Picayune,* 26 August 1973, sec. 6, p. 1.

6. *Student Printz,* 10 October 1972, p. 1.

7. Interview with Joe Brashier, 6 November 1972.

8. *Student Printz,* 19 December 1972, p. 1; *Student Printz,* 16 October 1973, p. 2.

9. *Perspective USM,* 21 September 1970, 4.

10. Hearing before Dean Rader Grantham for Stephen Pike, Hattiesburg, Mississippi, 5 May 1972.

11. *University of Southern Mississippi Bulletin,* 1971, 71.

12. The "blacklist" was a computer print-out (entitled "USM Suspensions, Winter 1970-71") of 880 students who were suspended for low grade-point averages. Eight of the names on the list—the same eight whose suspension appeals were denied—were circled in black ink. Grade-point averages of the blacklisted individuals in most cases were above levels of the uncircled names on the list. Students whose names were uncircled were not refused readmission.

13. "McCain's Military Mania," *Kudzu,* Vol. 4, No. 2, 3: personal interviews with Joe Davis and Michael Murphy, two of the students on the blacklist; personal interview with the "fired" dean.

14. *Student Printz,* 4 June 1970, p. 1; personal interview with Richard Peters, one of the "Southern Four."

15. *Sneake* v. *Grantham,* 317 F. Supp. 1253 (1970).

16. *Student Printz,* 14 December 1971, p. 1.

17. "ACLU Pursues Charter at U.S.M.," *Foundation Free Press,* I, No. 3, 1971, 7.

18. *Speake* v. *Grantham,* 317 F. Supp. 1253 (1970).

19. *Student Printz,* 14 December 1971, p. 1.

20. Hattiesburg *American,* 5 January 1972, p. 1.

21. Interview with Charles W. Moorman, Dean of the University, Fall 1971.

CHAPTER TEN

1. Powell, "Academic Martial Law at Southern: McCain Zips Dissenting Lips," 1.

2. Interview with a confidential source.

3. Interview with Mike Turner, editor of the *Student Printz,* Spring 1972. Incidentally, a feature article in the July 1972 issue of *McCall's* magazine was entitled, "Love Means Never Having to Say You're Starving." It was not about oral genital sex. Liz Carpenter, "Love Means Never Having to Say You're Starving," *McCall's* 94 (July 1972): 63.

4. *Drawl* (1972), 57. James A. Lewis, chief counsel of the Mississippi ACLU stated, "It's a ridiculous rule, it's very unconstitutional, and it gives..the right to pick and choose. Anything that says you have to have a permit has to tell the standards." *Student Printz,* 28 October 1969, p. 2.

5. *Student Printz,* 16 October 1969, p. 1.

6. Interview with Richard Peters, a USM student, Summer 1972.

7. *Student Printz,* 21 October 1969, p. 1. Three Southern students who participated in the Moratorium Day march were called before the University Disciplinary Committe. Following the hearing, the students received the following letter: "The Committee feels that since...you assumed positions of leadership only after the 'Moratorium Day' march of October 15 had begun, you cannot reasonably be held personally responsible for the fact that a permit for the march was not obtained three days in advance as required by University regulations. However...should you become involved later in incidents of a similar nature or in any incident involving an infraction of University regulations, [the Committee] would be forced to consider your actions in light of your active role in the 'Moratorium Day' demonstration." Letter from University Disciplinary Committee of the University of Southern Mississippi to William James Young, 14 October 1969, p. 1.

9. Letter from Pat Guyton, President of the Progressive Student Association to William D. McCain, president of the University of

Southern Mississippi, 5 May 1970.

10. *Student Printz,* 5 June 1974, p. 1.

11. Legal Brief for the plaintiff, *Wood v. University of Southern Mississippi* (1974).

12. The two were reprimanded but not fined. Hattiesburg *American,* 11 May 1967, p. 12.

13. *Student Printz,* 6 December 1966, p. 2.

14. *Ibid.*

15. Powell, "Academic Martial Law at Southern: McCain Zips Dissenting Lips," 4.

16. *Student Printz,* 12 January 1967, p. 2.

17. J. Allen Broyles, *The John Birch Society* (Boston: Beacon Press, 1964), p. 104.

18. General Walker alleged that the Supreme Court was the "control apparatus" of "International Communism," Nell McMillen, *The Citizens' Council: Organized Resistance to the Second Reco nstruction 1954-64* (Urbana, University of Illinois Press, 1971), pp. 344-45.

19. Benjamin R. Epstein and Arnold Forster, *The Radical Right* (New York: Random House, 1966), p. 66.

20. Letter from Robert F. Steele, President of the Young Democrats club to Claude Ramsay, President of the Mississippi AFL-CIO, 3 November 1967.

21. *Ibid.*

22. *Student Printz,* 9 February 1967, p. 1.

23. Evers spoke at Mississippi State University on 9 March 1970 and at Ole Miss on 7 October 1971.

24. In September 1970, General McCain confirmed reports that he was considering entering the 1971 race for governor of Mississippi. *Student Printz,* 24 September 1979, p. 1.

25. *Student Printz,* 14 October 1971, p. 1.

26. Report of Activities of Pre-Law Club of University of Southern Mississippi, submitted by Pat Guyton, 2 October 1969.

27. *Student Printz,* 16 May 1974, p. 1.

28. *Student Printz,* 9 September 1971, p. 8.

29. *Student Printz,* 18 May 1969, p. 1.

31. *Student Printz,* 12 September 1974, p. 1.

32. *Student Printz,* 16 May 1974, p. 1.

CHAPTER ELEVEN

1. The master of ceremonies for the luncheon was R.C. Cook, USM's president from 1945 to 1955. In introducing Enoch Powell, himself a noted racist, Cook boasted of former Mississippi Governor Bilbo's movement to send all blacks back to Africa. Later in the day, Cook presented Powell to the full faculty with this introduction: "Ladies and Gentlemen: You may wonder why I'm here instead of Dr. McCain. About ten days ago, I had the pleasure of calling on your Dr. Roger Pearson...He told me about the impending visit of the Right Honorable Enoch Powell, who's been a long-time friend of his, and he asked me if I would introduce him. And, 'Oh, no, I couldn't do it.' I got back to the office and the telephone rang. Dr. McCain told me that he was going to be out of town at a meeting and whether I could introduce our speaker. I said, 'Oh, yes, I'll introduce him,' just like you would have done." R.C. Cook, Introduction to speech by Enoch Powell before the meeting of the faculty of the University of Southern Mississippi, Hattiesburg, Mississippi, 5 October 1971.

2. Letter from a professor to William Hatcher, Chair of the department of political science, 31 May 1973. The quotation is a statement by a professor who was fired from the University of North Carolina in 1857 and was quoted in Silver, *Mississippi: The Closed Society*, p. 142.

CHAPTER TWELVE

1. Quoted in Brand Blanchard, *The Uses of a Liberal Education and Other Talks to Students* (LaSalle, Ill.: Open Court Publishing Co., 1973), p. 195.

2. Charles Moorman, "The Humanities in the Career University: A Local View," *The Southern Quarterly* 12 (January 1974): 117.

3. *Higher Education and National Affairs*, 24 (17 January 1975): 7.

4. Bowles and Gintis, *Schooling in Capitalist American: Educational Reform and Contradictions of Economic Life*, pp. 205-206.

5. Alan Wolfe, "Reform Without Reform: The Carnegie Commission on Higher Education," *Social Policy* 2 (May/June 1971): 20.

6. *Ibid.*

7. Carnegie Commission on Higher Education, *Priorities for Action: Carnegie Commission on Higher Education, Final Report* (New York: McGraw-Hill, 1973), p. 30.

8. Bowles and Gintis, *op. cit.*, p. 211.

9. Burton R. Clark, *The Open Door College* (New York: McGraw-Hill, 1960).

10. Rick Turner, "Cooling Out," *The Black Collegian* 7 (November-December 1976): 12.

11. Jerome Karabel, "Community Colleges and Social Stratification," in *The Educational Establishment*, eds. Elizabeth L. Useem and Michael Useem (Englewood Cliffs, N.J.: Prentice-Hall, 1974), p. 139.

12. Jencks and Riesman, *The Academic Revolution*, p. 26.

13. Quoted in Caroline Bird, *The Case Against College* (New York: David McKay Co., 1975), p. 107.

14. *Ibid.*, p. 117.

15. Frank Riesman, "The 'Vocationalization' of Higher Education: Duping the Poor," *Social Policy* 2 (May/June 1971): 4.

16. Beverly T. Watkins, "Vocational Education Found No Sure Way to Better Jobs," *The Chronicle of Higher Education*, 7 July 1980, p. 4.

17. V.O. Key, Jr., *Southern Politics in State and Nation* (New York: Vintage Books, 1949), p. 160.

18. Herber Ladner, "James Kinble Vardaman, Governor of Mississippi, 1904-1908," *Journal of Mississippi History, 2 (October 1940): 176-77.*

19. Jessie Parkhurst Guzman (ed.), *Negro Year Book: A Review of Events Affecting Negro Life 1941-1945* (Tuskegee, Ala.: Tuskegee Institute, 1947), p. 76.

20. The average salary for Mississippi's black teachers in 1948-49 was only $682 a year. Jessie Parkhurst Guzman (ed.), *1952 Negro Year Book: A Review of Events Affecting Negro Life* (New York: Wm. H. Wise & Co., 1952), p. 205.

21. Jackson *Clarion-Ledger*, 11 April 1972, p. 1.

22. The White Citizens' Councils led the movement to have the state's former compulsory school attendance law taken off the books in 1956, as part of the grand strategy to prevent desegragation of public education in Mississippi. In 1973, 33,500 youngsters, or 5.4 percent of the population, ages five to seventeen, were not in school. W.F. Minor, "Councils Oppose Attendance Law," New Orleans *Times-Picayune*, 16 December 1973, sec. 2, p. 2.

23. Despite all of the highly touted teacher pay raised in recent years, Mississippi teachers still stand at the very bottom in the nation. For 1973-74, the Mississippi teacher pay average was $7,506, compared to the southeastern average of $9,100 and the national average of $10,673. W.F. Minor, "Poorly Paid Teachers Said Using Food Stamps," New

Orleans *Times-Picayune,* 31 October 1974, p. 8.

24. The test was the California Achievement Test. The results showed that state norms for 35,227 students in grade five in the areas of reading, mathematics, language and spelling had a composite percentage of achievement of 23 compared with a national norm of 50 in the same grade level. For 32,630 students in grade eight in Mississippi tested in reading, mathematics, language and spelling, the composite rank was 27 compared with a national norm of 50. W.F. Minor, "Education Levels Low, Tests Show," New Orleans *Times-Picayune,* 14 October 1973, sec. 2, p. 2.

25. Jackson *Daily News,* 24 April 1959, p. 10.

26. Silver, *Mississippi: The Closed Society,* p. 67.

27. *Guardian,* 16 April 1980, p. 10.

28. Nunn, Crockett and Williams, *Tolerance for Nonconformity,* p. 176.

29. Carnegie Commission on Higher Education, *Priorities for Action Carnegie Commission on Higher Education, Final Report,* p. 47.

CHAPTER THIRTEEN

1. "Academic Freedon and Tenure in the Quest for National Security," *AAUP Bulletin* 42 (Spring 1956): 54.

2. *Keyishian* v. *Board of Regents,* 385 U.S. 589 (1967).

3. *Sweezy* v. *New Hampshire,* 354 U.S. 250 (1957).

4. Rodney T. Hartnett, *College and University Trustees: Their Backgrounds, Roles, and Educational Attitudes* (Princeton, N.J.: Educational Testing Service, 1969), pp. 19-40.

5. Lionel S. Lewis and Michael N. Ryan, "In the Matter of University Governance during the 1960's," *Social Problems* 19 (Fall 1971): 255.

6. David N. Smith, *Who Rules the Universities* (New York: Monthly Review Press, 1974), pp. 30-33.

7. Thomas R. Dye, *"Who's Running America? Institutionalized Leadership in the United States* (Englewood Cliffs, N.J.: Prentice-Hall, 1976), p. 118.

8. Reed Whittemore, "Faculty Survival: Coping with Managers," *Harper's* 260 (February 1980): 39.

9. "The Yeshiva Decision," *Academe* 66 (May 1980): 192-194.

10. Samuel Bowles, "Unequal Education and the Reproduction of the

Social Division of Labor," in *The Educational Establishment,* eds. Elizabeth L. Useem and Michael Useem (Englewood Cliffs, N.J.: Prentice-Hall, 1974, p. 17.

11. Jack Weston, "Do Radical Teachers Have a Progressive Effect?" *Radical Teacher* (March 1979): 10-11.

12. Ralph Miliband, *The State in Capitalist Society* (New York: Basic Books, 1969), p. 261.

13. Everett C. Ladd, Jr. and Seymour Martin Lipset, "Faculty Survey," *The Chronicle of Higher Education,* January 16, 1978, p. 9.

14. Nathan M. Pusey, *The Age of the Scholar; Observations on Education in the Troubled Decade* (Cambridge, Mass.: Harvard University Press, 1963), p. 171.

15. For an excellent discussion of the harassment of university professors during the McCarthy era, see "Academic Freedom and Tenure in the Quest for National Security," pp. 49-107.

16. Lionel S. Lewis, "The Academic Axe: Some Trends in Dismissals from Institutions of Higher Learning in America," *Social Problems* 12 (Fall 1964): 151-58; Lewis and Ryan, "In the Matter of University Governance during the 1960s," pp. 249-57.

17. Lewis and Ryan, "In the Matter of University Governance during the 1960s," p. 252.

18. Greg Mitchell, "The Inventor as Target: Ollman Plays 'Class Struggle' for Real," *The Nation* 227 (18 November 1978): 543.

19. David Rubin, *The Rights of Teachers: The Basic ACLU Guide to a Teacher's Constitutional Rights* (New York: Avon Books, 1972), pp. 86-88.

20. *Ibid.*

21. "Academic Freedom and Tenure: The University of California at Los Angeles," *AAUP Bulletin* 57 (September 1971): 405.

22. Rachelle Marshall, "The Bruce Franklin Affair," *The Progressive* 36 (May 1972): 24.

23. Paul M. Levitt, "The Trials of H. Bruce Franklin," *Change* 9 (August 1977): 24.

24. Bill Sonn, "H. Bruce Franklin: Another First," *The Progressive* 38 (September 1974): 36.

25. Gene Lyons, "A Case of 'Thoughtcrime,'" *The Progressive* 38 (May 1974): 40-41.

26. *The Chronicle of Higher Education,* July 9, 1979, p. 2.

27. "Academic Freedom and Tenure: University of Maryland," *Academe* 65 (May 1979): 218.

28. Mitchell, "The Inventor as Target: Ollman Plays 'Class Struggle' for Real," p. 542.

29. *Ibid.*

30. "Academic Freedom and Tenure: University of Maryland," p. 224.

31. Ronald Radosh, "The Rise of a Marxist Historian: An Interview with Eugene Genovese," *Change* 10 (November 1978): 32.

CHAPTER FOURTEEN

1. Richard H. de Lone, *Small Futures: Children, Inequality and the Limits of Liberal Reform* (New York: Harcourt Brace Jovanovich, 1979).

2. Bowles, "Unequal Education and Reproduction of the Social Division of Labor," p. 39.

3. Karabel, "Community Colleges and Social Stratification," pp. 117-145.

4. *Ibid.,* p. 120.

5. Lorenzo Middleton, "Enrollment of Blacks Doubled Since 1970," *Chronicle of Higher Education,* 29 January, 1979, p. 2.

6. Deborah S. Rosenfelt and Gloria DeSole, "Affirmative Action: The Verdict Is Still Out," *Radical Teacher* (March 1979): 4.

7. *Ibid.,* pp. 4-5.

8. Joel Dreyfuss, "The New Racism," *Black Enterprise* 8 (January 1978): 54.

9. "Unfinished Business," *Change* 11 (October 1979): 8.

10. Middleton, "Enrollment of Blacks Doubled Since 1970," p. 2.

11. Barry Phillips, "The Bakkelash," *Radical Teacher* (March 1979): 6.

12. "26 Million Black Americans—," *U.S. News & World Report* 86 (14 March 1979): 50.

13. Harry Edwards, "Edwards vs. the University of California," *The Black Scholar* 8 (May 1977): 32.

14. *Phi Delta Kappan* 60 (December 1978): 329; see Michael Olivas, *The Dilemma of Access: Minorities in Two Year Colleges* (Washington, D.C.: Howard University Press, 1979).

15. Barnard C. Watson, "Through the Academic Gateway," *Change* 11 (October 1979): 25.

16. Lorenzo Middleton, "Bakke Ruling Seen as Having Little Effect," *The Chronicle of Higher Education,* July 30, 1979, p. 13; *Guardian,* 20 December 1978, p. 10.

17. Middleton, "Bakke Ruling Seen As Having Little Effect," p. 13.

18. Manning Marable, "Black Colleges Are In Danger," *In These Times,* 3 October 1979, p. 8.

19. Robert C. Maynard, "The Black College: The Price of Excellence," *Black Enterprise* 9 (May 1979): 29.

20. Rosenfelt and DeSole, "Affirmative Action: The Verdict Is Still Out," p. 4.

21. Phillips, "The Bakkelash," p. 6,

22. Edwards, "Edwards vs. the University of California," p, 32.

23. *The Call,* 28 April 1980, p. 7.

24. Cheryl M. Fields, "Nursing Schools Get Low Marks for Efforts to Recruit Blacks," *The Chronicle of Higher Education,* 14 May 1979, p. 15.

25. Maynard, "The Black College: The Price of Excellence," p. 29.

26. Richard Rodriguez, "Beyond the Minority Myth," *Change* 10 (September 1978): 32.

27. *The Chronicle of Higher Education,* 19 March 1979, p. 5.

28. "Looking Out for No. 1," *Time* 113 (16 April 1979): 104.

29. Jesse L. Jackson, "I Am Somebody," New Orleans *Times-Picayune,* 13 January 1980, sec. 2, p. 8.

30. Bartley McSwine, "The Great American Whitewash," *Change* 11 (October 1979): 55.

31. "Looking Out for No. 1," p. 100.

32. McSwine, "The Great American Whitewash," p. 56.

33. Maynard, "The Black College: The Price of Excellence," p. 28.

34. "Looking Out for No. 1," p. 100. For a comprehensive documentation of racism at Harvard, see "A Study of Race Relations at Harvard College," a lengthy 1980 report prepared by a multiracial student-faculty committee. The report reveals blacks' anger over inadequate affirmative action policies and whites' doubts about minority students' academic abilities.

35. C. Eric Linclon, "Black Studies and Cultural Continuity," *The Black Scholar* 10 (October 1978): 13.

36. Harold Cruse, "Has Black Studies Failed?" *In These Times,* 3 October 1979, p. 8.

37. Lincoln, "Black Studies and Cultural Continuity," p. 13.

38. "Looking Out for No. 1," p. 100.

39. Phillips, "The Bakkelash," p. 7.

40. Biensen, Ostriker and Ostriker, "Sex Discrimination in the Universities," p. 370.

41. *Ibid.* Pusey's remark was in response to the realization that the draft was going to reduce the number of men applying to Harvard's graduate school.

42. U.S. Department of Education, *Women Faculty Still Lag in Salary and Tenure for the 1979-80 Academic Year,* National Center for Educa-

tion Statistics Bulletin No. 80-342 (1980), p. 1.

43. Biensen, Ostriker and Ostriker, "Sex Discrimination in the Universities," pp. 371-373.

44. U.S. Department of Education, *Women Faculty Still Lag in Salary and Tenure for the 1979-80 Academic Year,* p. 1.

45. Juanita Kreps, *Sex in the Marketplace: American Women at Work* (Baltimore: The John Hopkins Press, 1971), pp. 55-56.

46. Rosenfelt and DeSole, "Affirmative Action: The Verdict Is Still Out," p. 4.

47. See National Research Council, Office of Scientific Personnel, *Careers of Ph.D.'s Academic and Nonacademic: A Second Report of Follow-ups of Doctoral Cohorts 1935-1960* (Washington, D.C.: National Academy of Sciences-National Research Council, 1968).

48. Jane W. Loeb and Marianne A. Ferber, "Women on the Faculty at the Urbana-Champaign Campus," in *Academic Women on the Move,* eds. Alice Rossi and Ann Calderwood (New York, Russel Sage, 1973), p. 247.

49. Rita J. Simon, Shirley M. Clark and Kathleen Galway, "The Woman Ph. D.: A Recent Profile," *Social Problems* 15 (Fall 1967): 221.

50. Annette Kolodny, "Women Fight To Keep Hard Won Gains," *In These Times,* 3 October 1979, p. 9.

51. Rosenfelt and DeSole, "Affirmative Action: The Verdict Is Still Out," p. 5.

52. Ellen Cantarow, "Academic Gore," *Radical Teacher* (March 1979): 15.

53. Alice Rossi, "Discrimination and Demography Restrict Opportunities for Academic Women," in *And Jill Came Tumbling After: Sexism in American Education,* eds. Judith Stacey, Susan Bereaud and Joan Daniels (New York: Dell Publishing Co., 1974), p. 371.

54. Adrienne Rich, "Taking Women Students Seriously," *Radical Teacher* (March 1979): 41.

55. Harris, "The Second Sex in Academe," p. 285; Jo Freeman, "How to Descriminate Against Women Without Really Trying," in *Women: A Feminist Perspective,* ed. Jo Freeman (Palo Alto, California: Mayfield Publishing Co., 1979), pp. 217-218.

56. Martha S. White, "Women in the Professions: Psychological and Social Barriers to Women in Science," *Science* 170 (23 October 1970): 413-416.

57. Rich, "Taking Women Students Seriously," p. 42.

58. Bowles and Gintis, *Schooling in Capitalist America: Educational Reform and the Contradictions of Economic Life,* p. 49.

59. Page Smith, *Daughters of the Promised Land* (Boston: Little, Brown and Co., 1970), pp. 307, 318.

60. Ruth Rosen, "Sexism in History," in *And Jill Came Tumbling*

After: Sexism in American Education, eds. Judith Stacey, Susan Bareaud, and Joan Daniels (New York: Dell Publishing Co., 1974), p. 330.

61. I have been struck by the fact that in the hundreds of U.S. history and American government books I have scanned, I have not once seen Jeannette Rankin's name mentioned. Rankin was the first woman ever elected to the U.S. House of Representatives. Elected in 1916 from Montana, Rankin was the *only* representative to vote against U.S. entry into both World Ward I and II. In 1968, at the age of 87, Rankin led an antiwar march in Washington.

62. Smith, *Daughters of the Promised Land,* p. 313.

63. William O'Neill, *Everone Was Brave: The Rise and Fall of Feminism in America* (Chicago: Quadrangle Books, 1969), p. viii.

64. Rosen, "Sexism in History," p. 329.

65. Karen L. Adams and Norma Ware, "Sexism and the English Language: The Linguistic Implications of Being a Woman," in *Woman: A Feminist Perspective,* ed. Jo Freeman (Palo Alto, CA.: Mayfield Publishing Co., 1979), pp. 490-492.

66. This example appears in Mary Ritchie Key, *Male/Female Language* (Metuchen, New Jersey: The Scarecrow Press, 1975), p. 89. Italics added. As Adams and Ware explain, it is interesting to note that *he* has not always been considered the correct third-person pronoun for referring to a single human being of indeterminate sex. Until about the eighteenth century, the correct choice of pronoun for such a person was *they.* Adams and Ware, "Sexism and the English Language: The Linguistic Implications of Being a Woman," p. 502.

67. *Ibid.,* pp. 493-494.

68. Catherine R. Stimpson, "Sex, Gender, and American Culture," in *Women and Men: Changing Roles Relationships and Perceptions,* eds. Libby A. Cater, Anne Firor Scott and Wendy Martyna (New York: Praeger Publishers, 1977), p. 203.

69. Rich, "Taking Women Students Seriously," p. 41.

70. Manuel G. Mendoza and Vince Napoli, *Systems of Society: An Introduction to Social Science* (Lexington, Mass.: D.C. Heath and Co., 1977), pp. 492-493.

71. *The Call,* 28 April 1980, p. 7.

72. Grant McConnell, *Private Power and American Democracy* (New York: Vintage Books, 1970), p. 25.

73. John McDermott, "Campus Missionaries: The Laying on of Culture," *The Nation* 208 (10 March 1969): 301.

74. Willard Waller, "Social Problems and the Mores," *American Sociological Review,* 1 (December 1936): 926.

75. Jerome H. Skolnick and Elliott Currie, *Crisis in American Institutions* (Boston: Little Brown and Co., 1970), p. 14.

76. For an excellent analysis of how racism serves the capitalist system, see Michael Reich, "Economic Theories of Racism, in *Schooling in a Corporate Society,* ed. Martin Carnoy (New York: David McKay Co., 1973), pp. 80-92; and Frederick Stirton Weaver, "*Cui Bono? And the Economic Function of Racism,*" *The Review of Black Political Economy* 8 (Spring 1978): 302-13.

77. Bowles, "Unequal Education and Reproduction of the Social Division of Labor," pp. 40-41.

78. Kolodny, "Women Fight to Keep Hard Won Gains," p. 9.

CHAPTER FIFTEEN

1. Gunnar Myrdal, *An American Dilemma: The Negro Problem and Modern Democracy* (New York: Harper & Brothers, 1944), p. xiv.

2. Samuel DuBois Cook, "The Black Man and the American Political System: Obligation, Resistance, and Hope," *The Journal of Afro-American Issues* 5 (Summer 1977): 230.

3. Lyman Tower Sargent, *Contemporary Political Ideologies, A Comparative Analysis* (Homewood, Ill.: The Dorsey Press, 1975), pp. 33-38.

4. CBS Report, "Blacks in America: With All Deliberate Speed?", Part I, 24 July 1979.

5. U.S. Bureau of the Census, *Historical Abstract of the United States* (Washington, D.C.: U.S. Government Printing Office, 1971), Table 569.

6. Timothy McNulty, "Old Problems Persist in the 'New South,' " *Chicago Tribune,* 17 June 1978, p. 9.

7. Joint Center for Political Studies, *National Roster of Black Elected Officials* (Washington, D.C.: Joint Center for Political Studies, 1978), pp. *ix.* xii, 123.

8. W.F. Minor, "Election Plan to Outsmart Supreme Court 'Bombed Out,' " New Orleans *Times-Picayune,* 8 June 1975, p. 11.

9. JoAnn Klein, "Changing Politics in Mississippi," *Southern Changes* 2 (December 1979): 5-6.

10. Ron Harris, "The Myth of the 'New South,' " *Ebony* 24 (February 1979): 60.

11. CBS Report, "Blacks in America: With All Deliberate Speed?

12. W.F. Minor, "Waller Decision Points up Change," New Orleans *Times-Picayune,* 17 June 1973, sec. 2, p. 2.

13. *The Capitol Reporter,* 19 July 1979, p. 9.

14. Frederic Tulsky, "Standing Up to Fear in Mississippi," *Southern Exposure* 6 (Fall 1978): 68-69.

15. Harris, "The Myth of the 'New South,' " p. 55.

16. Tulsky, "Standing Up to Fear in Mississippi," p. 69.

17. *Ibid.*

18. *Guardian,* 17 May 1978, p. 4.

19. New Orleans *Times-Picayune,* 11 June 1978, p. 46.

20. CBS Report, "Blacks in America: With All Deliberate Spped?"

21. "Progress and Poverty in Two Cities," *U.S. News & World Report* 86 (14 May 1979): 54.

22. U.S. Department of Justice, *Capital Punishment 1974,* National Prisoner Statistics Bulletin No. SD-NPS-CP-3 (November 1975), p. 21.

23. 347 U.S. 483 (1954).

24. Kenneth Clark, "Vision: Cornerstone For Democracy," *Southern Exposure* 7 (Summer 1979): 143.

25. Linda Williams, "Finances: Short-Changing Equal Education," *Southern Exposure* 7 (Summer 1979): 104.

26. Ibid.

27. CBS Report, "Blacks in America: With All Deliberate Speed?"

28. *Guardian,* 20 September 1978, p. 3.

29. See Frederick A. Rogers, *The Black High School and Its Community* (Lexington, Mass,: Lexington Books, 1975).

30. CBS Reports, "Blacks in America: With All Deliberate Speed?"

31. McNulty, "Old Problems Persist in the 'New South,' " p. 9.

32. Williams, "Finances: Short-Changing Equal Education," p. 106.

33. McNulty, "Old Problems Persist in the 'New South,' " p. 9.

34. *Ibid.*

35. Gay Collins, "Who's Going to Help Black Farmers during Crisis?" New Orleans *Times-Picayune,* 11 March 1979, sec. 3, p. 13.

36. Leo McGee and Robert Boone, "Black Rural Land Decline in the South," *The Black Scholar* 8 (May 1977): 8.

37. Gay Collins, "Black Farmers: A Vanishing Breed," New Orleans *Times-Picayune,* 4 March 1979, sec. 2, p. 2.

38. Harris, "The Myth of the 'New South,' " p. 60.

39. CBS Report, "Blacks in America: With All Deliberate Speed?"

40. Sargent, *Contemporary Political Ideologies: A Comparative Analysis,* pp. 37-38.

41. CBS Report, "Blacks in America: With All Deliberate Speed?"

42. Harris, "The Myth of the 'New South,' " p. 62.

43. *Civil Liberties,* February 1979, p. 8.

44. Harris, "The Myth of the 'New South,' " p. 62.

45. CBS Reports, "Blacks in America: With All Deliberate Speed?"

46. Ivory Phillips, "1964 Freedom Summer and Rosedale Mississippi 1979," *Southern Changes* 2 (January 1980): 14.

47. David Treadwell, "Going Back Home to Dixie: Blacks' 'New Land of Hope,' " New Orleans *Times-Picayune,* 30 November 1977, p. 10.

48. Ellen Bravo, "2,000 Declare 'Slave Days Are Over,' " *The Call,* 16 May 1980, p. 11.

49. Laurel, Miss.: A Struggle for Justice and Dignity," Leaflet issued by Committee for Justice in Mississippi, c/o International Chemical Union, Akron, Ohio, 1980, p. 2.

50. William Serrin, "200 Mississippi Women Carry on a Lonely, Bitter Strike," *New York Times,* 27 February 1980.

51. "Laurel, Miss.: A Struggle for Justice and Dignity," p. 2.

52. *Ibid.*

53. Dennis Schaal, "Laurel Strikers Boosted by Ruling," *Guardian,* 11 February 1981, p. 8.

54. Judy Putnam, "Strikers at Laurel Chicken Plant Marshall Forces," Jackson *Clarion-Ledger,* 27 April 1980, p. 3.

55. "Laurel, Miss.: A Struggle for Justice and Dignity," p. 2.

56. Serrin, "200 Mississippi Women Carry on a Lonely, Bitter Strike."

57. Elizabeth M. Almquist, "Black Women and the Pursuit of Equality *Women: A Feminist Perspective,* ed. Jo Freeman (Palo Alto, Ca.: Mayfield Publishing Co., 1979), pp. 437, 441.

CHAPTER SIXTEEN

1. Joint Center for Political Studies, *National Roster of Black Elected Officials,* p. xiii.

2. *Focus,* December 1978, p. 4.

3. Joint Center for Political Studies, *National Roster of Black Elected Officials,* p. xi; *Guardian,* 28 January 1981, p. 11.

4. Ira Glaser, "Supreme Court Decision Sets Back Minority Voting Rights in the South," *Civil Liberties,* June 1980, p. 2.

5. Frank Elam, "Court Deals Blow to Black Suffrage," *Guardian,* 11 June 1980, p. 7.

6. New Orleans *Times-Picayune,* 27 April 1980, p. 24.

7. Glaser, "Supreme Court Decision Sets Back Minority Voting Rights in the South," p. 2. For a full discussion of the implications of the *Bolden* decision, see Laughlin McDonald, "The Bolden Decision

Stonewalls Black Aspirations," *Southern Changes* 2 (July-August, 1980): 11-17.

8. *Guardian,* 19 September 1979, p. 10.

9. Robert Staples, "Land of Promise, Cities of Despair: Blacks in Urban America," *The Black Scholar* 10 (October 1978): 5.

10. Jules Kroll, "Growth Industry, White Collar Crime," San Francisco *Examiner,* 3 August 1978, p. 9.

11. *Guardian,* 6 December 1978, p. 9.

12. Patrick Oster, "Find Black Men Most Likely to Be Shot by Cops," Chicago *Sun Times,* 16 May 1977, p. 4.

13. Dianne Herman, "The Rape Culture," in *Women: A Feminist Perspective,* ed. Jo Freeman (Palo Alto, Ca.: Mayfield Publishing Co., 1979), p. 44.

14. U.S. Department of Justice, *Capital Punishment* 1974, p. 20.

15. "Negroes Accuse Maryland Bench: Double Standard Is Charged in Report on Rape Cases," *New York Times,* 18 September 1967, p. 33.

16. M. Wolfgand and M. Riedel, "Rape, Racial Discrimination and the Death Penalty," in *Capital Punishment in the United States,* eds. H. Bedau and C. Pierce (New York: AMS Press, 1976), pp. 109-119.

17. Herbert Hoover, *American Individualism* (New York: Doubleday, Page, 1922), p. 9.

18. 418 U.S. 717 (1974).

19. *Civil Liberties,* February 1980, p. 6.

20. New Orleans *Times-Picayune,* 14 February 1979, p. 3.

21. New Orleans *Times-Picayune,* 18 May 1978, sec. 2, 3.

22. Clark, "Vision: Cornerstone For Democracy," p. 143.

23. Hal Gulliver, "Understanding Public Education," *The Atlanta Constitution,* 28 May 1978, p. 3-c.

24. This number is the difference between the actual number of minority teachers and the number that should exist if the ratio of minority-to-white teachers was the same as the ratio of minority-to-white students. Leon Hall, "The Implementors' Revenge," *Southern Exposure* 7 (Summer 1979): 125.

25. *Ibid.,* pp. 122-25.

26. James J. Shields, Jr., "The Return to Gray Flannel Thinking," *USA Today* 107 (January 1979): 51.

27. Pamela George, "Testing: The Competency Controversy," *Southern Exposure* 7 (Summer 1979): 115-16.

28. Clark, "Vision: Cornerstone For Democracy," p. 144.

29. George, "Testing, The Competency Controversy," pp. 115-16.

30. See de Lone, *Small Futures: Children, Inequality and the Limits of Liberal Reform.*

31. Gerald R. Gill, *Meanness Mania: The Changed Mood* (Washington,

D.C.: Howard University Press, 1980), pp. 29-31.

32. "The Election: Jimmy's Debt to Blacks—and Others," *Time* 108 (22 November 1976): 16.

33. Joint Center for Political Studies, *The Black Vote: Election '76* (Washington, D.C.: Joint Center for Political Studies, 1977), p. 2.

34. Charles V. Hamilton, "Blacks in the System: Finding a Reason to Vote," *The Nation* 227 (16 December 1978): 669.

35. Herbert Hill, "Falling Behind Again: White Myths of Black Economics," *The Nation* 227 (16 December 1978): 666-67.

36. Joanna Foley, "Urban League Finds 'New Negativism,' " *In These Times* 3 (7 February 1979): 4.

37. Hill, "Falling Behind Again: White Myths of Black Economics," p. 667.

38. Joseph Kraft, "California Message: Selfish Indulgence," New Orleans *Times-Picayune,* 12 June 1978, p. 12.

39. *Time* 111 (26 June 1978): 8.

40. Kraft, "California Message: Selfish Indulgence," p. 12.

41. Otto Kerner et al., *Report of the National Advisory Commission on Civil Disorders* (Washington, D.C.: U.S. Government Printing Office, 1968), p. 1.

42. Thomas L. Van Valey, Wade Clark Roof and Jerome E. Wilcox, "Trends in Residential Segregation: 1960-1970," *American Journal of Sociology* 82 (January 1977): 826-44.

43. U.S. Bureau of the Census, "Population Profile of the United States: 1977," *Current Population Reports,* Series P-20, No. 324 (Washington, D.C.: U.S. Government Printing Office, 1977).

44. National Commission on Urban Problems, *Building the American City* (Washington, D.C.: U.S. Government Printing Office, n.d.), p. 52.

45. Leonard F. Heulmann, "Housing Needs and Housing Solutions: Changes in Perspectives from 1968 to 1978," in *The Changing Structure of the City,* ed. Gary A. Tobin, Urban Affairs Annual Review Series, No. 16 (Beverly Hills, Ca.: Safe Publication, 1979), p. 252.

46. Mack H. Jones, "Blacks and Politics in Atlanta: Myth and Reality," (1972), p. 1.

Cited in Hanes Walton, Jr., "Black Politics in the South: Projections for the Coming Decade," in *Public Policy for the Black Community: Strategies & Perspectives,* eds. Marguerite Ross Barnett and James A. Hefner (New York: Alfred Publishing Co., 1976), p. 94.

47. CBS Report, "Blacks in America: With All Deliberate Speed?", Part II, 25 July 1979.

48. "A New Racial Poll," *Newsweek,* 93 (February 26, 1979): 48.

49. Dreyfuss, "The New Racism," p. 42.

50. William Watts and Lloyd A. Free, *State of the Nation III* (Lexington, Mass.: D.C. Heath and Co., 1978), p. 10.

51. Carl T. Rowan, "Whites and Blacks: Different Worlds," New Orleans *TimesPicayune,* 12 March 1979, p. 16.

52. Staples, "Land of Promise, Cities of Despair: Blacks in Urban America," p. 9.

53. Robert Lekachman, "Proposition 13 and the New Conservatism," *Change* 10 (September 1978): 26.

54. Dreyfuss, "The New Racism," p. 42.

55. The term "institutionalized racism" was first used by Carmichael and Hamilton. See Stokely Carmichael and Charles V. Hamilton, *Black Politics: The Politics of Liberation in America* (New York: Random House, 1967), pp. 4-5.

56. Ronald S. Edari, "White Attitudes Toward Busing: Segregation and the Life Cycle," *Journal of Black Studies* 10 (September 1979): 100-101.

SELECTED BIBLIOGRAPHY
BOOKS

Barnett, Marguerite Ross and James A. Hefner. *Public Policy for the Black Community: Strategies & Perspectives*. New York: Alfred Publishing Co., 1976.

Barrett, Russell. *Integration at Ole Miss*. Chicago: Quadrangle Books, 1965.

Bedau, H. and C. Pierce. *Capital Punishment in the United States*. New York: AMS Press, 1976.

Bird, Caroline. *The Case Against College*. New York: David McKay Co., 1975.

Blanchard, Brand. *The Uses of a Liberal Education and Other Talks to Students*. LaSalle, Ill.: Open Court Publishing, 1973.

Bowles, Samuel and Herbert Gintis. *Schooling in Capitalist America: Educational Reform and Contradictions of Economic Life*. New York: Basic Books, 1976.

Cabaniss, Allen. *The University of Mississippi: Its First Hundred Years*. Hattiesburg: University and College Press of Mississippi, 1971.

Carmichael, Stokely and Charles V. Hamilton. *Black Politics: The Politics of Liberation in America*. New York: Random House, 1967.

Carnegie Commission on Higher Education. *The Open-Door Colleges*. New York: McGraw-Hill Book Co., 1970.

————. *Priorities for Action: Carnegie Commission on Higher Education, Report*. New York: McGraw-Hill, 1973.

Clark, Burton R. *The Open Door College*. New York: McGraw-Hill, 1960.

deLone, Richard. *Small Futures: Children, Inequality and the Limits of Liberal Reform*. New York: Harcourt Brace Jovanovich, 1979.

Dye, Thomas R. *Who's Running America? Institutionalized Leadership in the United States*. Englewood Cliffs, New Jersey: Prentice-Hall, 1976.

Freeman, Jo. *Women: A Feminist Perspective*. Palo Alto, Ca.: Mayfield Publishing Co., 1979.

Gill, Gerald R. *Meanness Mania: The Changed Mood*. Washington, D.C.: Howard University Press, 1980.

Glazer, Nona and Helen Youngelson Waehrer. *Women in a Man-Made World: A Socioeconomic Handbook*. Chicago: Rand-McNally College Publishing Co., 1977.

Green, A. Winfall. *The Man Bilbo*. Baton Rouge: Louisiana State University Press, 1963.

Griffin, John Howard. *Black Like Me*. New York: Signet Books, 1961.

Hartnett, Rodney T. *College and University Trustees: Their Backgrounds, Roles, and Educational Attitudes.* Princeton, N. J.: Educational Testing Service, 1969.

Hickman, Alma. *Southern As I Saw It: Personal Remembrances of an Era.* Hattiesburg: University of Southern Mississippi Press, 1965.

Hook, Sidney. *Academic Freedom and Academic Anarchy.* New York: Cowles Book Co., 1969.

Jencks, Christopher and David Riesman. *The Academic Revolution.* New York: Doubleday & Co., 1969.

Joint Center for Political Studies. *National Roster of Black Elected Officials.* Washington, D.C.: Joint Center for Political Studies, 1978.

Kerner, Otto, et al. *Report of the National Advisory Commission on Civil Disorders.* Washington, D.C.: U.S. Government Printing Office, 1968.

Key, Mary Ritchie. *Male/Female Language.* Metuchen, N.J.: The Scarecrow Press, 1975.

Key, V.O., Jr. *Southern Politics in State and Nation.* New York: Vintage Books, 1949.

Kreps, Juanita. *Sex in the Marketplace: American Women at Work.* Baltimore: The John Hopkins Press, 1971.

Lord, Walter. *The Past That Would Not Die.* New York: Harper & Row, 1965.

McMillen, Neil R. *The Citizens' Council: Organized Resistance to the Second Reconstruction, 1954-64.* Urbana: University of Illinois Press, 1971.

Meredith, James. *Three Years in Mississippi.* Bloomington: Indiana University Press, 1966.

Miliband, Ralph. *The State in Capitalist Society.* New York: Basic Books, 1969.

Myrdal, Gunner. *An American Dilemma: The Negro Problem and Modern Democracy.* New York: Harper & Brothers, 1944.

Nunn, Clyde Z., Harry J. Crockett Jr. and J. Allen Williams, Jr. *Tolerance for Nonconformity.* San Francisco: Jossey-Bass, 1978.

Olivas, Michael. *The Dilemma of Access: Minorities in Two Year Colleges.* Washington, D.C.: Howard University Press, 1979.

O'Neill, William. *Everyone Was Brave: The Rise and Fall of Feminism in America.* Chicago: Quadrangle Books, 1969.

Pusey, Nathan M. *The Age of the Scholar: Observations on Education in a Troubled Decade.* Cambridge: Harvard University Press, 1963.

Rossi, Alice and Ann Calderwood. *Academic Women on the Move.* New York: Russell Sage, 1973.

Rubin, David. *The Rights of Teachers: The Basic ACLU Guide to a Teacher's Constitutional Rights.* New York: Avon Books, 1972.

Seatre, Gilbert T. *The Pride 1920-1970.* Hattiesburg: University of Southern Mississippi Press, 1969.

Sargent, Lyman Tower. *Contemporary Political Ideologies, A Comparative Analysis.* Homewood, Ill.: The Dorsey Press, 1975.

Silver, James W. *Mississippi: The Closed Society.* New York: Harcourt, Brace & World, 1963.

Skolnick, Jerome H. and Elliott Currie. *Crisis in American Institutions.* Boston: Little, Brown and Co., 1970.

Smith, David N. *Who Rules the Universities.* New York: Monthly Review Press, 1974.

Smith, Page. *Daughters of the Promised Land.* Boston: Little, Brown and Co., 1970.

Stacey, Judith, Susan Bereaud and Joan Daniels. *And Jill Came Tumbling After: Sexism in American Education.* New York: Dell Publishing Co., 1974.

Versey, Laurence R. *The Emergence of the American University.* Chicago: University of Chicago Press, 1965.

Watts, William and Lloyd A. Free. *State of the Nation III.* Lexington, Mass.: D.C. Heath and Co., 1978.

Woodward, C. Van. *The Burden of Southern History.* Baton Rouge: Louisiana State University Press, 1960.

ARTICLES

"Academic Freedom and Tenure in the Quest for National Security," *AAUP Bulletin* 42 (Spring 1956): 49-107.

"Academic Freedom and Tenure: The University of California at Los Angeles," *AAUP Bulletin* 57 (September 1971): 382-405.

"Academic Freedom and Tenure: University of Maryland," *Academe* 65 (May 1979): 213-227.

"Academic Freedom in Mississippi," *AAUP Bulletin* 51 (Autumn 1965): 341-356.

"The American Historical Association and the AAUP: A Joint Inquiry into an Issue of Attribution," *AAUP Bulletin* 57 (Winter 1971): 528-532.

Bennett, Lerone Jr. "Old Illusions and New Souths." *Ebony* 26 (August 1971) 35-40.

Bond, Julian. "Better Voters, Better Politicians," *Southern Exposure* 7 (Spring 1979): 68-70.

Cantarow, Ellen. "Academic Gore," *Radical Teacher* (March 1979): 15-16.

Carter, John N. "A Boll Weevil Six Feet Long," *Library Journal* (15 October 1969): 3615-3618.

. "The Return of the Boll Weevil," *Library Journal* (15 May 1970): 1817.

Cason, Clarence. "The Mississippi Imbroglio," *Virginia Quarterly Review* 7 (April 1931): 123-125.

Caudill, Orley B. "The Americans, the World and the Future," *The Southern Quarterly* 9 (October 1970): 12-23; (January 1971): 163-190.

Clark, Kenneth. "Vision: Cornerstone For Democracy," *Southern Exposure* 7 (Summer 1979): 143-145.

Commager, Henry Steele. "Our Schools Have Kept Us Free," *Life* 29 (16 October 1950): 46-47.

Cook, Samuel Dubois. "The Black Man and The American Political System: Obligation, Resistance, and Hope," *The Journal of Afro-American Issues* 5 (Summer 1977): 228-243.

. "Democracy and Tyranny in America: The Radical Paradox of the Bicentennial and Blacks in the American Political System," *Journal of Politics* 38 (August 1976): 276-294.

Daniel, Bradford and John Howard Griffin. "Why They Can't Wait: An Interview with a White Negro," *The Progressive* 28 (July 1964): 15-19.

Dent, Tom. "Portrait of Three Heroes," *Freedomways* 5 (Spring 1965): 250-262.

Dreyfuss, Joel. "The New Racism," *Black Enterprise* 8 (January 1978): 41-44.

Edari, Ronald S. "White Attitudes Toward Busing: Segregation and the Life Cycle," *Journal of Black Studies* 10 (September 1979): 98-118.

Edwards, Harry. "Edwards vs. the University of California," *The Black Scholar* 8 (May 1977): 32-33.

Frady, Marshall. "Discovering One Another in a Georgia Town," *Life* 70 (12 February 1971): 46C-52.

George, Pamela. "Testing: The Competency Controversy," *Southern Exposure* 7 (Summer 1979): 114-118.

Hall, Leon. "The Implementors' Revenge," *Southern Exposure* 7 (Summer 1979): 122-125.

Hamilton, Charles V. "Blacks in the System: Finding a Reason to Vote," *The Nation* 227 (16 December 1978): 668-671.

Harris, Ann Sutherland. "The Second Sex in Academe," *AAUP Bulletin* 56 (Fall 1970): 283-295.

Harris, Ron. "The Myth of the 'New South,' " *Ebony* 24 (February 1979): 54-62.

Hill, Herbert. "Falling Behind Again: White Myths of Black Economics," *The Nation* (16 December 1978): 666-668.

Hill, Robert. "The Illusion of Black Progress," *The Black Scholar* 10 (October 1978): 18-24.

Hollander, Ronald A. "One Mississippi Negro Who Didn't Go to College," *The Reporter* 17 (8 November 1962): 30-34.

Hudson, John B. "The Spoils System Enters College: Governor Bilbo and Higher Education in Mississippi," *New Republic* 69 (17 September 1930): 123-125.

Klein, JoAnn. "Changing Politics in Mississippi," *Southern Changes* 2 (December 1979): 5-6.

Ladner, Heber. "James Kimble Vardaman, Governor of Mississippi, 1904-1908," *Journal of Mississippi History* 2 (October 1940): 175-205.

Lekachman, Robert. "Proposition 13 and the New Conservatism," *Change* 10 (September 1978): 22-27.

Levitt, Paul M. "Trials of H. Bruce Franklin," *Change* 9 (August 1977): 21-24.

Lewis, Lionel S. "The Academic Axe: Some Trends in Dismissals from Institutions of Higher Learning in America," *Social Problems* 12 (Fall 1965): 151-158.

Lewis, Lionel S. and Michael N. Ryan. "In the Matter of University Governance during the 1960s," *Social Problems* 19 (Fall 1965: 249-257.

Lincoln, C. Eric. "Black Studies and Cultural Continuity," *The Black Scholar* 10 (October 1978): 12-17.

Lyons, Gene. "A Case of Thoughtcrime," *The Progressive* 38 (May 1974): 40-41.

Marable, Manning. "The Post-Movement Reaction," *Southern Exposure* 7 (Spring 1979): 60-64.

———. "Tuskegee and the Politics of Illusion in the New South," *The Black Scholar* 8 (May 1977): 13-24.

Marshall, Rachelle. "The Bruce Franklin Affair," *The Progressive* 36 (May 1972): 27-29.

Maynard, Robert C. "The Black College: The Price of Excellence," *Black Enterprise* 9 (May 1979): 26-38.

McCain, William D. "The Administration of David Holmes, Governor of the Mississippi Territory, 1809-1817," *Journal of Mississippi History* 24 (November 1967): 328-347.

———. "History Is Being Made in Mississippi Now," *The Citizen* 7 (November 1967): 328-347.

. "Reminiscences of the United States Archivist in Italy, 1944-1945—Director William D. McCain on Military Leave from Mississippi Department of Archives and History," *Journal of Mississippi History* 39 (February 1972): 1-28.

McDermott, John. "Campus Missionaries: The Laying on of Culture," *The Nation* 208 (10 March 1969): 296-301.

McDonald, Laughlin. "The Bolden Decision Stonewalls Black Aspirations," *Southern Changes* 2 (July/August 1980): 11-17.

McGee, Leo and Robert Boone. "Black Rural Land Decline in the South," *The Black Scholar* 8 (May 1977): 8-11.

McSwine, Bartley. "The Great American Whitewash," *Change* 11 (October 1979): 54-57.

Miles, Michael. "The Triumph of Reaction," *Change* 4 (Winter 1972-73): 30-36.

Mitchell, Greg. "The Inventor as Target: Ollman Plays 'Class Struggle' for Real," *The Nation* 227 (18 November 1978): 541-543.

Moorman, Charles. "The Humanities in the Career University: A Local View," *The Southern Quarterly* 12 (January 1974): 113-119.

Murchland, Bernard. "The Eclipse of the Liberal Arts," *Change* 8 (November 1976): 22-26.

Phillips, Barry. "'Bakkelash," *Radical Teacher* (March 1979): 6-7.

Phillips, Ivory. "The 1964 Freedom Summer and Rosedale Mississippi 1979," *Southern Changes* 2 (January 1980): 12-16.

Radosh, Ronald. "The Rise of a Marxist Historian: An Interview with Eugene Genovese," *Change* 10 (November 1978): 31-35.

Rich, Adrienne. "Taking Women Students Seriously," *Radical Teacher* (March 1979): 40-43.

Reissman, Frank. "The 'Vocationalization' of Higher Education: Duping the Poor," *Social Policy* 2 (May/June 1971): 3-4.

Rodriguez, Richard. "Beyond the Minority Myth," *Change* 10 (September 1978): 28-34.

Rosenfelt, Deborah and Gloria DeSole. "Affirmative Action: The Verdict Is Still Out," *Radical Teacher* (March 1979): 3-5.

Schrag, Peter. "A Hesitant South: Fragile Promise on the Last Frontier," *Saturday Review* 105 (12 February 1972): 51-58.

Shields, James J., Jr. "The Return to Gray Flannel Thinking," *USA Today* 107 (January 1979): 49-52.

Silver, James W. "Mississippi: The Closed Society," *Journal of Southern History* 30 (February 1964): 3-34.

Simon, Rita J., Shirley M. Clark and Kathleen Galway. "The Woman Ph.D.: A Recent Profile," *Social Problems* 15 (Fall 1967): 221-236.

Sonn, Bill. "H. Bruce Franklin: Another First," *The Progressive* 38 (September 1974): 36-37.

Staples, Robert. "Land of Promise, Cities of Despair: Blacks in Urban America," *The Black Scholar* 10 (October 1978): 2-11.

Tulsky, Frederic. "Standing Up to Fear in Mississippi," *Southern Exposure* 6 (Fall 1978): 68-72.

Turner, Rick. "Cooling Out," *Black Collegian* 7 (November-December 1976): 10-16.

"The University of Mississippi," *AAUP Bulletin* 56 (Spring 1970): 75-86.

Van Valey, Thomas L., Wade Clark Roof and Jerome E. Wilcox. "Trends in Residential Segregation: 1960-1970," *American Journal of Sociology* 82 (January 1977): 826-844.

Vinson, Ken. "Mississippi's Master Racist," *Change* 2 (September-October 1970): 23-24.

Watson, Bernard C. "Through the Academic Gateway," *Change* 11 (October 1979): 24-28.

Weaver, Frederick Stirton. *"Cui Bono?* And the Economic Function of Racism," *The Review of Black Political Economy* 8 (Spring 1978): 302-13.

Weston, Jack. "Do Radical Teachers Have a Progressive Effect?" *Radical Teacher* (March 1979): 10-11.

White, Martha S. "Women in the Professions: Psychological and Social Barriers to Women in Science," *Science* 170 (23 October 1970): 413-416.

Whittemore, Reed. "Faculty Survival: Coping with Managers," *Harper's* 260 (February 1980): 38-41.

Wilkie, Curtis. "Mississippi Muzzle," *Nation* 208 (3 February 1969): 132-133.

Williams, Linda. "Finances: Short-Changing Equal Education," *Southern Exposure* 7 (Summer 1979): 103-106.

Wolfe, Alan. "Reform Without Reform: The Carnegie Commission on Higher Education," *Social Policy* 2 (May/June 1971): 18-27.

"The Yeshiva Decision," *Academe* 66 (May 1980): 188-197.

INDEX

Southern California Edison, 130
Southern Historical Association, 35
Southern Politics (Key), 123
Southern Political Science Association, 113-114
Southern Quarterly, The, 55-56, 113, 223n
Southern Regional Council, 179
Stacey, Jedy, 229n-230n
Stalin, Joseph, 76
Stanford University, xii, 73, 127, 137-139, 150, 201
Staples, Robert, 191, 234n, 236n
Starsky, Morris, 134
State University of New York at Albany, 157
Steele, Robert F., 222n
Stimpson, Catharine R., 230n
Stouffer, Samuel A., 205n-206n
Structional-functionalism, 164
Student Government Association, xi, 50, 107-110
Student Printz, xviin, 61, 102-103, 108, 206n, 212n-215n, 217, 219n-222n
Student Senate, 11, 19-20, 96, 103, 106-109, 114
Students for a Democratic Society (SDS), 11
Suitts, Steven, 179
Sweezy v. *New Hampshire,* 128, 225n

"Tax revolt," 197, 201
Temple University, 148
Texas A&M University, 152
Texas Christian University, 35
The Times (of London), 47
Theory and Methods of Scaling (Torgerson), 47
Thurmond, Strom, 200
Time, 6, 46, 196
Time, Inc., 119
Tobin, Gary A., 235n
Tocqueville, Alexis de, 163
Toll, John, 142-143
Treadwell, David, 233n
Trister, Mike, 39
Truman, David, 121
Tuition tax credit, 193-194
Tulane University, 47, 111-112
Tulsky, Frederic, 232n
Turner, Mike, 221n
Turner, Rich, 224n
Tuskegee Institute, 153

United California Bank, 130
United League of North Mississippi, 172

United Nations, 16, 191
University of Alabama, 51
University of Arkansas at Little Rock, 139, 141
University of California at Berkeley, xii, 130, 134-136, 148, 151, 159
University of California at Davis, 150
University of California at Los Angeles, 44, 130, 135-136
University of Chicago, 22, 27, 31, 130, 141
University of Colorado, 13, 137, 139
University of Connecticut, 62
University of Maryland, xii, 141-143
University of Massachusetts at Boston, 154
University of Michigan, 113, 153-154
University of Mississippi, 25, 28, 30-36, 38-41, 49, 62, 106, 182, 209n, 222n
University of North California, 81, 233n
University of Pennsylvania, 81, 119, 149
University of Southern Mississippi (USM), ix, xi-xii, xv-xvi, 3-5, 10-15, 17-22, 27-28, 38, 40-52, 54-57, 60-62, 65-68, 71-73, 75-77, 79-82, 84-87, 89-96, 99-109, 111-114, 117-118, 127, 206n-207n, 212n-223n
University of Texas, 152
U.S. Army Reserve, 206n
U.S. Bureau of the Census, 231n, 235n
U.S. Civil Rights Commission, 169, 174, 193, 200
U.S. Congress, 15, 189, 194, 200, 230n
U.S. Constitution, 37, 55, 92, 136, 140, 167
U.S. Department of Defense, 138
U.S. Department of Education, 228n-229n
U.S. Department of Health, Education and Welfare, 33-34, 41, 156
U.S. Department of Justice, 34, 190, 232n, 234n
U.S. Senate, 60, 189, 200
U.S. Supreme Court, 78-79, 113, 128, 131-132, 151, 168-169, 189-192, 210n, 222n
Useem, Elizabeth, 224n, 226n
Useem, Michael, 224n, 226n

Van Valey, Thomas L., 235n
Vanderbilt University, 29
Vardaman, James K., 123, 224n
Veterans of Foreign Wars (VFW), 63, 140, 182
Veysey, Laurence R., 205n
Vietnam War, 35, 56, 134, 164
Vinson, Ken, 34, 211n-212n